Dining on

Cook Book

How to Eat Better and Spend Less!

Mixes, Gift Baskets and Jars

Kids

- Cleaning Cents

Pretty for Pennies

Menu Ideas

and more!

Includes
1,000
Money Saving
Recipes & Tips

by Tawra Kellam and Jill Cooper

Save $10,000
SEE PAGE 3

D0435349

2.00

Dining on a Dime

(Formerly published as **Not Just Beans**)

First Printing: August 2004. Reprinted 2005
ISBN: 0-9742552-1-1
Copyright 2004 Tawra Jean Kellam

Also by Tawra Jean Kellam and Jill Cooper

Pretty for Pennies	(ISBN: 0-9676974-1-7)	(Copyright 2003)
Halloween on a Dime	(ISBN: 0-9676974-4-1)	(Copyright 2003)
Menus on a Dime	(ISBN: 0-9676974-5-x)	(Copyright 2003)
Moving on a Dime	(ISBN: 0-9676974-3-3)	(Copyright 2003)

Designed, Produced and Published by
T&L Group
3802 Antelope Trail
Temple, TX 76504

888-458-1229
email: mkttx2@hot.rr.com

Book design production by Thao Vo, Arlington, Texas

Anecdotes are author unknown unless specified. Recipes used with permission from the Complete Tightwad Gazette by Amy Dacyczyn are noted on the acknowledgement page.

For additional copies of Dining on a Dime, send $19.95 plus $3.50 shipping and handling to:

Living On A Dime
PO Box 4252
Wichita KS 67204

Order by credit card online: *www.LivingOnADime.com*

Printed in China

How it adds up*

Look how much you would save in a year if you cut out just **ONE** thing.

Item	Price	How often	Cost per year
1 bag potato chips	$2.99/bag	1/week	$155.48
6-pack soda	$2.00	1/week	$104.00
Reduce meat	1.5 lbs.	2 nights/week	$468.00
1 box granola cereal	$4.00	1/week	$208.00
1 cup juice/family of 4	$1.50	1/day	$547.50
Fruit leather	$2.50	1/week	$130.00

At convenience store/coffee shop

1 liter soda	$1.00	1/day	$365.00
1 gourmet coffee	$3.65 each	1/day	$1332.25
Bottled water	$1.25	1 liter/day	$456.25
1-2 pk. snack cake	$1.25	1/day	$456.25

Eating out for a family of 4:

Dinner	@$30.00	1/week	$1560.00
Dinner	@$40.00	1/week	$2080.00
Lunch	$5.00/person	20 days/month	$1200.00
Pizza-delivered	$20.00	1/week	$1040.00

TOTAL IF YOU CUT ALL THESE OUT   **$10,102.73**

*2004 prices

Table of Contents

> *If you want to see a cup runneth over,*
> *let a child pour his own soda*

> *Early to bed and early to rise makes a man healthy,*
> *wealthy and good at making his own breakfast*

> *Man cannot live by bread alone....*
> *he needs peanut butter and jelly to go with it*

> *You have two choices for dinner. Take it or leave it*

> *Real families don't eat shitake mushrooms*

> *Life is too short to stuff a cherry tomato*

The Origin of Dining on A Dime

My first book was called Not Just Beans. I wanted to give people ideas and recipes for saving money in the kitchen without just "eating beans". Dining on a Dime is the third edition of that book. I learned most of my "living on a dime" tips from my mother, Jill. She was a single parent who raised two kids on a limited income, without sacrificing our comfort or sense of security and well being. The lessons she taught served me in my adult life, when my husband and I struggled to raise our young family. We managed to pay off more than $20,000 in debt over a period of five years on an average income of $22,000. This book tells you how we got out of debt by saving on our grocery bills.

Whether you can cook like a pro, or are just starting out, we hope you'll check out our ideas as presented in this book. Stop eating out. Eat at home and you'll eat better and spend less.

Keep your kitchen clean so you can prepare meals easily and have a comfortable place for your family to gather for fun and food.

Organize your home - get rid of the junk you don't need. Have your kids help and you can spend time together while teaching them life skills.

Shop wisely with a little planning and organization. We've included pantry organization lists to get you started.

Share your homemade gifts with family and friends. The mixes and jars we have in this book are easy to make and give you an opportunity to have some fun in the kitchen - again, a place for you to spend time with the kids.

Pamper yourself with our "Pretty for Pennies" ideas. You deserve it!

Tawra

Basics

of

Frugal

Cooking

Use it up, wear it out, make it do, or do without.

Basics of Frugal Cooking

Remember the ideas in this book are only suggestions.

I know some of these things might seem radical to some people but they are just things to get you thinking of new ways to save on your groceries.

Try not to take the book too seriously! But don't forget!!!! If you don't feed the sourdough starter it will die-but you can always make more.

Don't become overwhelmed. Read the book, try to do one or two things and then go back over it and try the next thing.

Cooking frugally is a mind set. You have to change your cooking and eating habits.

Don't get discouraged if one idea fails. Try another one. Some things take time and practice but in the end you save money by learning new skills.

Cooking frugally is like changing your diet. You need to gradually learn how to save money and how to cook frugally. Don't expect that you will get your food bill down to $150 for 4 people in the first month if you are spending $600 a month right now.

Try cutting just $25.00 or $50.00 a month. Even if you cut back $50.00 a month that is $600.00 a year you would save. If you saved only $1.00 a day that is $365.00 a year. You can put that $365.00 a year toward your credit card debt and work on paying it off. At 21% interest, you save more than $70 a year. There will eventually be a snowball effect and it will keep growing and growing.

Make cooking frugally a challenge. Make it a game to see how low you can get you grocery budget and still have delicious, exciting food **without feeling deprived.** If you start feeling deprived then change the way something is cooked or add something back in.

If you have young children, it is easy to instill these ideas.

If you have teenagers and husbands, they may complain.
Start by changing the way you cook your meals. Use home
cooked beans instead of canned in dishes. Use homemade
sauces and cut back on the meat in a dish. Start serving more
soup and pasta dishes. They probably won't notice any
difference. Then start cutting back on the juices, milk and pop.
Make the kids spend their allowance on extras like candy bars,
pop and potato chips if they still want these things.

**If your family is unsure of eating or say they don't like
homemade foods:** Try putting them in the name brand package.
Then if they like it tell them later that was the homemade item. At
least try it . . . you or your family may not like some off brands or
homemade foods but even if you try one product and they like it, it
is better than not saving anything at all.

Drink water with your meals. If your family is used to drinking
milk, juice or pop for every meal then start by cutting out juice
and only drinking water for one meal or snack a day. Then
increase it until you drink water for every meal and snack.

Another idea is after the food is eaten **offer one glass of milk,**
juice or pop, or allow one glass of juice at mealtimes and then
water after it is gone.

If you don't have the money to stock up on items that are a
great deal, start by eating one or two meatless meals a week
and culling out unnecessary Items. Take the savings and stock
up on 1 item on sale. Then take the additional savings and buy
something else on sale the next month. There will be a snowball
effect and you will be saving every month on your grocery bill.

Use dry milk for baking if you don't like it for drinking. Be sure
it is cheaper by the gallon than buying whole milk.

Also try mixing half whole milk and half dry milk.

Dry milk tastes best when it is chilled after mixing.

Try generic or off brands. If you don't think they taste as good as your old brand then stick with your old brand, but a lot of off brand products taste as good as or better than the name brand. Many off brand products are made by the same company as the name brand, but are relabeled and sold at lower prices.

Most foods have satisfaction guarantees on the products. If you don't like a product, return it to the store or call the toll free number on the back of the box. A lot of companies will either give you your money back or send you a coupon for another product.

Think of storing items found on sale in places other than the pantry. Try shelves in the garage, under the bed, under a crib, unused drawer space or under an open-bottom end table (no one will see canned goods stored under there with a tablecloth on top).

Stop buying things like toaster pastries and breakfast bars for breakfast. Eat oatmeal, pancakes, granola and fruit instead.

If you have a source for free or inexpensive walnuts, pecans, etc. in your area, purchase or collect nuts there and use them in recipes calling for them. If not, then omit this type of expensive ingredient.

If you get a VERY GOOD deal on chocolate chips and ingredients for candies then it is cheaper than buying them pre-made. But make sure you do the calculations. If not purchased on sale, homemade candies can be more expensive than those purchased at the store.

Planning Your Meals

Keep your pantry and kitchen cabinets organized. You lose money when your kitchen isn't organized and you keep re-buying items that you already have. Make sure everything is in neat rows and easy to see. Also make sure everything in your freezer is labeled. I use tape with a red permanent marker. Make sure you have the date, the item description and cooking instructions on every package in the freezer.

Clean your refrigerator the day before going to the grocery store. This way you can see what you have and you can plan menus around leftovers. This also saves on a huge once-a-month cleaning job.

Plan meals around what is on sale for the week.

Serve smaller portions. Use smaller plates for the illusion of more food.

Check the food pyramid. Don't overeat. Most people eat way too much. One serving of fruit is half of a banana but most people eat the whole thing.

Make do with what you have. If you run out of regular bread use corn bread instead.

Use fewer convenience foods. It really does not take any more time to bake a cake from scratch than it does to use a mix. Time yourself one day and see.

Keep a master list of menus. For one month keep track of what you have for every dinner. You then have a list to go by. That way you don't always have to sit down and plan.

It doesn't always save to plan menus two weeks in advance. This doesn't take into account unexpected good deals and the need to use leftovers. Instead, try planning one or two days in advance.

Make a habit of planning the next day's dinner after the evening meal's dishes are cleaned. Usually it only take 5 to 10 minutes.

Menu Ideas

I don't plan meals one or two weeks in advance. I prefer to do it only a couple of days in advance. If I planned too far ahead I wouldn't be able to take advantage of deals that I find. (I just found 14 avocados for .99 on the clearance shelf. I didn't plan for this but it was a great treat!) I hope these menu suggestions help you get started. Enjoy!

#1
Slow Cook Roast *
Brown Gravy *
Onions, Carrots, Potatoes *
(cooked with roast)
Tossed Salad & Dressing *
Buttermilk Muffins *

#2
Barbecued Beef *
Potato Salad *
Baked Beans *

#3
Macaroni Salad *
Green Beans *
Pineapple-Orange Gelatin *
Oatmeal Muffins *

#4
Pizza *
Tossed Salad
Ranch Dressing *

#5
Maidrites *
Cucumbers & Tomatoes *
Macaroni Salad *

#6
Cheese Enchiladas *
Sopapillas *
Refried Beans *
Baked or Fried Tortilla Chips *

#7
Ham & Potatoes *
Minty Peas & Onions *
Mom's Sweet Muffins *

#8
Maple Glazed Chicken *
Glazed Carrots *
Cucumber Salad *
Ninety Minute Rolls *

#9
Beef Stroganoff *
Garden Salad *
Dinner Rolls *

#10
Mexican Chicken *
Spanish Rice *
Broccoli
Sliced Tomatoes

Picky Eaters

#1
Hamburger Casserole *
Sliced Tomatoes or
Corn on the Cob

#2
Macaroni and Cheese
Sliced Apples and Oranges

#3
Sloppy Joes *
French Fries *
Sliced Orange, Kiwi
or Banana

#4
Chicken Fried Steak *
Mashed Potatoes *
Green Beans *
Mom's Sweet Muffins *

#5
Sliced Ham
Scrambled Eggs *
Fried Potatoes *
Orange Juice

#6
Chicken & Dumplings *
Toss Salad
Green Beans *

#7
Chef Salad
Ninety Minute Rolls *

Quick Dinners

#1
Tacos *
Refried Beans *
Tortilla Chips w/ Honey *
Giant Peanut Butter Cookies *

#2
BBQ Ribs in crock pot *
Cole Slaw *
Relish Dish
Ranch Dressing Mix *
Corn Bread *

#3
Grilled Cheese Sandwiches *
Tomato Soup *
Carrot Sticks

#4
Waffles *
Eggs, scrambled or fried *
Bacon or Sausage
Fresh fruit, sliced

#5
Chicken Sandwich on
Whole Wheat Bread with
Lettuce, Tomato,
Tater Tots with Cheese
Cantaloupe Slices

* <u>Check Index for page
 number.</u>

How to Eat Better and Spend Less

Make a price list. Keep track of prices on the items you buy most frequently in a small pocket notebook. Then set a goal to only buy those items when they are at their cheapest.

Don't buy everything at one store. Prices vary greatly from one store to the next. Go to different stores to buy only their sale items. You will save more than the cost of your gas. It usually only takes a half hour or so per store to get the items that are on sale including driving time. If you save a minimum of $20-$30 per trip, that is like "earning" $40-$60 an hour. If I saved $60 spending one hour going to two different stores then that is five extra hours my husband would have had to work for us to pay for that same food if it wasn't purchased on sale. I would rather have him home with us.

Warehouse stores aren't always cheaper. Use warehouse stores only for things that you know are cheaper. Not every item in the store is less expensive than the grocery store.

Do not buy non-food items at the grocery store: Items such as diapers, wipes, over-the-counter medications, shampoos, etc. are almost always more expensive at the grocery store than at a discount store.

Shop at the dollar store for spices, dressings, over-the-counter medications, shampoo and conditioner.

Shop discount stores for non-food items and canned goods.

Ask for rain checks when a sale item is sold out. If they don't have a limit on quantity tell them you want DOUBLE what you think you will need. You can always buy less but you can't get more if you need it.

Ask if there are limits on sale items at the store. Sometimes there are no limits and you can stock up on a good deal.

If something's a great buy, stock up. When there is a really good price on something, I get as many of the item as I can if I use it often.

Don't assume that bulk is cheaper. Compare cost by the ounce or pound.

Don't assume homemade is cheaper.

Only use coupons if you can double them or get the name brands for next to nothing. In most cases you can make the item from scratch or get a generic brand for less.

When using coupons it's not how much you save but how much you spend. The same is true with sales. You don't save anything by buying something you could do without just because it is on sale.

Never shop hungry.

Try to shop alone. If you do take the kids, have them spend their allowance if they want extras such as candy bars and potato chips.

Buy the smallest packages of meats like chicken, turkey and pork chops for cooking. Buy small fruits. When you eat a banana or apple, you almost always eat a whole one so make it a small one. They weigh less, so they cost less.

Don't buy fruit in bulk. If you can't eat it all, it goes to waste and you lose money.

Wash and reuse freezer and storage bags <u>except</u> those that have been used to store meat.

Make your own baby food.

Steam vegetables in a small amount of water.

Puree vegetables and leftovers with water in a blender or food processor until smooth. Freeze in ice cube trays. When frozen, place in a freezer bag. Take as many cubes as you need for a meal. Defrost and serve.

How to Save on Herbs

✦ **Buy spices in bulk** from spice shops or from mail order companies. Sometimes they have minimum orders. If so, split the order with your friends and family.

✦ Here's a good company:

> The San Francisco Herb Company
> 250 14th Street,
> San Francisco, CA 94103
> www.sfherb.com

✦ **Grow your own herbs.** One herb plant is enough to supply you for a year with dried herbs. Place one herb plant in a 6-inch pot or two or three herb plants in a 15-inch pot. Fill to two inches from the top with dirt. Place in a sunny window or in a sunny spot in the yard. Water when the soil becomes dry as needed. Do not over water and do not fertilize herbs.

✦ **To use fresh herbs:** Harvest one or two stems from the plant. Strip leaves from stem and cut leaves into small pieces. Discard stems.

✦ **To dry herbs:** In the fall before the first frost, cut the stems at the base of the plant. Tie the bottom of the stems together with a rubber band. Hang to dry upside down in a cool dark place for several weeks. When dry, strip the leaves from the stems and crush leaves to desired consistency. Store in an airtight container.

✦ **Chives do not dry well** but you can wash them, let them dry and then cut into small pieces and freeze in a freezer bag. Just use as many as you need.

✦ **Chop a large quantity of parsley** and pack into freezer bags. Freeze. Take out a tablespoon as needed.

Herb Guide:

Beef: thyme, celery, marjoram, coriander, sage, rosemary, oregano, garlic

Chicken: garlic, marjoram, tarragon, oregano, coriander

Fish, fried: mustard, oregano, tarragon, sage

Fish, grilled: thyme, coriander, fennel, rosemary

Pork: marjoram, mustard, oregano, sage, rosemary, thyme, garlic

Roast Beef: basil, oregano, thyme, mustard, rosemary, garlic

Turkey: basil, rosemary, cumin, oregano, thyme, sage

Basil: tomatoes, tomato sauces, peas, squash, lamb, fish, eggs, tossed salad, cheese, potatoes, pasta

Bay leaf: vegetable and fish soups, tomato sauces, poached fish and meat stews

Dill: fish, cream and cottage cheese, potatoes, fish, vegetable salads, pickles, tomatoes

Marjoram: fish, vegetable soups, cheese dishes, stew, roast chicken, beef, pork, stuffing

Mint: jellies, fruit juices, candies, frosting, cakes, pies, pork, potatoes, peas and chocolate

Oregano: tomato sauces, pork, pizza, vegetable, fish, salads, chili

Parsley: meats, vegetables, soups, eggs, cheese

Rosemary: poultry stuffing, potatoes, cauliflower, fish

Sage: stuffing, pork roast, sausage, poultry and hamburgers

Savory: eggs, meats, salads, chicken, soups and stuffing

Tarragon: fish sauces, egg and cheese dishes, green salads, pickles, chicken, tomatoes, sauces for meats and vegetables

Thyme: soups, stuffing, beef, pork dishes, eggs, cheese, fish, bean and vegetable soups

What's in Tawra's Pantry?

An essential element of cooking frugally is keeping a well stocked pantry. The concept of a pantry is more than storage. Your pantry should be a place where you always have a good supply of basic ingredients and a few less expensive convenience foods.

When you have the opportunity to buy something that you use frequently at a great price, buy a lot of extra and keep it in the pantry until the next time you can get such a good price. This allows you to opt not to buy an item except when the price is very low, "flexing" your pantry.

Here is a list of items that we keep stocked in our pantry virtually all the time. I plan meals around what I have in the pantry and I buy what is on sale to keep my pantry well stocked.

You may want to copy the pantry list for your Grocery Shopping List.

Just about the time
you can make ends meet,
someone moves the end.

Pantry/Shopping List

Baking Supplies

___ baking powder
___ baking soda
___ chocolate chips
___ cocoa
___ coconut
___ cornstarch
___ eggs
___ food coloring
___ lemon juice
___ salt
___ unflavored gelatin
___ vinegar
___ yeast

Beverages

___ coffee
___ flavored drink mix
___ orange juice
___ tea

Breads

___ croutons (we make our own)
___ graham crackers
___ saltines
___ wheat bread
___ white bread

Cereals

___ cold cereal (on sale)
___ cream of wheat
___ grits
___ oatmeal

Cheeses

___ american
___ Cheddar
___ cream cheese (occasionally)
___ mozzarella
___ Parmesan

Cooking Oil

___ cooking spray
___ margarine
___ olive oil
___ shortening
___ vegetable oil

Dairy

___ butter
___ buttermilk (canned or recipe p.301)
___ dry milk
___ evaporated milk
___ margarine
___ sour cream
___ sweetened condensed milk (occasionally)
___ whole & skim milk yogurt

Fruits

__ apples
__ grapefruits
__ oranges
__ peaches (fresh and canned)
__ pears (fresh and canned)
__ pineapple (canned)
__ raisins
__ *seasonal fruit that is
         on sale or free

Grains

__ cornmeal
__ popcorn
__ wheat flour
__ white rice
__ white flour

Meats

__ bacon
__ beef roast
__ chicken (whole or parts,
    occasionally boneless
         chicken breast)
__ ground beef
__ ground turkey
__ ham
__ pork chops
__ round steak

Pasta

__ egg noodles
__ macaroni

__ macaroni and cheese,
         pre-packaged
__ spaghetti

Vegetables

__ broccoli (frozen)
__ carrots
__ corn (canned and frozen)
__ green beans (canned)
__ green peppers
__ instant mashed potatoes
__ lettuce
__ mushrooms (purchased
                  on sale)
__ onions
__ potatoes
__ tomatoes, diced, whole,
         paste and sauce

Misc. Canned goods

__ coffee creamer, powdered
__ dried beans
__ mushrooms, canned
__ peanut butter
__ pork and beans
__ pumpkin
__ Ramen noddles
__ spaghetti sauce
__ soup,
   _ cream of mushroom
   _ cream of chicken soup
   _ tomato soup

Sugars

___ brown sugar
___ corn syrup- dark and light
___ honey
___ powdered sugar
___ white sugar

Condiments

___ BBQ sauce
___ ketchup
___ jelly
___ mayonnaise
___ mustard
___ pickles
___ salad dressing
___ salsa

Seasonings/Flavorings

___ bouillon-beef, chicken
___ maple extract
___ peppermint extract
___ vanilla (recipe p.303)

Spices and herbs

_ allspice
_ basil
_ chili powder
_ cinnamon
_ cinnamon sticks
_ cloves, ground and whole
_ cream of tartar
_ cumin
_ garlic powder and salt

_ ginger
_ marjoram
_ meat tenderizer
_ nutmeg
_ onion powder and salt
_ oregano
_ pepper
_ rosemary
_ salt
_ thyme
___ soy sauce
___ Tabasco® sauce
___ worcestershire sauce

Misc. Optional Items

___ flavored gelatins
___ frozen pizzas
___ ice cream
___ nuts (pecans, etc)
___ olives
___ puddings, boxed
___ whipped topping

_____
_____
_____
_____
_____
_____
_____
_____

FREEZER GUIDE:

How long will food keep?

Beef . . . . 12 months

Butter, pasteurized . . . . 6 months

Cakes, Cookies and Breads . . . . 3 to 4 months

Cheese . . . . 6 months

Coconut . . . . 12 months

Cream Cheese . . . . 4 months

Cooked Meats . . . . 3 months

Egg whites, out of shell . . . . 12 months

Egg yolks, out of shell . . . . 3 months
(Add ⅛ tsp. salt or ½ tsp. sugar
            for every 4 egg yolks)

Fruits and Juices . . . . 12 months

Ground Meats . . . . 3 months

Ice Cream . . . . 4 months

Lamb . . . . 9 months

Liver . . . . 2 months

Nuts . . . . 12 months

Pork . . . . 6 months

Poultry, raw . . . . 6 months

Vegetables . . . . 12 months

Whipping Cream . . . . 3 months

Recipes that freeze well

+ Barbecued Beef (p.177)
+ Barbecued Meatballs (p.177)
+ Bean Goulash (p.185)
+ Cheeseburger Rolls (p.182)
+ Chicken Pot Pie (p.199)
+ Green Chile (without the tortillas) (p.215)
+ Ham and Beans (p.210)
+ Hamburger Casserole (p.185)
+ Hash (p.186)
+ Maidrites (p.187)
+ Pizza (p.217)
+ Shepherd's Pie (p.192)
+ Sloppy Joes (p.117)

Foods that <u>DO NOT</u> freeze well

+ canned cinnamon rolls*
+ canned croissant dough*
+ canned Danish rolls*
+ canned refrigerator biscuits*
+ cooked egg whites
+ cream pies with meringue
+ custards
+ grapes (unless eating frozen)
+ mayonnaise
+ salad dressings
+ salad greens
+ raw tomatoes

*These items can be baked and then frozen

Freezer Tips

+ **To vacuum seal your freezer bags:** zip up your freezer bag almost all the way. Leave a hole and put a straw in it. Suck out all the air, quickly remove the straw and seal the bag the rest of the way.

+ **To freeze one serving of leftovers.** Place plastic wrap or foil in a muffin tin. Put the leftovers on the plastic wrap, seal and label. Freeze. Remove from muffin tin and store several in a freezer bag. Keep frozen until you need an instant "TV dinner".

+ **Fill milk cartons,** water bottles or soft drink bottles three quarters full with water and place in the freezer to fill up extra space. This makes the freezer use less energy and makes things stay frozen better. These can also be used in coolers or while camping.

+ **If there is a power outage,** do not open the freezer unless absolutely necessary. Should you need food, know what you need to get out of the freezer ahead of time, leaving the door open for just a few seconds and quickly shut the door securely. During a power outage, a full freezer of food will usually stay frozen for three days. In a half-full freezer, food will usually stay frozen for a couple days.

+ **If you need to remove** the package from frozen food such as hamburger without defrosting: Dip it in warm water for a couple of minutes just until the plastic loosens. Remove from package. Brown the frozen hamburger right away.

+ **To freeze milk:** Remove ½ cup to allow for expansion and then freeze. When thawed shake well before using.

+ **To freeze cheese:** Grate it and then spread on a cookie sheet. Put in the freezer for one hour and then transfer to a freezer bag. When grating chesse, place a little oil on the grater to make it easier to grate and easier to clean the grater.

+ **Freeze grains** (such as flour and oatmeal) for 24 hours and then store in an airtight container. This helps eliminate pests.

✦ **Store nuts in a bag in the freezer.** Remove directly from the freezer and use as needed.

✦ **Brown hamburger and store in ½ -pound and 1-pound portions** in freezer bags or containers. Then make chili, casseroles and such more conveniently.

✦ **Slow cook a roast,** shred, add barbecue sauce and divide it into individual containers and have barbecue sandwiches anytime!

✦ **Cook chicken, pork chops,** lasagna or meatloaf and freeze. When you need a quick meal, simply reheat it. (350° is a reliable oven temperature.) Be sure to consider the amount/thickness of the dish when heating.

✦ **When meat has reached its limit of freezer time,** defrost and cook it. Then freeze cooked meat for meals.

✦ **To freeze a casserole:** Line the casserole dish with double thick aluminum foil. Prepare dish in the foil-lined casserole. When finished, cover and freeze. Then remove the casserole from the dish and put it in a large freezer bag. When you want to serve it just slip it and the foil in the dish to bake.

✦ **Cheese or crumb toppings** are best added after the food has been reheated.

✦ **Freeze bananas** for breads, cakes and shakes. Just peel and throw in a freezer bag. Mash after defrosting. Two to three large bananas are enough for one loaf of banana bread. Bananas can also be frozen whole in the peel. To use: defrost, cut off the end and squeeze banana out. It is already mashed.

✦ **For foods that will darken (like bananas),** add ⅛ tsp. lemon juice to keep them from browning in the freezer.

✦ **To freeze apples:** Peel, quarter, and slice a few at a time. Drop immediately into cold salt water. Place in freezer bags. The salt water prevents them from darkening. Use for pies, applesauce and apple butters.

✦ **When you have several oranges or lemons,** wash them thoroughly. Grate the peel before using and freeze the zest.

✦ **When onions or green peppers are on sale,** buy a large quantity and chop into pieces. Freeze on a tray and then put into freezer bags. Later, take out what you need and return the rest to the freezer. Use for cooked dishes only!

✦ **To freeze corn on the cob:** Clean ears by trimming ends and removing silks. Do not wash. Freeze in freezer bags. To serve: Drop ears in boiling water and cook 6-8 minutes after water returns to a boil.

✦ **Collect all the odds and ends from the garden** at the end of the season. Wash, dry and freeze together for vegetable soup.

✦ **Buy ketchup in the gallon cans and freeze** all but one "bottle" full. Save salad dressing bottles for this. Do the same with hot sauce and whole tomatoes.

✦ **Place all pre-made meals in one part of the freezer.** That way your husband and kids can easily find the meals when you aren't home.

Keep a container in the door of the freezer:

1- Dump 1 or 2 tablespoons of hamburger into the container every time you brown hamburger. At the end of a week or two you will have a "free" meal.

2- Add to a container any leftovers like small pieces of meat, sauces or gravies, soups and vegetables that could be used for a soup or stew. Everything but fruit and bread can go in it, even leftover hot breakfast cereal. This is much easier than fighting about eating leftovers. Thaw and add some spices for a hot stew in the winter.

3- Keep another container for things that would make a good pot pie. This is especially good for vegetables that get overripe before you use them. Place everything in a baking dish and top with a crust or dumplings. Bake at 350° until done.

Lunch Ideas

Granola

Quesadillas

Omelets

Spaghetti

Cereal/Oatmeal with Fruit

Grilled cheese sandwich

Tuna, egg or chicken salad sandwich

Tuna salad and crackers

Soup and Cracker

Scrambled egg with cheese

Turkey sandwiches

Macaroni and cheese

Hot dogs (not for children 3 and under)

Pizza cut into bite-size pieces

Salad

Refried beans: Spread on toast and sprinkle with cheese. Broil until cheese bubbles.

Toast with some spaghetti sauce & cheese melted on top

Rice with a vegetable, mixed with teriyaki sauce

Hot ham and cheese sandwich. Toast bread. Melt cheese and warm the ham on the bread in the microwave.

Ants on a log: celery with peanut butter inside and raisins on the peanut butter

Canned baked beans. Hot dog slices or a spoon of plain yogurt may be added.

Noodles with cream-of-something soup (mushroom or broccoli)

✦ **To keep drinks cold in lunch boxes, pour a small amount in the bottom of the container (not glass) and then set the cap loosely on top. Put it in the freezer overnight. The next day fill with the rest of the drink. The ice should slowly melt all day long, keeping the beverage cool.**

✦ **Save the ketchup, mustard packets and napkins you don't use from fast food restaurants. Use them in lunch boxes.**

Snack Ideas

Fresh fruit

Apples, cut into quarters

Apples, quartered with 1 tsp. peanut
butter on each

Dried apples or bananas

Oranges, peeled and quartered

Bananas

Bananas sliced in half and spread
with peanut butter

Frozen grapes (p.371)

Veggies with ranch dressing
(p.168)

Celery sticks, spread with
peanut butter

Cherry tomatoes

Strawberry leather (p.377)

Puddings (p.294-295)

Homemade granola bars (p.290)

Pretzels, (p.82)

Peanut butter snacks (p.372)

Cinnamon sugar toast with tea

Chocolate milk

Cocoa

Creamy Orange Shake (p.39)

Milk shake

Fruit shakes (p.39-42)

Hard-boiled eggs

Popcorn balls

Popcorn

Bagels (p.84)

Muffins

Breadsticks

Banana bread (p.102)

Zucchini bread

Pumpkin bread (p.100)

Crackers and cheese

Crackers spread with peanut
butter and jelly or jam

Cheese

Cookies

Yogurt Popsicles (p.373)

Beef jerky (p.179)

Tortillas with cream cheese

Yogurt with fruit or
wheat germ added

Bread or toast spread with
jelly, jam, peanut butter,
spiced honey (p.325)
or honey butter (p.322)

Snack Tips

✦ **Have a snack sitting at the kitchen table** for the kids when they come home from school. This way they won't be grouchy from being hungry. This will also prevent them from digging though the kitchen cabinets looking for something themselves and messing up your neat, well-organized pantry. It is also the perfect time for you to sit and visit with them about their day at school.

✦ **To discourage bad snack habits,** don't buy unhealthy snacks or keep them in the house.

✦ **Present your snacks with a plate,** place mat, napkin and maybe a flower from the garden. This way your snacks always look inviting.

✦ **Have jars sitting on the counter** with sunflower seeds, raisins, granola, prunes or peanuts for the children. If they see healthy snacks they're more likely to want them.

✦ **Pre-bag chips, cookies and snacks.** Place in a basket for easy access for kids.

✦ Try **"out of the box" snacks** such as popcorn balls, Chex Mix™ chocolate dipped fruit, etc.

✦ **Kids whine and fuss because they are either hungry or tired.** Make sure they are given snacks to keep them from being grouchy.

Leftovers?

✦ Hearty Chili Pie-Pour 4 cups extra **chili** in a deep pie dish. (Add one can corn if you have a little less than 4 cups.) Prepare cornbread recipe according to directions. Drip batter over chili. Bake at 375° for 30 minutes or until the cornbread is done. Sprinkle with shredded Cheddar cheese.

✦ Cut leftover **meat loaf** into chunks and add them to a jar of spaghetti sauce to make speedy spaghetti and meatballs.

✦ Spicy Hash. Dice leftover **roast beef, roasted potatoes, carrots and onions.** Add bread crumbs until the consistency is such that you can shape into cakes. Cook over medium heat in a greased skillet until pancakes are light brown and heated through.

✦ Dice leftover **chicken and mixed vegetables** and toss with a well-seasoned white sauce. Enclose mounds of the mixture in flattened refrigerator biscuits and bake to make delicious turnovers.

✦ Freeze leftover **mashed potatoes** in small portions in freezer containers or freezer bags. Use to thicken soups and stews in place of flour.

✦ Use leftover **pork and beans** to make an open-faced sandwich. Put the bean mixture on hamburger bun halves or bread, top each with a slcce of American cheese and broil until the cheese is melted and bubbly.

✦ Mash any leftover **beans** and make refried beans. Serve with rice or tortillas.

✦ Mash leftover **beans** and add to meatloaf.

✦ Fried meatloaf: Cut left over **meat loaf** into bite sized pieces. Set aside. Saute 1 large onion in a frying pan. Add one 8-ounce can of tomato sauce and meat loaf pieces. Add a can of peas. Heat through.

✦ Grind leftover **roast beef**, stew meat, etc. in your food processor. Add to scrambled eggs along with leftover potatoes for an easy and hearty breakfast.

✦ Add leftover cooked **rice** to pancake batter for a hearty breakfast. Top with butter and syrup.

Time Saving Tips

✦ **Have family members help:**

There is no reason why the kids can't help with the cleaning, including dishes and other chores, so that you have time to prepare meals. Have everyone remove his or her own dirty place setting from table and put away 4 or 5 additional items. The table will be cleared quickly using this method. Wash your dishes right away. If you don't let them sit, the food will not get stuck on them. This will save you a lot of time and you won't have to clean the kitchen before the next meal.

✦ **Try exchanging meals with another family.**

Set up a system where you cook double the amount and take half over to another family. Later, they cook double and bring it to you. This means a night off for the cook and brings variety to your menu.

✦ **When unloading the dishwasher, set the table for the next meal.**

✦ **Make simple meals.** One-dish meals can contain your meat, your vegetable and your bread.

✦ **Put away containers and clean up as you cook.**

✦ **Things to do the night before:**

*Plan your meals.

*Put things in the refrigerator to defrost.

*Pack lunches.

*Set the table for breakfast and prepare breakfast foods. For pancakes, mix dry ingredients the previous night. In the morning, add wet ingredients and cook.

Time Saving Tips
(Continued)

✦ **Cook Once, Cook Big:**

*Make large batches of beans and store in 1- or 2-cup portions.

*Make a large batch of granola and store in an airtight container. If used in lunches or snacks, divide into single-serving plastic bags or containers

*Brown a large portion of ground beef and store in 1-cup portions. This can also be done with roast, pork and round steak.

*Cut extra ingredients for another meal when using onions, green peppers, etc.

*Cook double batches of rice or pasta to be reheated later in the week.

✦ **Buy staples that you use often in quantity.**

✦ **Make double or triple the amount when you prepare main dishes.** Freeze. Label with the name of the dish and cooking instructions. Later when you are too busy to cook, put in the crockpot on low or set the timer for the oven to start dinner before you get home.

✦ To **fill flour and sugar canisters** without making a mess, place them in your kitchen sink first. Any spills can easily be rinsed away.

✦ Store **cooking oil in a plastic squeeze bottle** like the kind used for ketchup in restaurants. This way you don't have to stop to unscrew the cap in the middle of making a recipe.

Beverages

If you want to see a cup runneth over,
Let a child pour his own soda.

Beverage Tips

✦ **Be careful to shop wisely.** Sometimes buying name brand flavored or specialty coffees on sale costs less than making your own.

✦ **Drink water.** One quarter to one third of most American's grocery bill is spent on drinks, drink mixes and sugar for the mixes. Cut down on the amount of coffee, tea, juice, milk and pop your family drinks. Kids don't need juice, pop or a lot of milk. They can drink water. It is just a matter of teaching them to drink water instead of other things.

✦ **Use powdered milk** instead of creamer in coffee or tea or try mixing your creamer half and half with dry milk.

✦ **Buy regular grind coffee and regrind it** into a powder at home. You need to use much less to achieve the same flavor as regular grind coffee.

✦ **If you run out of coffee filters** use a paper towel until you can get to the store to buy more.

✦ **You don't always have to make a full pot of coffee.** Just make one or two cups at time.

✦ **Save extra coffee in a thermos** instead of making a new batch or buy a smaller coffee maker.

✦ **Use 1 tea bag to make 2 or 3 cups of tea** if you don't like it strong. Keep the tea bag in a cup in the refrigerator.

✦ **Put 1 tea bag in a thermos or teapot** and fill with water. Then you can have hot tea all day long.

✦ **Put 1 mint leaf or lemon balm leaf** in each ice cube tray section. Pour water over the top and freeze. Then you will have a decorative ice cube for your tea.

✦ After making coffee **save the coffee filter and the coffee grounds in the maker**. Add your coffee for the next day on top of the old grounds. This way you can use each filter 2 or 3 times. Buy a reusable coffee filter. They last for years.

Hot Cocoa

¼ cup plus 1 Tbsp. cocoa
½ cup sugar
   dash of salt
4 cups hot milk
¾ tsp. vanilla

Combine cocoa, sugar and salt in a saucepan. Add milk and vanilla and then warm. Serves 4.

Extra Rich
Hot Cocoa Mix

10⅔ cups dry milk
6   ounces non-dairy coffee creamer
16   ounces Nestle's Quik™
⅓   cup powdered sugar

Mix the ingredients in a large bowl and store in covered container.

To prepare hot cocoa, mix ½ cup of the mix with 1 cup of hot water. This is double the cost of the plain cocoa mix but it is very good and still cheaper than the little packets.

Mexican Hot Chocolate

1/2	cup sugar
1/3	cup unsweetened cocoa
2	Tbsp. flour
1	tsp. ground cinnamon
1/2	tsp. salt
1 1/2	cups cold water
6	cups milk
1	Tbsp. vanilla

Combine sugar, cocoa, flour, cinnamon, and salt in a large saucepan. Stir in cold water and bring to a boil, stirring constantly. Reduce heat and simmer, stirring often. Slowly stir in milk and heat almost to boiling. Remove from heat and add vanilla. Beat until frothy with an electric mixer or whisk. Serve by garnishing with a cinnamon stick or a dollop of whipped cream. Serves 6.

Orange Cinnamon Coffee

1/3	cup ground coffee
1 1/2	tsp. orange peel, grated
1/2	tsp. vanilla
1/2	tsp. cinnamon

Blend coffee and dry ingredients in a blender. Blend in vanilla. Scrape sides and blend 15 seconds more. Place coffee mix in the center of a coffee filter. Place a filter on a square of plastic wrap. Draw together with a ribbon.

Makes one 8-cup pot of brewed coffee.

Recipes reprinted with permission from The Complete Tightwad Gazette by Amy Dacyczyn.

Spiced Tea

4   cups boiling water
4   tsp. loose black tea
6   whole cloves
$\frac{1}{2}$ tsp. dried orange peel
$\frac{1}{8}$ tsp. cinnamon

Mix all the ingredients in a teapot and pour boiling water on top. Let steep 3-5 minutes. Stir, strain and serve. Serves 4.

Double Berry Tea

2   cups hot water
2   Tbsp. seedless raspberry or strawberry jam
2   tsp. sugar
3   blackberry tea bags
1   tsp. lemon juice

In a small saucepan, bring water and jam to a boil. Remove from heat and add tea bags. Steep 5 minutes covered. Remove tea bags and stir in lemon juice and sugar. Pour into tea cups and garnish with lemon twists. Serves 4.

✦ **To get the most juice from an orange, lemon or lime. Punch a couple of times with a fork. Microwave for 20 seconds or put in boiling water for 3-4 minutes or try rolling on the counter with the palm of your hand.**

Wassail

8	cups apple cider
1/4	cup brown sugar
1	tsp. whole cloves
1	tsp. whole allspice
1	cinnamon stick

Heat all the ingredients to boiling; reduce heat. Cover and simmer 20 minutes. Strain and pour into a punch bowl. Serves 8.

Iced Tea

3	regular sized tea bags
1½	qts. boiling water
½	cup sugar

In a pitcher combine tea bags, water and sugar. Let steep 10-20 minutes depending on desired strength. Stir well and chill. Serve over ice cubes. This will be strong but when you put the ice cubes in, the tea will be the right strength. Add a sprig of mint to your glasses. Or try replacing 1 regular tea bag with a flavored tea bag for variety. Makes 1½ quarts.

✦ **To make flavored tea add a package of flavored drink mix to each pot of tea.**

Orange Slush

1   cup orange juice
1   Tbsp. honey
½   banana
4   ice cubes
1   tsp. vanilla (optional)

Blend all ingredients until smooth in a blender. Serves 1.

Creamy Orange Shake

Taste like Orange Julius®

⅓   cup frozen orange juice concentrate
½   cup milk
¼   cup sugar
½   cup water
½   tsp. vanilla
5-6 Ice cubes
2   scoops vanilla ice cream (optional)

Combine ingredients in blender until smooth. Can be kept in the refrigerator up to 1 day. Serves 4.

✦ **Use small juice glasses. ½ cup of juice is one serving of fruit.**

Smoothies

2   cups milk or 1 cup milk and 1 cup yogurt
1   cup ice cubes
3   Tbsp. sugar
1   tsp. vanilla

In a blender combine all ingredients and blend until smooth.
Makes 2 smoothies.

You can make any combination of the following for your smoothies. When using juices replace juice for milk in recipe.

+ top off any smoothie with ginger ale or sparkling water.
+ strawberries, blueberries, peaches and a sprig of mint
+ strawberries, blueberries, raspberries and blackberries
+ strawberries, raspberries and banana
+ orange juice, pineapple juice, banana
+ crushed pineapple, $\frac{1}{4}$ tsp. coconut flavoring
+ apple juice, coconut and $\frac{1}{4}$ tsp. grated ginger
+ banana and 2 Tbsp. peanut butter
+ banana, strawberries, 2 Tbsp. chocolate syrup
+ strawberries, banana, peaches and apple
+ mixed berries and peaches or pears
+ bananas and kiwi fruit
+ watermelon
+ cantaloupe
+ peaches and $\frac{1}{4}$ tsp. cinnamon
+ $\frac{1}{4}$ cup mint extract, $\frac{1}{4}$ cup chocolate syrup
+ 4 tsp. malted milk powder
+ $\frac{1}{4}$ cup chocolate syrup
+ $\frac{1}{3}$ cup unsweetened grape juice
+ $\frac{1}{4}$ cup chocolate syrup and $\frac{1}{4}$ cup coffee (don't use with fruit)

Smoothies
(Continued)

Other add ins:

+ ¼ cup oatmeal
+ 1 Tbsp. wheat germ
+ ¼ cup bran cereal
+ flaxseed oil
+ bee pollen
+ breakfast powder
+ protein powder
+ powdered milk
+ cocoa mix
+ instant coffee
+ instant pudding mix
+ powdered soft drink mix
+ 2 Tbsp. fruit juice concentrate
+ cinnamon
+ nutmeg
+ any flavorings such as cherry, strawberry, peppermint etc.
+ whipped cream

Banana Milkshake

3   bananas, frozen
4   cups milk
1   tsp. vanilla
¼   cup sugar
6   crushed ice cubes

Place all the ingredients in a blender and process until smooth. Serve immediately. Serves 4.

Other stir-ins
✦ cocoa powder
✦ jams or jellies
✦ coconut
✦ other fruits

Fruit Slush

6   cups water
4   cups sugar
5   bananas, mashed
1   (46 ounce) can pineapple juice
1   (6 ounce) small can frozen
     lemon juice
1   (6 ounce) small can frozen
     orange juice

Bring water and sugar to a boil. Boil 3-5 minutes. Cool. Add all the other ingredients to the water and sugar mixture. Freeze overnight. Put a scoop in a glass and pour lemon-lime soda on top. Serves 50.

David's Punch

1   qt. cranberry juice
2   lemons, squeezed, or 2 ounces lemon juice
1   pint orange juice
4   qts. ginger ale

Combine juices and chill. Pour into a punch bowl over a block of ice and add ginger ale. Garnish glasses with mint sprigs. Orange sherbet scoops may be added.

When making punch for a party freeze part of it in a mold. Float the block of frozen punch in the punch bowl. This prevents diluting. Makes 44 servings.

✦ **Store lemons in a sealed jar of water. You will be able to get more juice out of them**

✦ **Combine 2 cups of flat soda with 1 package of unflavored gelatin to make a great flavored gelatin. This is particularly good with root beer, orange and grape sodas.**

Chocolate Soda

2   Tbsp. chocolate syrup
½   cup club soda
1-2 large scoops vanilla ice cream

Mix syrup and club soda in a tall glass. Add ice cream. Pour in more soda. Stir to blend and serve at once. Serves 1.

Cherry Syrup

1   pkg. cherry-flavored drink mix
1½   cups water
½   cup sugar

Stir ingredients together until sugar is dissolved. Keep refrigerated. Add 2 to 3 tablespoons to your favorite glass of soda. Works especially well for lemon-lime soda and colas. Makes 2 cups.

Daily Prayer

O God, help me to keep my big mouth shut until I know what I am talking about.

Breakfast

Early to bed and early to rise makes a man healthy,
wealthy and good at making his own breakfast.

Breakfast Tips

✦ **Add a pinch of salt** to your oatmeal, cream of wheat, grits and cracked wheat. It will bring out the sweetness of the sugar, so you use less.

✦ **Spread some peanut butter and honey** or corn syrup on a pancake and roll up for a snack. This is great for **leftover pancakes.**

✦ **Mix all the dry ingredients for pancakes** and muffins the night before. Mix all the wet ingredients and keep in the refrigerator. Then simply mix the two in the morning.

✦ Make a **double or triple batch of pancakes,** waffles or French toast on the weekend and freeze the leftovers. Put them in the toaster and they are ready to eat!

✦ **Mix cinnamon and sugar together** and keep in a shaker bottle. This works great for toast or when making cinnamon bread. An old spice bottle works great.

✦ **Compare the price of breakfast cereals by servings or portions and not by the ounce.** Cold cereal may be cheaper than oatmeal by the ounce but if you eat more per serving then it may actually cost more.

✦ **Whip a teaspoon of mayo into eggs BEFORE scrambling** them. They don't dry out that way (it's hard to overcook eggs with a spoonful of mayo in them). They are very tasty. Use about a spoonful per 2 medium eggs. I've had people say "yuck!" to this, until they tried it.

✦ **If muffins brown around the outside before the centers are cooked,** try partly filling one section of the muffin pan with water. The extra steam will keep the edges from cooking.

✦ Use a **meat baster to "squeeze" your pancake batter** onto the hot griddle. You'll have perfectly shaped pancakes every time.

✦ **Teach kids to like oatmeal** and cream of wheat.

Overnight Refrigerator Pancakes

1	pkg. yeast
¼	cup warm water (110°–115°)
2	Tbsp. sugar
4	cups flour
2	Tbsp. baking powder
2	tsp. baking soda
1	tsp. salt
6	large eggs
4	cups (1 qt.) buttermilk
¼	cup vegetable oil

Combine yeast, water and sugar. Let stand 5 minutes. Combine remaining dry ingredients in a large bowl. Combine eggs, buttermilk and oil. Make a well in the center of the dry ingredients. Pour in egg mixture, stirring just until moistened. Stir in yeast mixture. Cover and refrigerate overnight. When ready to use mix batter well. Can be stored 1 week in refrigerator. The recipe can be cut in half. Makes 36 medium pancakes.

✦ **Lightly salt melons to bring out their sweetness.**

✦ **If you need to measure 1 cup of shortening, fill a 2-cup measuring cup with 1 cup of water. Then spoon in shortening until the water level reaches 2 cups. Pour off water and you have exactly 1 cup of shortening.**

✦ **Mix prepared pancake batter in a pitcher. Pour batter directly from the pitcher into the skillet for no drips or mess. Cover and refrigerate extra batter to use later.**

Mom's Buttermilk Pancakes

2   eggs
½   tsp. salt
¼   cup sugar
2   cups buttermilk
½   tsp. soda
1½ tsp. baking powder
2   cups flour

In a bowl, mix first 3 ingredients together. Stir soda into buttermilk in a measuring cup. Add to bowl. Lightly stir in baking powder and flour, just enough to moisten dry ingredients. Mixture will be thick and lumpy. Heat a griddle or frying pan over medium heat and lightly grease. Cook on a hot greased griddle. Flip when bubbles break on the surface and the edges begin to dry.

Makes 18-20 medium pancakes.

Stir any of the following into pancakes or for an added treat or for more nutrition:

✦ blueberries or chopped apples
✦ bacon
✦ nuts
✦ grated cheese
✦ cinnamon
✦ chocolate chips
✦ corn meal, wheat or soy flour, in place of equal amount flour

✦ **For lump free pancakes or waffles, mix all ingredients in a blender, then pour batter onto the griddle or waffle iron.**

Pancakes

2   eggs
2   cups flour, all-purpose or wheat
1½   cups milk
2   Tbsp. sugar
¼   cup vegetable oil
5   tsp. baking powder
¼   tsp. salt

In a boowl, mix ingredients just enough to moisten dry ingredients. Mixture will be thick and lumpy. Heat a griddle or frying pan over medium heat and lighly grease. Cook on a hot greased griddle. Flip when buble break on the surface and the edges begin to dry. Makes 15-18 pancakes.

Waffles

2   eggs
2   cups flour or wheat flour
2   Tbsp. sugar
½   cup vegetable oil, margarine or butter, molted
4   tsp. baking powder
¼   tsp. salt
1⅔   cups milk

Heat waffle iron. Beat eggs in a medium bowl until fluffy. Beat in remaining ingredients just until smooth. Do not over mix. Pour batter onto center of hot waffle iron. Bake 5 minutes or until steaming stops. Remove carefully.

Makes twelve 4 inch waffles.

Baking Mix

9   cups flour
2/3   cup dry milk
3   Tbsp. baking powder
2   tsp. salt
1   cup shortening or ½ shortening and ½ butter*

Mix flour and other dry ingredients. Cut in shortening. Use a mixer on low to cut in the shortening to save time. Store in an airtight container up to 6 months.

This recipes uses a 5-pound sack of flour when doubled.

*Refrigerate if using butter.

Baking Mix Pancakes

2¼   cups baking mix (see above)
¼   cup sugar
1   egg
1½   cups water
2   Tbsp. vegetable oil

Mix ingredients until moist. The batter should be lumpy. Cook on a hot greased griddle. Flip when bubbles break on the surface and the edges begin to dry.

Makes 15-18 medium pancakes.

Baking Mix Biscuits

2¼ cups baking mix (p.50)
⅔   cup water or milk

Mix lightly until dough forms a ball. Turn onto a lightly floured surface. Knead 10-12 times. Roll dough about ½ inch thick. Cut with a 2-inch cutter or the rim of a glass dipped in flour. Bake at 450° for 10-12 minutes on an ungreased cookie sheet. For drop biscuits, use 1 cup water and drop by tablespoonfuls onto a baking sheet. Makes one dozen.

*For cheese biscuits, add ¼ cup Cheddar cheese.

Baking Mix Muffins

2¼ cup baking mix (p.50)
¼   cup sugar
1   egg
¾   cup water
⅓   cup vegetable oil

Mix dry baking mix and sugar. Add egg, water and vegetable oil to dry ingredients. Mix only enough to moisten flour. The batter will be lumpy. Fill greased muffin tins two-thirds full. Bake at 400° for 20 minutes.

*For an added surprise fill muffin cup halfway and then add a spoonful of jelly. Top with more batter. Add raisins, cinnamon or nuts for gourmet muffins. Makes 12-15 muffins.

✦ **Use the ring from a canning jar if you don't have a biscuit cutter or cookie cutter.**

Breakfast Puffs

2   cups baking mix (p.50)
¼   cup sugar
¼   tsp. nutmeg
2   Tbsp. butter or margarine, softened
½   cup milk
1   egg
½   cup butter or margarine, melted

Topping

⅔   cup sugar
1   tsp. ground cinnamon

Heat oven to 400°. Grease 24 mini muffin cups. Mix baking mix, sugar, nutmeg, margarine, milk and egg. Beat vigorously for 30 seconds. Fill muffin cups about ⅔ full. Bake 10 minutes. Mix sugar and cinnamon in a bowl. Quickly roll the puffs in melted margarine, then in the cinnamon and sugar mixture. Makes 24 puffs.

Overnight Bubble Bread

1   pkg. frozen rolls or 1 batch basic bread dough (p.71)
1   cup nuts (optional)
½   cup margarine, melted
1   cup sugar
1   Tbsp. cinnamon

If using frozen rolls, thaw rolls for 15 minutes. Mix sugar and cinnamon. Dip rolls in margarine and sugar mix. Sprinkle ½ cup nuts in bottom of a greased bundt pan. Layer rolls, nuts, rolls, etc. Pour remainder of sugar mix and margarine over rolls. Let rise in the refrigerator over night. Bake 350° for 25 minutes. When done, invert onto a plate or serving platter. Serves 6-8.

Butterfly Ring

2½ cups baking mix (p.50)
1 Tbsp. sugar
1 egg, beaten
⅔ cup milk
¼ cup butter, room temperature

Grease a jellyroll sheet and preheat over to 375°. Mix first four ingredients until well blended. Dough will be sticky. Knead on a lightly floured surface 18 times. Roll out into an 11×14 inch rectangle. Spread butter on the dough, then the filling on the dough. Serves 12.

Filling:

2 Tbsp. butter, melted
½ cup sugar
¾ cup nuts (optional)
¼ cup cherry jelly (raspberry, strawberry or any other jam or jelly will work)
¼ tsp. cinnamon
1 Tbsp. flour

Add the ingredients to the melted butter. Blend until smooth. If necessary, heat jelly 30 seconds in the microwave if you need to make it smooth. Spread filling onto dough. Roll the dough lengthwise, like a jelly roll and seal the edges by pinching them together. Form into a circle on the jellyroll pan. Cut 4 to 5 slits in the top to release steam. Bake for 20 minutes. Cool and frost with butter cream frosting (p.241).

Mike's Baking Powder Biscuits

2   cups flour
2½   tsp. baking powder
1   tsp. salt
5   Tbsp. margarine
1   scant cup milk

Mix flour, baking powder and salt in a bowl. Cut in margarine with a fork or pastry blender until it resembles cornmeal. Add milk, stirring enough to combine ingredients. Do not over stir. Put dough on a lightly floured surface and gather into a ball. If the dough is sticky add a little flour to help form the ball. Knead lightly 5-10 times. Roll out ½ inch thick and cut with a biscuit cutter or a glass rim that has been dipped in flour. Put onto an ungreased cookie sheet and bake at 425° for 15-20 minutes or until golden brown. Makes 10-12 biscuits.

Drop Biscuits

2   cups flour
1   Tbsp. baking powder
½   tsp. salt
1   cup milk
¼   cup shortening

Mix ingredients together. Batter will be lumpy. Drop by spoonfuls onto an ungreased baking sheet. Bake at 450° for 10-12 minutes. Makes 10-12 biscuits.

✦ **To make biscuits in a hurry, pat or roll the dough into a rectangle and cut out square biscuits with a pizza cutter. This way the dough only needs to be rolled out once.**

French Toast

1½	cups milk
1	Tbsp. sugar
½	tsp. vanilla
¼	salt
½	tsp. cinnamon
1	egg, slightly beaten
10-12	slices day-old bread

Put egg in a shallow dish and beat. Mix in milk, sugar, vanilla, salt and cinnamon. Heat griddle over medium heat and grease. Dip bread slices into egg mixture and cook on each side until golden brown. Serve with syrup or powdered sugar and butter. If you don't have day-old bread, lightly toast the bread and then dip in the batter so it doesn't get soggy. Tastes great fried in bacon grease. Makes 10-12 slices.

French Toast Sticks

After cooking french toast cut each piece into 4 strips. Kids love to dip these in syrup.

Banana French Toast

In a blender combine all the ingredients except bread for french toast with 1 ripe banana. Blend until smooth. Use as you would regular french toast batter.

✦ **Put powdered sugar in a spice bottle to sprinkle on cakes and French toast.**

Basic Muffins

2   cups flour
¼   cup sugar
1   Tbsp. baking powder
½   tsp. salt
1   egg, beaten
1   cup milk
¼   cup oil

Mix ingredients together; batter will be lumpy. Spoon into greased muffin cups ⅔ full. Bake 425° for 20-25 minutes. Makes 12-15 muffins.

Mom's Sweet Muffins

1   egg
½   cup buttermilk
¼   cup vegetable oil
1½   cups flour
½   cup sugar
1½   tsp. baking powder
½   tsp. salt
½   tsp. soda

Mix all the ingredients in a bowl. The batter will be slightly lumpy. Place in greased muffin tins ⅔ full and bake at 400° for 15-20 minutes. Makes 1 dozen.

Jam Muffins

Basic muffin mix (p.56)
6   Tbsp. jam

Prepare basic muffin mix according to recipe.

Fill greased muffin cups ¼ full. Place 1 teaspoon jam on top of batter and fill with more batter until muffin cup is ⅔ full.

Amish Bran Muffins

5   cups flour
5   tsp. baking soda
2   tsp. salt
2   tsp. allspice
3   cups sugar
4   eggs
1   cup oil
2   tsp. vanilla
4   cups (1 qt.) buttermilk
1   (20 ounce) box raisin bran flakes

Mix together; batter will be lumpy. Fill muffin cups ⅔ full or tin and bake at 375° for 20 minutes. Batter can be kept refrigerated for up to 6 weeks. Because these muffins include cereal as an ingredient, you should buy cereal on sale, use coupons or buy generic to keep it inexpensive. I included it because it keeps in the refrigerator a long time so it is great if you are short on time. Makes 30-35 muffins.

Oatmeal Muffins

1   cup quick oats
1   cup buttermilk
1   egg
½   cup brown sugar, packed
½   cup vegetable oil
1   cup flour
1   tsp. baking powder
½   tsp. salt
½   tsp. baking soda
½   tsp. cinnamon (optional)
1   cup raisins (optional)

Mix all ingredients; batter will be lumpy. Spoon batter into greased muffin tins ⅔ full. Bake at 400° for 15-20 minutes. Makes 1 dozen.

Buttermilk Muffins

1   cup butter or margarine
1   cup sugar
2   eggs
1   tsp. soda
1   cup buttermilk
2   cups flour, sifted

Cream butter and sugar. Add eggs and beat well. Stir soda into buttermilk and add alternately with flour to batter mixture. Fill lined or greased muffin tins ⅔ full and bake at 400° for 20-25 minutes. Remove from pan immediately. Makes 12-15 muffins.

Cinnamon Muffins

1½ cups flour
¾   cup sugar
2   tsp. baking powder
¼   tsp. salt
½   cup milk
1   egg, beaten
⅓   cup butter or margarine, melted

Topping

⅓   cup butter, melted
1   tsp. cinnamon
½   cup sugar

Mix flour, sugar, baking powder and salt. Add milk, egg, and ⅓ cup melted butter. Mix well. Fill greased muffin tins ⅔ full and bake at 400° for 20 minutes. Remove while still hot. Dip in melted butter, then in mixture of sugar and cinnamon. Makes 12-15 muffins.

The best sellers in many bookstores
are Cookbooks and Diet Books.
One tells you how to prepare your food...
the other tells you how not to eat it.!

Raised Donuts

1   pkg. or 1 Tbsp. yeast
1/4   cup water, lukewarm
3/4   cup milk, scalded
4-5   cups flour
3/4   cup sugar
2   eggs, well beaten
2   tsp. lemon rind (optional)
1/2   cup shortening, melted
3/4   tsp. nutmeg
1/2   tsp. salt
      vegetable oil for frying

Dissolve yeast in water. Add cooled milk. Add 1/2 cup flour and 2 tablespoons sugar. Beat until smooth. Let rise 1/2 hour. Add eggs, lemon rind, shortening, flour, sugar, nutmeg and salt. Beat 4 or 5 minutes with mixer. Gently knead with a small amount of flour Let rise 1 hour. Roll 1/2-inch thick and cut with a biscuit cutter. Let rise 1 hour. Fry in hot vegetable oil until golden brown on each side. Frost with chocolate frosting, or coat with powdered sugar or cinnamon and sugar. Makes 2 dozen.

Formal education
will make you a living
Self-education
will make you a fortune.

Refrigerator Donuts

1   can refrigerator biscuits
     oil for frying
1   cup powdered sugar
or
1   cup granulated sugar and 1 tsp. cinnamon

Punch a hole in the center of each biscuit. Fry in hot oil until donut puffs and is golden brown. Turn and fry the other side. Drain on a paper towel. In a paper sack, put about 1 cup of powdered sugar or 1 cup granulated sugar and 1 teaspoon cinnamon. Drop donuts into bag and toss until coated. Serve warm. Makes 10 donuts.

*A 1-inch-diameter piece of clean metal pipe cut down to 3 inches is a good donut hole punch.

* The powdered sugar or cinnamon and sugar may be saved to use again.

Cinnamon Biscuits

1   can refrigerator biscuits
¼   margarine, melted
1   tsp. cinnamon
½   cup sugar

In a bowl, mix cinnamon and sugar. Dip each biscuit into margarine. Dip into cinnamon mixture until coated on both sides. Place in an 8×8 pan. When all the biscuits are in the pan, pour the leftover margarine on top. Bake at 375° for 10-12 minutes. Serve warm. Makes 10 biscuits.

Egg Brunch

2½ cups milk
8 eggs
1 (10¾ ounce) can cream of mushroom soup
¾ lb. Cheddar cheese, shredded
12 slices bread
1 (16 ounce) pkg. sausage, bacon or ham, cooked

Whisk eggs and milk together. Add cream of mushroom soup. Layer bread in the bottom of a greased 9×13 pan. The bread will overlap slightly. Then add meat and top with cheese. Pour egg mixture on top and refrigerate overnight. Bake uncovered at 350° for 45 minutes. Serves 18.

Scrambled Eggs

8 eggs
1 tsp. salt
¼ tsp. pepper
4 Tbsp. milk or water (optional)
4 tsp. margarine or bacon drippings

Stir all the ingredients except margarine in a bowl until well blended. Heat a skillet on medium heat. Add margarine. Pour egg mixture into skillet. Stir constantly about 4 minutes until eggs are fluffy and set. Serves 4.

✦ **To test eggs for freshness: Place in a glass of cold water; if they float, do not use them.**

Poached Eggs

4   eggs
    water

In a large saucepan, heat water to boiling. Reduce to a simmer. Break each egg into a cup. Hold cup over the water and slip the egg into the water. Cook 3 minutes until whites are set. Remove eggs with slotted spoon and allow to drain briefly. Serve on buttered toast or English muffins. Serves 4.

Golden Morning Sunshine

2   cups white sauce (p.143)
4   eggs, hard boiled and chopped

Make white sauce. Once the white sauce has thickened, add eggs. Serve on toast. Serves 4-8.

✦ **Save your bacon grease: use it for frying eggs, flavoring corn bread, muffins or for greasing pans.**

✦ **When frying bacon, sprinkle a little sugar in the skillet. Your bacon won't stick to the pan.**

Broiled Grapefruit

2   grapefruit
2   Tbsp. brown sugar
½   tsp. cinnamon
1   Tbsp. margarine

Cut grapefruit in half. Mix cinnamon and brown sugar and sprinkle a little on each grapefruit. Dot a little bit of margarine on top of the brown sugar and margarine. Broil 10 minutes. Serve warm. Serves 4.

Cantaloupe Balls

1   cantaloupe
¼ -½ cup sugar
¼ -½ cup corn syrup

Halve and seed cantaloupe. Then scoop out the flesh with a melon baller or cut into chunks. Add corn syrup and sugar, to taste. Let sit in the refrigerator overnight. Serves 4-6.

Applesauce

5   lbs. apples, peeled, cored and chopped
2   cups water
1½ cups sugar
¼   tsp. each salt, cloves, nutmeg
½   tsp. cinnamon
1   tsp. vanilla

Mix everything in a saucepan and boil until apples are tender. Add vanilla. Serve warm or chilled. Serves 8.

Rice Cereal

2	cups leftover rice
1/2	tsp. cinnamon
2	Tbsp. sugar
2	cups milk
1	tsp. butter or margarine

Combine all the ingredients in a saucepan. Cook on medium heat until warmed but not boiling. You can adjust the cinnamon and sugar to your taste. This can also be microwaved very easily. Serves 4

Oatmeal Ideas

Cook oatmeal according to instruction on package

Stir any of the following into oatmeal:

+ sugar
+ applesauce
+ cinnamon and sugar
+ chopped fruit
+ brown sugar
+ dried apples
+ margarine
+ raisins
+ molasses
+ berries
+ maple syrup

+ bananas
+ jam or jelly
+ chopped peaches
+ plain or fruit yogurt
+ wheat germ
+ honey
+ dark brown sugar and 1 drop of maple extract makes oatmeal taste just like the store bought instant oatmeal

+ **Melt peanut butter in hot oatmeal and top with chocolate chips**
+ **Present oatmeal in a fancy glass such as a sundae dish. Sprinkle granola, fruit, honey, brown sugar or nuts on top.**

Granola

3/4	cup brown sugar
1/3	cup vegetable oil
1/3	cup honey
5	cups oatmeal
1/2	cup dry milk
3/4	tsp. cinnamon
	pinch of salt
1/2	cup raisins

Mix brown sugar, oil and honey in a saucepan. Bring to a boil and heat until the sugar is dissolved. Combine dry ingredients in a large cake pan. Pour syrup over dry mixture and mix well. Bake at 375° for 10 minutes. Stir occasionally. Let cool in pan. Add raisins and stir. Store in an airtight container. You can also add wheat germ, coconut, nuts, dates and other dried fruit but this will increase the cost of the granola. Makes 5 cups.

Recipes reprinted with permission from The Complete Tightwad Gazette by Amy Dacyczyn.

Homemade Grape Nuts®

3	cups whole wheat flour
1/2	cup wheat germ
1	cup brown sugar or 3/4 cup corn syrup
2	cups buttermilk or sour milk
1	tsp. soda
	pinch salt

Combine all the ingredients in a mixing bowl and beat until smooth. Spread dough on 2 large cookie sheets. Bake at 350° for 25-30 minutes. Crumble by breaking into chunks while still warm and then grating or briefly chopping in the blender or food processor one cupful at a time. Crisp in the oven at 250° for 20-30 minutes. Store in an airtight container. Makes 2½ pounds.

Maple Syrup

1   cup water
2   cups sugar
¼   tsp. maple flavoring

Stir ingredients together. Bring to a boil. Simmer for 2-3 minutes, and cool. Pour into serving container. Makes 1 pint.

Grandma's Maple Syrup

1   cup brown sugar, packed
¼   tsp. maple flavoring (vanilla may be substituted)
½   cup water

Stir ingredients together. Bring to a boil. Simmer for 2-3 minutes, and cool. Pour into serving container. Makes 1 cup.

A. Jamie Syrup

2   cups water
1   cup granulated sugar
2   cups dark corn syrup
¼   tsp. salt
1   tsp. maple flavoring

Combine the first four ingredients in a saucepan over medium heat. Stir occasionally, until the mixture comes to a full boil. Boil for 7 minutes. Remove the syrup from the heat and let it cool for 15 minutes. Stir in the maple flavoring. When completely cool, transfer the syrup to a covered plastic or glass container. Makes 1 quart.

Honey Syrup

½   cup water
1   cup honey
1   tsp. vanilla

Heat water in a saucepan over medium heat. Add honey just before boiling. Stir well until combined- do not boil. Remove from
heat and stir in vanilla. Store covered in the refrigerator. Honey
can be used straight from the jar on pancakes however this
syrup pours nicely and dilutes the overwhelming sweetness of
honey. Makes 1 cup.

Fruit-Flavored Syrup

2   cups water
¾   cup sugar
1   pkg. flavored drink mix (strawberry or cherry are great)
2   Tbsp. cornstarch

Mix ingredients and bring to a boil while stirring. Boil several
minutes to thicken. Pour into a pitcher and serve hot. Makes 2
cups.

Can be used to flavor milk or over pancakes and waffles.

✦ **When you need to measure honey, first oil the measuring
cup. The honey will pour out easily**

Breads

Man cannot live by bread alone...he needs
peanut butter and jelly to go with it.

Bread Tips

✦ **Buy yeast in bulk.** Split it with a friend. Buying in bulk uses less packaging which is less expensive and better for the environment. Yeast is approximately $2.70 a pound bulk compared to $25.00 a pound buying the little packets. If you don't have someone to split it with buy bulk anyway. Even if half is wasted it is still less expensive than the small packets. Extra yeast may be frozen for longer storage.

✦ **When cutting bread,** freeze the crumbs in a freezer bag. Use when a recipe calls for bread crumbs.

✦ **Save and freeze dried bread slices and heels.** When you need bread crumbs, grind them in the blender or food processor. Toss with seasonings and melted margarine, or use in stuffing, croutons, or bread pudding.

✦ **Buy bread at the day-old bread store** and freeze all of it even if you plan to use it in just a few days.

✦ **When you are baking** something in the oven and you are using a burner on the range at the same time, use the burner that has the vent for the oven. The heat from the oven will cause the burner to use less energy, thus saving money.

✦ **Use powdered milk for baking.** Pour some in a small container and leave in your "baking center" with the rest of your baking supplies.

✦ **To check and see if the baking powder** in your pantry is still active, stir one teaspoon into one-third cup hot water. There should be immediate vigorous bubbling. If no bubbling occurs or bubbling is sporadic, the baking powder is past its prime.

✦ **Use a cutting board with a no-slip pad** underneath to knead bread.

✦ **To glaze bread:** For a dark, shiny glaze, brush on one beaten egg yolk and bake as usual.

✦ **For a shine but no color,** brush on one egg white mixed with one tablespoon water.

Basic Bread Dough

1   cup warm water (110°-115°)
1   pkg. or 1 Tbsp. yeast
½   cup sugar
1   tsp. salt
¼   cup oil or margarine (melted)
1   cup water or milk
6-7 cups flour

Combine water and yeast until yeast dissolves. Add sugar, salt, oil, and water. Stir in flour. Knead on floured surface until smooth. Let rise until double in size. Form into desired shape, place in greased loaf pans. Bake at 350° 20-30 minutes until loaves are golden brown and hollow-sounding when tapped. Remove from pan and cool. Makes 2 loaves.

*This dough can be used for bread, pizza crust, cinnamon rolls, dinner rolls, etc.

Cinnamon Bread

¼   cup sugar
2   tsp. cinnamon
¼   cup margarine, softened

Mix sugar and cinnamon together. Spread each dough rectangle with margarine and ½ the cinnamon mixture before rolling. Raisins may be added for Cinnamon Raisin Bread.

Herbed Bread

Add 6 tablespoons fresh herbs right before the second addition of flour. Chives, sage and thyme work well.

Herbed Cheese Bread

Add ½ cup shredded cheese and 6 tablespoons fresh herbs.

French Bread

1	pkg. or 1 Tbsp. yeast
1	Tbsp. sugar or honey
1	cup warm water (110°-115°)
2	Tbsp. olive or vegetable oil
1	tsp. salt
3-3½	cups flour
1	egg, beaten
2	Tbsp. milk

In a bowl, dissolve yeast and sugar in warm water. Add oil and salt and enough flour to make a stiff dough. Knead 10 minutes on a floured board. Place in a greased bowl, turning once. Let rise until doubled about 1½ -2 hours. Punch down and let rest 15 minutes. Divide dough in half. Roll each half on a floured surface into a 15-inch long log. Place on greased cookie sheets sprinkled with cornmeal and make 5 slashes diagonally across tops. Mix egg and milk and brush on top. Let rise until double about 1 hour. Bake at 375° for 25 minutes or until loaves are golden brown and sound hollow when tapped. Makes 2 loaves.

Garlic Bread

Spread garlic butter (p.323) onto bread or French bread and then broil until golden brown. If using French bread loaf, cut the loaf of bread in half lengthwise. Spread garlic butter onto both halves and wrap in aluminum foil. Bake at 375° for 15 minutes until heated through. Slice before serving.

Whole Wheat Bread

3	cups whole wheat flour
1/3	cup honey
1	Tbsp. salt
1/4	cup shortening
2	pkgs. or 2 Tbsp. yeast
2 1/4	cups warm water (120°-130°)
3-4	cups all-purpose flour
3	Tbsp. margarine, melted

Mix whole wheat flour, honey, salt, shortening and yeast in a large bowl. Add warm water. Beat with a mixer 3 minutes, scraping bowl frequently. Beat on medium speed for 1 minute, stirring frequently. Stir in enough all-purpose flour to make dough easy to handle. Turn dough onto lightly floured surface. Knead until smooth (10 minutes). Place in a greased bowl. Turn dough to grease other side of dough. Cover and let rise in a warm place until double (45 minutes). Grease 2 loaf pans.

Punch down dough and divide in half. Flatten dough for each loaf into a rectangle with your hands or a rolling pin. Roll dough tightly starting from the narrow end. Place dough with seam side down in the pans. Brush lightly with margarine. Let rise until double (about 30 minutes). Place in oven at 375° and bake for 40-45 minutes or until loaves are golden brown and hollow-sounding when tapped. Remove from pans and cool. Makes 2 loaves.

Round Herb Bread

2   pkgs. or 2 Tbsp. yeast
½   cup warm water (110°-115°)
3   Tbsp. cooking oil
½   cup onion, chopped or 2 Tbsp. instant onion flakes
1⅔ cup (1 can) evaporated milk or
     1½ cup milk plus ½ cup dry milk powder
½   cup parsley, chopped
3   Tbsp. sugar
1   tsp. salt
½   tsp. dill, dried
¼   tsp. thyme
1   cup cornmeal
4½ cups whole wheat flour

Dissolve yeast in warm water. Saute onion in oil until tender. In a bowl mix onion, evaporated milk, parsley, sugar, salt, dill, and thyme. Add yeast mixture and beat in cornmeal and 2 cups whole wheat flour. Stir in 2½ cups flour by hand. Turn out onto a lightly floured board. Knead 5 minutes. Place in greased bowl, turning once. Cover and let rise until double (about 1 hour). Punch down and divide in half. Make round loaves out of dough. Place on a greased cookie sheet. Cover and let rise until double, 30-45 minutes. Bake at 350° for 45 minutes. Cover bread loosely with foil if it becomes too brown. Makes 1 loaf.

Dinner rolls bake a lot faster
when the oven is on.

Ninety-Minute Rolls

2-2½ cups flour
½   tsp. salt
2   Tbsp. sugar
1   pkg. or 1 Tbsp. yeast
½   cup milk
¼   cup water
2   Tbsp. margarine

Mix ¾ cup flour, sugar, yeast, and salt. Heat milk, water and margarine until very warm (120°-130°). Add to dry ingredients and beat 2 minutes on medium speed. Add ¼ cup flour. Beat 2 minutes on high. Stir in enough flour to make a stiff dough. Knead 2-3 minutes. Place in greased bowl and let rise 15 minutes. Divide dough into 12 pieces and shape into balls. Place in 8-inch round cake pan. Let rise 15 minutes. Bake at 375° for 20-25 minutes. Makes 12 rolls.

Cinnamon Rolls

To make cinnamon rolls: Roll dough out after rising the first time and spread with 2 tablespoons margarine. Combine 1 teaspoon cinnamon and ¼ cup sugar and sprinkle on dough. Roll jelly-roll style and cut into 1 inch pieces. Place In pan and bake as above.

✦ **Reuse aluminum foil. To store: flatten and save in a file folder.**

Cinnamon Rolls

2   pkgs. or 2 Tbsp. yeast
1   Tbsp. granulated sugar
1   tsp. salt
1   cup warm water (110°-115°)
1   cup milk
6   Tbsp. margarine
½   cup granulated sugar
3   eggs, well beaten
7   cups flour, sifted

Filling

2   Tbsp. margarine
½   cup brown sugar, packed
½   cup raisins (optional)
1   Tbsp. cinnamon

Dissolve yeast, 1 Tbsp. granulated sugar and salt in water. Scald milk and add 6 Tbsp. margarine and ½ cup granulated sugar. Cool. Add eggs. Add 2 cups flour to the yeast mixture. Beat until smooth. Add the milk mixture to the batter and stir in remaining flour. Knead to make a smooth dough and place dough in a greased bowl. Cover and allow to rise to double the bulk. Divide dough into four sections and roll each ½ inch thick. Spread each section with margarine. Sprinkle with brown sugar, cinnamon, and raisins. Roll jelly-roll fashion and cut into ½ inch slices. Place cut side down in two greased 9x13 inch pans. Allow to rise until double (about 1 hour), then bake at 350° until golden brown (about 20-25 minutes). Cool and frost with butter cream frosting (p.241). Makes 2 dozen.

Dinner Rolls

3   heaping Tbsp. shortening
1   Tbsp. salt
½   cup sugar less 1 Tbsp.
1   cup hot water
6   cups flour
1   cup warm water (110°-115°)
2   pkgs. or 2 Tbsp. yeast

Combine shortening, salt, and sugar in large bowl. Pour hot water over mixture and stir until shortening melts. Add enough flour to make a paste. Add 1 cup warm water in which yeast has been dissolved. Mix in remaining flour to form a soft dough. Knead dough well. Place in a bowl and cover with a damp towel; let rise. Punch dough down when doubled and roll to 1/2 inch thickness. Cut with cookie cutter and place on greased pans about 1/2 inch apart. Let rise until doubled. Bake at 400° for 20 minutes or until golden brown. Makes 3 dozen.

Popovers

2   eggs
1   cup flour
1   cup milk
½   tsp. salt

Preheat oven to 450°. Grease 6 custard cups or popover pans well. In a bowl lightly beat eggs. Add remaining ingredients and beat until smooth (do not over beat). Fill cups ½ full and bake 20 minutes. Decrease oven temperature to 350° and bake an additional 20 minutes until golden brown. Remove from cups and serve hot. Makes 6 popovers.

Easy Hamburger Buns

5-6	cups flour
2	pkgs. or 2 Tbsp. yeast
1	cup milk
¾	cup water
½	cup oil
¼	cup sugar
1	Tbsp. salt
	butter or margarine, melted

Stir together 2 cups flour and yeast. In a saucepan over medium, heat milk, water, oil, sugar and salt to very warm (120°-130°). Add liquid all at once to flour mixture. Beat until smooth (about 3 minutes) on medium speed with electric mixer or 300 strokes by hand. Add enough additional flour to make a soft dough; mix well. Let rest 10 minutes. Roll out on well-floured surface to ½ inch thickness. Cut with 3-inch round cutter, coffee can or the rim of a glass. Place rounds on greased baking sheets. Let rise in warm place (80°) for 30 minutes. Preheat oven to 425° and bake 12-15 minutes or until lightly browned. Brush melted margarine or butter on the tops while still warm. Makes 12-15 buns.

✦ **Spread margarine on leftover hamburger and hot dog buns. Broil. Serve with jelly for a different toast. You could also spread with garlic butter and/or Parmesan cheese and broil.**

Buttermilk Yeast Buns

1	pkg. or 1 Tbsp. yeast
1/4	cup warm water (110°-115°)
3	cups buttermilk (room temp.)
1/2	cup sugar
1/2	cup butter or margarine, melted
1	tsp. baking soda
1	tsp. salt
2	eggs
9 1/2-10	cups flour

Sprinkle yeast over warm water in large bowl. Add buttermilk and sugar. Let stand 15 minutes. Add melted butter and eggs. Sift soda, salt and 4 cups flour into the buttermilk mixture. Mix well and add additional flour (about 4 1/2 cups) to make a stiff dough. Knead. Place in a bowl and let rise about 1 hour. Punch down, make into golf ball-sized balls. Place on a greased baking sheet. Flatten slightly with hand. Rise about 30 minutes. Bake at 400° 15-20 minutes. When finished brush the tops with melted butter. Makes 4 dozen rolls.

Half the dough can be made into 24 buns and the other half into 2 loaves of cinnamon bread. Bake the cinnamon bread at 350° for 45 minutes.

✦ **Make roll dough and put into baking pans. Cover and freeze. When you leave for church, leave rolls out at room temperature. When you return they will have risen and be ready to bake for Sunday dinner. Then you have fresh rolls. Do not freeze longer than 3 weeks.**

Crazy Bread

2   pkgs. or 2 Tbsp. yeast
1   cup warm water (110°-115°)
1   cup shortening
¾   cup sugar
1½ tsp. salt
1   cup boiling water
2   eggs, beaten
6   cups flour
1   stick butter, melted

Dissolve yeast in warm water. Mix together shortening, sugar, and salt. Add boiling water and mix well. Add eggs and stir. Add flour and dissolved yeast to shortening mixture, alternately, until well blended. Knead well. Let rise until double in bulk. Roll to ¼ to ½ inch thickness. Cut into various shapes and sizes. Dip in melted butter and place in tube pan until half full; let rise until doubled. Bake at 350° for 35-45 minutes or until brown. After mixing and rising once, dough may be punched down and refrigerated to be used later. Cover with a damp cloth. Do not use regular loaf pans. Makes 1 loaf.

Face powder may catch a man
but
baking powder will keep him!

Butterhorns

1	pkg. or 1 Tbsp. yeast
1/4	cup warm water (110°-115°)
3/4	cup scalded milk
1	tsp. salt
1/4	cup margarine, softened
3-4	Tbsp. sugar
1	egg
3 1/4-4	cups flour
	margarine, melted

Sprinkle yeast in warm water. Let stand 5-10 minutes. Cool milk and stir in next 4 ingredients. Stir yeast and add to milk mix. Add 1/2 cup flour. Beat smooth. Add rest of flour to make a stiff dough. Place in greased bowl, cover, and let rise until double. Turn on floured board and knead until smooth and elastic. Add more flour if needed. Divide into balls the size of a tennis ball. Roll out in a circle and spread with butter. Cut in small pie-shaped pieces and roll up into crescents. Let rise again. Bake at 425° for 15 minutes. Remove from oven and brush with melted margarine. Makes 16 rolls.

Cornbread

2	cups baking mix (p.50)
1/2	cup cornmeal
1/2	cup sugar
1/2	cup butter, melted
1	tsp. baking powder
2	eggs
1	cup milk

Preheat the oven to 350°. In a large bowl, stir all the ingredients together. Blend until smooth. Pour into a greased 8x8 inch baking pan and bake for 30 minutes. Serves 9.

Pretzels

2   cups warm water (110°-115°)
1   pkg. or 1 Tbsp. yeast
½   cup brown sugar
5-6 cups flour
6   cups water
½   tsp. baking soda

Topping

1   large egg
1   Tbsp. water
    coarse salt
    sesame seed
    poppy seed
    Parmesan cheese, grated
    hot mustard sauce (p.312)

Dissolve yeast and brown sugar in warm water. Add flour slowly, stirring until mixture does not stick to the side of the bowl. Knead dough. Make into pretzel shapes, circles or hearts on a lightly floured surface. In a large frying pan place 6 cups water and ½ tsp. baking soda and bring to a boil. Cook each pretzel 1 minute. You have to change the water when it gets full of flour. Lightly beat egg and water and brush on the top of the pretzels. Sprinkle salt, sesame seed, poppy seed or Parmesan cheese on top if desired. Place on a greased baking sheet, salt, and bake at 475° until golden (about 10 minutes). Serve with hot mustard sauce. Makes 16-18 pretzels.

Dessert Pretzels

Brush with butter, sprinkle with cinnamon and sugar

Zwieback

½ cup milk
1 pkg. or 1 Tbsp. yeast
¼ cup sugar
¼ cup butter, melted
¼ tsp. salt
½ tsp. ground cinnamon
⅛-¼ tsp. anise or 1-2 drops anise flavoring
3 eggs
3 cups flour

Scald the milk. Cool to lukewarm. Add yeast and stir until dissolved. Add the sugar, butter, salt, cinnamon, anise, the unbeaten eggs, and enough flour to handle. Knead lightly. Let rise until light. Make into 3-inch oblong rolls. Place on a greased pan in rows, two inches apart. Let rise again and bake at 400° for 20 minutes. When cold, cut into ½ inch slices. Brown evenly in an oven at 400° for 8-10 minutes. You can frost with a vanilla glaze or dust with powdered sugar if desired. Makes 40-50 crackers.

Be careful how you live. You may be the only Bible some people read.

Bagels

2   cups warm water (110°-115°)
2   pkgs. or 2 Tbsp. yeast
3   Tbsp. sugar
3   tsp. salt
5¼   cups flour
3   qts. water
1   Tbsp. sugar
     cornmeal
1   egg yolk
1   Tbsp. water

Combine warm water, yeast and 3 tablespoons sugar. Let stand 5 minutes. Stir in salt. Gradually mix in 2 cups of flour, beat at medium speed for 5 minutes with an electric mixer. Add rest of flour to make a stiff dough. Turn out on a floured board and knead until smooth, elastic, and no longer sticky (about 15 minutes), adding more flour as needed. Dough should be firmer than for most yeast breads. Place in a greased bowl, cover and let rise until almost doubled, (about 45 minutes). Knead dough lightly and divide into 12 equal pieces. To shape, knead each piece, forming it into a smooth ball. Holding ball with both hands, poke your thumbs through the center. With one thumb in hole, work around perimeter, shaping bagel like a doughnut 3 to 3½ inches across. Place shaped bagels on lightly floured board. Cover loosely and let stand in a warm place for 20 minutes. Bring the 3 quarts of water and 1 tablespoon sugar to boiling in large saucepan. Adjust heat to keep it boiling gently. Lightly grease baking sheet and sprinkle with cornmeal. Heat oven to 400°. Gently lift one bagel at a time and drop into water. Boil about 4 bagels at a time, turning often, for 5 minutes. Lift out with slotted spatula. Drain briefly on a towel and place on baking sheet. Brush with glaze made with 1 egg yolk and 1 Tbsp. water. Bake 35-40 minutes or until well browned and crusty. Cool on a wire rack. Makes 12 bagels.

Whole Wheat Bagels

Follow basic recipe but omit sugar and use 3 tablespoons of honey instead. In place of flour, use 2 cups whole wheat flour, ½ cup wheat germ, and about 2¾ cup all-purpose flour, blended together. Knead with white flour.

Onion Bagels

Use the basic recipe but add ½ cup instant toasted onion to the yeast, water and sugar in basic dough.

Poppy Seed Bagels

Sprinkle boiled bagels with poppy seed after using egg wash and before baking.

Sesame Seed Bagels

Sprinkle boiled bagels with sesame seed after using egg wash and before baking.

Blueberry Bagels

Use 1 (16 ounce) can bluberries in light syrup, drained. Reserve 2 Tbsp. juice. Add reserved juice with warm water. Add ½ tsp. ground cinnamon with salt. Mix well. Stir in blueberries with flour.

Croissants

2	pkgs. or 2 Tbsp. yeast
1	cup warm water (110°-115°)
5	cups flour, unsifted, divided
¾	cup evaporated milk
1½	tsp. salt
1	egg
⅓	cup sugar
¼	cup butter, melted
1	cup butter, chilled
1	egg, beaten with 1 Tbsp. water

Sprinkle yeast over warm water in large bowl. Add 2 cups flour, evaporated milk, salt, egg, sugar and melted butter. Beat until smooth. In separate bowl, cut chilled butter into remaining flour until butter particles are the size of peas. Pour yeast batter over the top. Fold in until all flour is moist. Cover bowl with plastic wrap. Chill 3 hours. Dough may be refrigerated up to 5 days.

Work dough as little as possible. Divide in half, keeping other half cool until ready to work. Knead 6-7 times and roll ¼ of the dough into a ¼ inch thick circle on a floured board. Cut dough circle into pie-shaped wedges. Roll each loosely towards point. Place on an ungreased cookie sheet. Cover lightly. Let rise until doubled. When doubled, brush with egg and water mixture. Bake in oven preheated to 400° for 12-15 minutes. Makes 3 dozen.

Pita Bread

1 pkg. or 1 Tbsp. yeast
2 cups warm water (110°-115°)
1 Tbsp. shortening
1 Tbsp. sugar
2 tsp. salt
6-7 cups flour

In a mixing bowl, dissolve yeast in warm water. Blend in shortening. Add sugar, salt and flour. Knead dough until no longer sticky. Add more flour if needed. Place in a greased bowl. Cover and let rise in a warm place 30- 40 minutes. Divide dough into 24 pieces. Work into smooth balls. Let rest 20 minutes. Preheat oven to 450°. Flatten balls. Roll into a 7-inch circle, turning ¼ turn once. *Do not* stretch, puncture or crease. Place on an ungreased cookie sheet. Bake 3-4 minutes until dough puffs. Turn and bake 2 minutes more. Makes 24 rounds.

English Muffin Bread

6 cups flour
2 pkgs. or 2 Tbsp. yeast
2 tsp. salt
1 Tbsp. sugar
¼ tsp. baking soda
2 cups milk
½ cup water
½ cup cornmeal (to coat pan)

Combine 3 cups flour, yeast, salt, sugar and soda in a large mixing bowl. Heat milk and water until very warm (120°). Add dry ingredients and beat well. Stir in the rest of the flour to make a stiff batter. Spoon into two loaf pans that have been well greased and sprinkle the top with cornmeal. Cover and let rise in a warm place for 45 minutes. Bake at 400° for 25 minutes. Remove from pan and cool. Makes 2 loaves.

Potato Flake Starter Bread

Starter

1   pkg. or 1 Tbsp. yeast
1   cup warm water (110°-115°)
½   cup sugar
3   Tbsp. instant potato flakes

Bread

⅓   cup sugar
½   cup oil
1½   cups warm water (110°-115°)
1   Tbsp. salt
1   cup starter
6   cups flour

To make starter:

Mix ingredients in a glass jar or container. Cover loosely and let stand 24 hours at room temperature. Put in the refrigerator for three to five days. On the fourth day, feed it with ½ cup sugar, 3 tablespoons potato flakes and 1 cup water. Stir and keep at room temperature for 24 hours. You will use 1 cup of the starter to make the bread. Store remaining starter in the refrigerator and feed every 4 days. (If you don't make bread, discard 1 cup starter at each feeding.)

Potato Flake Starter Bread
(Continued)

To make bread:

Stir together all the ingredients except flour in a 4-quart mixing bowl. Add flour a little at a time to the other ingredients, mixing well. Knead 5 minutes. Put dough into a large, greased bowl. Turn dough to grease the top. Cover bowl with aluminum foil. Let rise at room temperature overnight for at least 8 hours. Punch dough down. Turn out onto a floured board and knead. Divide into 3 parts and shape into loaves. Put in 3 greased loaf pans. Brush tops with oil. Cover with a paper towel and let rise 4 -5 hours longer. Bake at 350° for 30-40 minutes. Brush with butter and remove from pan. Cool and keep covered. Cinnamon rolls, pizza dough and rolls can also be made with this dough. Makes 3 loaves.

Never be discouraged.
Remember, Noah was an amateur.
The experts built the Titanic.

Hush Puppies

1½ cups cornmeal
½ cup flour
2 tsp. baking powder
½ tsp. salt
1 egg, well beaten
¾ cup milk
1 small onion, grated or 1 tsp. onion powder
    vegetable oil for frying
    dash Tabasco® (optional)

Mix together cornmeal, flour, baking powder, and salt in a bowl.
Mix egg, milk, onion and Tabasco® in another bowl. Combine
with dry ingredients. Drop a teaspoonful at a time into hot oil.
When hush puppies are crisp and golden (about 1 minute),
remove from oil and drain on a paper towel. Serve hot.
Serves 4-6.

Spoon Bread

1 cup cornmeal
1 tsp. salt
2 cups boiling water
1 cup cold milk
4 eggs
5 Tbsp. butter or margarine, melted

Preheat oven to 425°. Combine cornmeal and salt in a bowl and
stir in boiling water until smooth. Let stand several minutes, then
stir in milk. Add the eggs, one at a time, beating well after each
one. Stir in the melted butter last. Pour batter into a hot 2½ quart
baking dish and bake 25-30 minutes. Serve hot with extra butter.
Serves 4-6.

Dumplings

2 cups baking mix (p.52)
⅔ cup milk

Stir until mixed. Drop by spoonfuls into simmering soup. Cook for 10 minutes. Cover and cook for 10 more minutes. *Do not lift the lid.* You can also add herbs, spices or shredded cheese in with the baking mix. This can be used with any soup instead of noodles. Makes 10-12 small dumplings.

Scratch Dumplings

1 cup flour, sifted
1½ tsp. baking powder
½ tsp. salt
2 Tbsp. shortening
⅓ cup milk
1 egg, beaten

Sift together in a bowl flour, baking powder, and salt. Cut in shortening with a pastry blender until mixture is crumbly. Pour in milk and add egg. Mix only until flour is dampened. Dough should be lumpy. Drop by spoonfuls on top of boiling meat or soup. Cover tightly and steam 12 minutes without removing cover. Makes 6 dumplings.

Dessert Dumplings

Add: 3 Tbsp. sugar, 1 tsp. vanilla and substitute margarine or butter for shortening. Great with fruit cobblers. Use on top of pie filling instead of using pie crust.

Parmesan Bread

1   slice bread
     margarine or butter
     Parmesan cheese

Spread a thin layer of margarine on bread and lightly sprinkle with Parmesan cheese. Broil until golden brown. Garlic may be substitute for or used with Parmesan cheese.

Restaurant-Style Breadsticks

1   batch white bread, pre-made but not baked (p.71)
1   Tbsp. dry oregano leaf (rub into a powder between fingers)
     spray vegetable oil
     garlic powder

Grease your fingers with vegetable oil and knead bread dough just until you can shape into cigar-sized pieces. Place these 3" apart on lightly greased cookie sheets. Let rise in a warm place until doubled (about 1½ hours). Then, holding spray vegetable oil about 8" from sticks, lightly spray top of each and then dust with garlic powder and oregano. Bake at 375° 20 to 25 minutes or until golden brown. Cool in pan on rack to serve within a day or two. Makes 1 dozen.

Optional stir-ins might be diced onions, onion flakes, or Parmesan cheese.

Cheddar Puffs

These taste like goldfish crackers!

1   cup Cheddar cheese, shredded
½   cup flour
¼   cup margarine
½   tsp. ground mustard

Combine all ingredients in a bowl and mix well. Roll into 1-inch balls. Place on an ungreased baking sheet 1 inch apart. Bake at 400° for 12-15 minutes until lightly browned. Serve warm. Makes 2 dozen.

Cheddar Muffins

1½   cups milk (if using mashed potatoes omit milk)
¾   cup mashed potato flakes or 2 cups mashed potatoes
1   egg
⅓   cup vegetable oil
1   cup Cheddar cheese, shredded
1⅔   cups flour
3   Tbsp. sugar
2   Tbsp. chives, cut into small pieces
1   Tbsp. parsley, dried
1   Tbsp. baking powder
1   tsp. salt

Bring milk to a boil in a saucepan. Remove from heat and stir in potato flakes. Let stand for 2 minutes. Whip with a fork until smooth and let cool slightly. Into mashed potatoes beat in egg, cheese and oil. Combine remaining ingredients in a separate bowl. Stir into potato mixture just until moistened. Fill greased or lined muffin cups ¾ full. Bake at 400° for 20-25 minutes. Cool for 5 minutes. Remove from pan. Makes 1 dozen.

Onion-Cheese Bread

2   cups flour
1   tsp. salt
1   Tbsp. sugar
3   tsp. baking powder
1   tsp. dry mustard
¼   cup margarine
2   Tbsp. Parmesan cheese
½   cup Cheddar cheese,
       shredded
1   cup milk
1   egg
       paprika
½   cup onion, finely chopped

Combine the first 5 ingredients in a bowl and mix well. Cut in margarine until it is a coarse meal. In seperate bowl combine cheeses, milk and eggs and stir. Add to the flour mixture and mix with a fork just until dry ingredients are moistened. Put into a greased loaf pan and sprinkle onions and paprika over the batter. Bake at 350° for 1 hour. Makes 1 loaf.

Cheese Bread

Use recipe above, simply omit onions.

✦ **Moldy cheese: Trim off the mold and use. It is perfectly safe.**

Garlic-Cheese Biscuits

2   cups flour
2½ tsp. baking powder
1   tsp. salt
1   tsp. garlic powder
2   Tbsp. chives (optional)
¾   cup Cheddar cheese, finely grated (more or less to taste)
4   Tbsp. shortening
1   cup milk or sour milk

Mix flour, baking powder, salt, garlic powder, chives and Cheddar cheese in a bowl. Cut in shortening with a pastry blender or fork until it resembles cornmeal. Add milk, stirring just enough to combine ingredients. Do not over stir. Drop by tablespoonfuls onto an ungreased cookie sheet and bake 450° for 15-20 minutes or until golden brown. Makes 10 biscuits.

✦ **Hard, dry cheese: Grate finely and use as you would any grated cheese. Wrap cheese in a cloth soaked with vinegar to keep it from drying out.**

Crepes

1½ cups flour
1 Tbsp. sugar
½ tsp. baking powder
½ tsp. salt
2 cups milk
2 eggs
½ tsp. vanilla
2 Tbsp. butter or margarine, melted

Toppings

jelly
whipped topping (p.294)

Mix dry ingredients. Stir in remaining ingredients. Beat until smooth. Heat pan as you would for pancakes. For each crepe, pour scant ¼ cup of the batter into skillet. Immediately rotate skillet until thin film covers bottom. Cook until light brown. Turn with a spatula and cook other side until light brown. Spread some of your favorite jelly or fresh fruit on each crepe. Roll and top with whipped topping. Makes 12 crepes.

Flour Tortillas

3   cups flour
1   tsp. salt
½   tsp. baking powder
½   cup shortening
¾   cup warm water

Blend all the ingredients except water until the consistency of oatmeal. Add water and blend with fingers. Knead on a floured board 5 minutes. Cover, let rest ½ hour. Roll into 8 balls. Let rest 45 minutes. Flatten balls until very thin and cook in hot ungreased skillet until each side is slightly browned. Makes 8 tortillas.

Sopapillas

1   pkg. or 1 Tbsp. yeast
¼   cup water
1½   cups milk
3   Tbsp. shortening, melted
1½   tsp. salt
2   Tbsp. sugar
5   cups flour
      oil for frying
½   cup sugar
½   tsp. cinnamon
      honey

Combine ingredients. Knead, about 10 times, until smooth. Cover with a dish towel and let rise 1 hour. Roll dough to ⅛ inch thickness. Cut into squares or triangles. Fry one at a time in hot oil (385° to 400°), turning once until brown. Drain on paper towels. Mix ½ cup sugar with ½ tsp. cinnamon in a bowl. Roll sopapillas in cinnamon and sugar and serve with honey. Make sure your oil is hot enough and the dough is ⅛ inch thick or your sopapillas won't puff. Makes about 20.

Coffee Cake

2   cups flour
2   tsp. baking powder
1   tsp. salt
¾   cup sugar
2   rounded Tbsp. shortening
1   cup milk

In a bowl, mix flour, baking powder, salt, sugar and shortening. Set aside ¾ cup of the mixture for the topping. Add milk to remainder of flour mixture and mix until smooth. Pour batter into an 8x8 inch buttered pan and sprinkle topping over the top. Bake at 350° for 30 minutes. Serves 9.

Topping

2   Tbsp. butter, melted
½   tsp. cinnamon
3   Tbsp. brown sugar

Combine all ingredients for the topping with the flour mixture that was set aside and mix well.

Graham Gems

1 cup sifted flour
¼ tsp. salt
¼ cup brown sugar, packed
3 tsp. baking powder
1 cup whole wheat flour
1 egg
1 cup milk
3 Tbsp. shortening, melted

Mix flour, salt, brown sugar, and baking powder. Stir in whole wheat flour thoroughly. Beat egg in a separate bowl. Add milk and melted shortening. Stir into flour mixture until blended well. Not all the lumps will come out. Pour into a greased muffin tin and bake at 400° for 15-20 minutes or until a toothpick put in the center comes out clean. Serve warm with butter. Makes 1 dozen.

Cinnamon Puff Bread

1 cup water
½ cup butter + 2 Tbsp. butter or margarine, melted
1 cup flour
3 eggs
½ cup sugar
1 Tbsp. cinnamon

Bring ½ cup butter and water to a boil in a large saucepan. Add flour and stir until dough forms a ball. Let cool until just warm to the touch. Add eggs one at a time. Beat with mixer 5 minutes. Spread on a 10x15x1 greased pan. Brush top with about ½ cup melted butter. Sprinkle with cinnamon and sugar. Bake at 400° for 30 minutes. Will puff during baking. Serves 4-6

Pumpkin Bread

1½   cups sugar
2   eggs, slightly beaten
½   cup oil
1   cup pumpkin
1¾   cups flour
1   tsp. baking soda
¼   tsp. baking powder
1   tsp. salt
½   tsp. cinnamon
½   tsp. cloves
½   tsp. nutmeg
¼   tsp. allspice
⅓   cup water
½   cup raisins (optional)

Mix sugar, eggs, oil and pumpkin in a bowl. Add dry ingredients and water in order given. Mix well. Stir in nuts and raisins if desired. Pour into a greased and floured loaf pan and bake at 350° for 1 hour or longer if needed. Makes 1 loaf.

To test doneness put a knife in the center of the bread. If it comes out clean it is finished.

Serve with Honey Butter (p.322).

Apple Bread

1	egg
½	cup milk
¼	cup applesauce
1½	cups flour
½	cup sugar
2	tsp. baking powder
½	tsp. cinnamon
1	cup apples, peeled, cored and diced

Topping

⅓	cup brown sugar
½	tsp. cinnamon

Mix ingredients. Batter will be lumpy. Pour into a well-greased and floured loaf pan. Mix topping and crumble over top of mixture. Bake at 375° for 55 minutes. Makes 1 loaf or 12-15 muffins.

For Muffins: Bake in greased muffin tins at 400° for 25-30 minutes.

One reason computers do so much work, they don't have to stop and answer the phone.

Banana Bread

1½   cup sugar
½   cup shortening
2   eggs, beaten
1   tsp. vanilla
¼   cup sour milk
2   cups flour
½   cup raisins (optional)
1   tsp. baking powder
½   tsp. baking soda
½   tsp. salt
1   cup bananas, (3 large) mashed
½ -1 cup nuts, chopped (optional)

Mix all the ingredients until smooth. Pour into a greased and floured loaf pan. Bake at 350° for 50-60 minutes. Makes 1 loaf.

✦ **If you have problems with the dough in your bread machine rising properly. Try rinsing out the bread machine container with hot tap water before adding the ingredients. This way the cold container doesn't cool down the warm water for the bread.**

Soups

&

Sandwiches

You have two choices for dinner-

Take it or leave it.

Soup and Sandwich Tips

✦ **When making sandwiches** use only one slice of lunch meat or for items like tuna, spread thin on the bread.

✦ **Use vegetable scraps to make vegetable stock.** Save onion peels, carrot peels and celery tops. Tie in a cheese cloth and use to make vegetable, chicken, or beef stock.

✦ **Use soy granules** for more protein in soups and casseroles.

✦ **Fry 1 pound of bacon.** When cool, crumble into pieces and freeze. When you need a little for flavor, simply take out a tablespoon or two.

✦ **When a recipe calls for parsley,** use the leaves from celery instead. Dry celery leaves and use in place of parsley flakes.

✦ **If you accidentally over-salt a dish:** While it's still cooking, drop in a peeled potato-it absorbs the excess salt for an instant fix.

✦ **Cut sandwiches into quarters** to make them "fancy". Even bologna sandwiches look tasty when cut like this.

✦ **Most soups only need ½ to 1 cup meat** even for a large pot of soup. Don't use more even if the recipe calls for it.

✦ **Adjust vegetables in your soup** to what you have on hand or what is on sale.

✦ **Stretch soup** with potatoes, pasta or rice.

✦ **Don't throw out leftover or soggy salad.** Grind it up and add to vegetable soups.

✦ **Freeze broth in ice cube trays.** Each cube equals about ¼ cup. Easy measuring when you need just a little broth.

✦ **Instant mashed potatoes** make a great thickener for soups and stews.

Basic Soup Seasoning

¼	cup basil
6	Tbsp. seasoned salt (p.305)
⅛	cup thyme
⅛	cup onion salt
⅛	cup garlic powder
⅛	cup sage
⅛	cup pepper
⅛	cup celery salt

Mix well. Store in an airtight container. Use 2-2½ teaspoons seasoning mix for each pot of soup.

Tomato Soup

2	Tbsp. flour
1	Tbsp. sugar
1	Tbsp. butter
2	cups milk, divided
4	cups tomato juice, heated
	parsley, chopped

In a large saucepan, combine flour, sugar and ¼ cup milk; stir until smooth. Add remaining milk and butter. Bring to a boil over medium heat, stirring constantly. Cook and stir for 2 minutes or until thickened. Slowly stir in hot tomato juice until blended. Sprinkle with parsley. Serves 10-12.

Broccoli Soup

2½	cups broccoli, frozen*
¼	cup onion, chopped or 1 tsp. onion powder
2	cups chicken broth
1	Tbsp. flour
½	tsp. garlic powder
1½	tsp. salt
	dash pepper
2	cups milk
¼-½	lb. cheese

In a saucepan combine broccoli, onion and chicken broth. Bring to boil. Simmer for 10 minutes or until broccoli is tender. Add flour, garlic powder, onion powder (if using instead of onion), salt and pepper. Slowly stir in milk and add cheese. Cook, stirring constantly until cheese is melted. *Do not boil.*

*2½ cups fresh broccoli stems or flowers, in bite size pieces may be used instead. This is a great way to use broccoli stems so they don't go to waste. Serves 6-8.

Broccoli Rice Soup

Add 2 cups of cooked rice to the broccoli soup.

Chicken Barley Soup

½ cup barley
1   stalk celery, sliced
½ carrot, diced
¼ cup chopped onion
4   cups chicken broth
1   cup chopped chicken
¼ tsp. turmeric (optional)
    salt and pepper (to taste)

Rinse and cook barley in broth as instructed on package.
Halfway through, add vegetables, chicken and seasonings.
Makes 2 quarts.

Beef Barley Soup

¾   cup barley
6   cups beef stock
½-1 lb. meat (or less), leftover roast or round steak
     are good choices
½   cup onion
3   cups carrots
2   lbs. mushrooms
½   tsp. rosemary
½   tsp. thyme
1   bay leaf

In a Dutch oven, brown meat and saute onions. Add stock and
bring to a boil. Add barley and boil 1 hour. Add the vegetables
and seasonings and simmer at least 30 minutes. Makes 3 quarts.

Lentil Soup

2   cups cubed ham
2   cups lentils, washed thoroughly
5   cups hot water
1   stalk celery, chopped
1   medium onion, chopped
1   bay leaf
⅛   tsp. garlic powder
2   tsp. salt
⅛   tsp. pepper

Combine all ingredients and simmer for 2 hours. Remove bay leaf. Puree in a food processor or blender. This is a great meal in the winter with sandwiches or salads. Makes 2 quarts.

Turkey Soup

turkey bones
water
salt (to taste)
garlic salt (to taste)
onion salt (to taste)
pepper (to taste)

Simmer turkey bones and water in a large pot following directions for Basic Chicken Soup (p.109). Season with salts and pepper to taste.

Basic Chicken Soup

2-3 chicken necks
2-4 chicken wings
3   qts. water
4   chicken bouillon cubes
1   tsp. salt
1   bay leaf
2   medium carrots, sliced
2   medium onions, diced
2   stalks celery, chopped

Bring first 6 ingredients just to boil in a large pot. Skim off foam and discard. Reduce heat and simmer, uncovered, 2½ hours or until the chicken is very tender. Strain the liquid. Cool and refrigerate so the fat can be removed easily. Let the meat cool until it can be handled. Remove meat from bones. Discard bones. Skim fat. Bring to a boil and add last 3 ingredients. Simmer 30 minutes and serve. Makes about 12 cups broth or soup. Half the broth may be removed before adding vegetables and frozen up to 6 months. Makes 12 cups.

Elephant Soup

1 Elephant
salt and pepper
2 rabbits (optional)

Cut the elephant into bite sized pieces. This will take about 3 months. Salt and pepper to taste. Cook over a kerosene fire at 470 degrees for about 8 days. This will serve 3,800 people. If more are expected, add 2 rabbits. Do this only if necessary since most people do not like to find hare in their stew.

Mom's Stew

½	lb. round steak, cubed
6	cups water
1	bay leaf
1	tsp. salt
1	tsp. sugar
1	tsp. garlic salt, (or to taste)
1	tsp. onion salt, (or to taste) or 1 onion, chopped
¼	tsp. allspice
1	tsp. Worcestershire sauce
1	tsp. lemon juice
2	carrots, peeled and sliced
6	potatoes, peeled and diced
1	Tbsp. cornstarch or flour
2	Tbsp. water

Brown meat in a large saucepan. Add all the other ingredients except vegetables, cornstarch and 2 tablespoons water and simmer for 1-2 hours, until meat is tender. Add the vegetables and cook for 15-20 minutes, until tender. Mix cornstarch and 2 Tbsp. water. Add to boiling stew and simmer for 15 minutes, until thickened. Makes 2 quarts.

Great with corn bread or Ninety-Minute Rolls (p.75).

✦ **If a recipe calls for herbs that don't dissolve, such as loose tea, whole cloves, bay leaves and garlic cloves, tuck them into a metal tea ball and hook the chain over the side of the pot. This way it's easy to remove seasonings after cooking or before cooking is finished if the flavor is strong enough.**

Potato Soup

6   medium potatoes, peeled and cubed
    water
2   chicken bouillon cubes
2   slices bacon, fried and crumbled or 1 Tbsp. bacon grease
    pepper (to taste)
    salt (to taste)
2   cups American cheese
1   tsp. onion salt
4   cups milk*

In a Dutch oven, add potatoes. Add enough water to cover. Boil until potatoes are tender. Drain and add rest of ingredients. Cook just until heated through. *Do not boil.*

*Dry milk may be used in place of milk. Do not drain water if dry milk is used. Just add the dry milk to the water. Makes 2 quarts.

French Onion Soup

4   onions, thinly sliced (yellow works best)
4   Tbsp. butter or margarine
1   qt. beef stock
1   bay leaf
4   slices day-old French bread
1   cup mozzarella or Swiss cheese, grated

Melt butter in a skillet. Saute onions until slightly brown. Add onions to beef broth in saucepan. Simmer slowly for 10 minutes. Pour into four bowls. Place bread on top of each bowl of soup, and sprinkle the cheese on top. Then set under broiler and cook until cheese is melted and brown. Serves 4.

This soup will simmer in the crockpot on low overnight.

Bacon-Bean Soup

8	slices bacon, diced
1/2	onion, chopped
2	cloves garlic, crushed
2	(16 ounce) cans ranch-style beans
1/2	cup cooked rice
1	(8 ounce) can stewed tomatoes
2	tsp. salt
	dash of pepper and paprika
4	cups water

Fry diced bacon in saucepan. Drain. Saute onions and garlic in bacon fat until onions are golden. Add remaining ingredients and simmer 1½ hours to allow flavors to blend. Add water as needed during cooking. Serves 4.

Vegetable Soup

1	beef soup bone
2	qts. water
2	bay leaves
2	Tbsp. salt
	pepper (to taste)
2	(16 ounce) cans whole peeled tomatoes
4	medium potatoes, pared and chopped
3	stalks celery, sliced
1	large onion, chopped
3	large carrots, peeled and sliced
1/3	cup barley

Place soup bone in large Dutch oven and cover with water. Add bay leaves. Simmer 2 hours. Remove the soup bone. Let stock cool. Skim fat. Add remaining ingredients and simmer 2 more hours. Remove bay leaf. Adjust seasoning. This soup is best if eaten the next day. Makes 3 quarts.

Chili

½   lb. ground beef
1   onion, chopped
1   green pepper, chopped
1-3 Tbsp. chili powder (to taste)
1   (15 ounce) can kidney beans, drained or
     2 cups cooked kidney beans (optional)
1   (8 ounce) can tomato sauce
1   (28 ounce) can tomatoes
1   tsp. salt
⅛   tsp. paprika
⅛   tsp. cayenne pepper
1   tsp. garlic powder

Cook and stir ground beef, onion and green pepper in a large
10-inch skillet until beef is brown and the onion is tender. Drain.
Stir in tomato sauce, tomatoes (with liquid), salt, paprika,
cayenne pepper, chili powder and garlic powder. Heat to boiling.
Reduce heat. Simmer uncovered 30 minutes. If using, add beans
to chili. One can of tomato juice may be added to make more
chili. Serves 4.

✦ **Grease the inside of the crockpot for easy cleanup.**

✦ **Place a few oyster crackers in salt and pepper shakers to
   prevent caking.**

✦ **If you prefer not to make your own ketchup, buy it in
   large containers. Freeze in 2½ cup portions, which is the
   amount that will fill an empty standard bottle.**

Tuna Chowder

2   carrots, shredded
1   onion, chopped, or 1 tsp. onion powder
1   Tbsp. butter or margarine
¼   cup flour
2   cups chicken broth
2   cups milk
6   ounce tuna, drained and flaked
½   tsp. celery seed
½   tsp. Worcestershire sauce
¼   tsp. salt
1   cup Cheddar or American cheese
       parsley

In a large saucepan, saute carrots and onion in the butter until tender. Mix in the flour. Add chicken broth and milk and heat until thick, stirring constantly. Add the rest of the ingredients and stir until heated through. Garnish with parsley if desired. Serves 6-8.

Egg Flower Soup

1   green onion, chopped (top included)
2   eggs, slightly beaten
3   cups chicken broth
¼   tsp. salt
       dash pepper

Stir onion into eggs. Heat broth to boiling in a 3-quart saucepan. Add salt and pepper. Pour egg mixture slowly into broth, stirring constantly with a fork. Boil about 5 minutes until eggs are done. Serves 4-6.

Onion Soup Mix

¾ cup instant minced onion
4 tsp. onion powder
⅓ cup beef bouillon powder
¼ tsp. celery seed, crushed
¼ tsp. sugar

Mix all ingredients, and store in an airtight container.

To use: Add 2 tablespoons mix to 1 cup boiling water. Cover and simmer 15 minutes.

This makes a stronger soup than the store-bought mix, so you can use less.

Cream Soup Mix

2 cups dry milk
1¼ cups cornstarch or 2½ cups flour
¼ cup chicken bouillon powder
2 Tbsp. dried onion flakes
½ tsp. pepper
1 tsp. thyme (optional)
1 tsp. basil (optional)

Mix all the ingredients and store in airtight container. If the mix is made with cornstarch, add ⅓ cup mix to 1¼ cups water; if made with flour, add ½ cup mix to 1¼ cups water.

This makes a concentrated casserole consistency. For soup consistency, double the water.

Recipes reprinted with permission from The Complete Tightwad Gazette by Amy Dacyczyn.

Chicken Salad

1½   cups chopped, cooked chicken or turkey
½   cup mayonnaise or salad dressing
1   small stalk celery, chopped
1   small onion, chopped, or 1 tsp. onion powder
¼   tsp. salt
¼   tsp. pepper

Mix all ingredients. Best if chilled for 1 or 2 hours.
Makes 4 sandwiches.

Ham Salad

Substitute ham for chicken or turkey. Omit salt and pepper and
add 1 tsp. prepared mustard.

Egg Salad

Substitute 6 hard-boiled eggs, chopped, for the chicken.

Tuna Salad

Substitute 1 can tuna, drained, for the chicken.

✦ **To help keep eggs from cracking while boiling, add
    vinegar to the water.**

Fried Egg Sandwich

1   egg
1   tsp. margarine*
2   slices bread

Heat margarine in a large skillet. Crack egg into a cup and beat slightly. Pour into hot skillet and let cook 3 to 5 minutes until it sets. Carefully turn egg over with a spatula and fry on the other side. Serve between 2 pieces of bread. Makes 1 sandwich.

*If on a low fat diet, fry egg in non-stick pan. Omit margarine.

Sloppy Joes

1   lb. ground beef
1   medium onion, chopped, or ½ tsp. onion powder
½   tsp. garlic powder
5   Tbsp. ketchup
2   tsp. brown sugar
⅛   tsp. lemon juice
1   Tbsp. Worcestershire sauce
½   tsp. salt
6   hamburger buns

Brown meat and onion until onion is tender. Drain fat. Add other ingredients and heat thoroughly. Serve on hamburger buns. Serves 6.

✦ **Spread leftover sloppy joe meat in a casserole dish. Place sliced American cheese over the meat and top the cheese with homemade or refrigerator biscuits. Bake at 350° until the biscuits are done.**

Hot Roast Beef Sandwich

1-2 cups leftover roast beef
2 cups leftover roast gravy (p.190)
4 pieces bread

Warm roast and gravy. Pour over bread or toast. Serve warm. Serves 4.

French Dip

Roast, slow cooked and sliced thin
Use juice from roast or make your own with beef bouillon cubes
French rolls or toasted bread

Layer thin pieces of roast on rolls or bread. Warm juice in bowls and serve for dipping sandwiches. Juice may be extended by adding some water and bouillon to suit your taste. An onion could be added to the roast while cooking; place a slice or two on the sandwich.

Hamburger Gravy On Toast

½   lb. ground beef, browned*
    white gravy (p.183)
    bread

Make white gravy from hamburger drippings and add hamburger. Cook until warmed through. Serve on bread or toast. Serves 4.

Pocket Sandwiches
(Hot Pockets ™)

2¼   cups Baking Mix
⅔   cup milk
1   cup ground beef
1   onion, chopped
2   tsp. chili powder
1   tsp. garlic powder
1   tsp. salt
1   cup cheddar cheese, grated

Make a dough out of baking mix and milk. Roll out into a rectangle. Cut out large squares and fill with meat filling. Bake 350° for 30 minutes. Ham and cheese, broccoli and cheese, taco meat or just cheese can be used as fillings.

Calzones

1   batch pizza dough (p.218)
    pizza sauce
2   cloves garlic, chopped
½   lb. mozzarella
    desired toppings:
    pepperoni, onions, olives, green peepers, mushrooms,
    sausage, browned ground beef

Divide dough into half. Roll each half in a circle. On half of one circle spread pizza sauce, toppings, ½ mozzarella and 1 clove garlic. Fold other half over and seal the edges. Repeat with other circle of dough. Bake at 350 for 15-20 minutes. When done brush with butter.

French Bread Pizza

loaf French bread
pizza sauce (p.217)
mozzarella cheese
Toppings of your choice: olives, mushrooms, peppers,
hamburger, sausage, or onions

Cut bread lengthwise, top with sauce, then cheese, then topping or toppings. Bake in oven at 350° until thoroughly warmed and cheese begins to bubble and brown, about 15 minutes. Serves 4.

Vegetables, Beans, Pasta & Rice

Real families don't eat shitake mushrooms.

Vegetable and Bean Tips

✦ **To make peeling vegetables and fruits** like tomatoes and peaches easier, carve an x on the bottom of them and place in the microwave. Microwave on high for 35-45 seconds. Remove from microwave and peel.

✦ **Peel broccoli stems.** It makes them very tender. You could use them for soup or in any dish calling for broccoli.

✦ **If potatoes get eyes,** cut them into halves or fourths (as long as they have about 3-4 eyes on each chunk) and plant them in the garden or flower bed. In a couple months you can dig them up and have new potatoes.

✦ **Keep a container in the freezer** for the leftover water from steaming vegetables. Then when you have enough, use it as vegetable broth.

✦ **Save bacon grease for flavoring** your dishes instead of butter or margarine.

✦ **Save your frying oil** in the refrigerator and use again later.

✦ **To keep hot oil from splattering,** sprinkle a little flour or salt in the pan before frying.

✦ **To store onions:** put one onion in a pantyhose leg, tie a knot, then put another onion and tie another knot until the pantyhose leg is full. To remove an onion, cut at the top of the next knot.

✦ **Wrap celery in aluminum foil** when putting it in the refrigerator. It will keep for weeks.

✦ **Use beans instead of meat in dishes.**

✦ **Renew limp celery** by soaking in ice water.

✦ **When boiling corn on the cob,** add a pinch of sugar to help bring out the corns natural sweetness.

Baked Beans

1   (16 ounce) can of pork and beans
1   tsp. mustard
1   Tbsp. bacon grease
4   Tbsp. brown sugar
2   Tbsp. onion, chopped or ½ tsp. onion powder

Put all the ingredients in a saucepan and mix thoroughly. Let simmer on medium heat 15-30 minutes. These can simmer longer if needed. Serve warm. You can also bake these in the oven for 1 hour at 250° until thickened. Serves 4.

Green Beans

1   pound green beans or 1 (16 ounce) can green beans
4   slices bacon*
1-2   Tbsp. onion chopped
1   tsp. salt
¼   tsp. pepper

Snip off ends and slice green beans into thin slivers. (If using canned, open can and drain.) Fry bacon until crisp. Remove bacon from pan and drain on paper towels. Cool and break into pieces. Remove all but 2 tablespoons bacon grease. Chop scallions and saute until limp. Add beans, stir thoroughly and cook over moderate heat for about 1 minute. Add 1 tablespoon water. Cover and cook 4 additional minutes. Remove cover. Continue to cook and stir until beans are tender but still crisp. Season with salt and pepper and add bacon bits. Serves 4.

*You may substitute 2 Tbsp. bacon grease for the bacon.

Herbed Broccoli

1   lb. broccoli
2   Tbsp. vegetable oil
1   tsp. fresh oregano, chopped or ¼ tsp. dried oregano
½   tsp. salt
1   tsp. fresh basil, chopped or ¼ tsp. dried basil
1   clove garlic, crushed
2   plum tomatoes, chopped

Steam broccoli until done. Heat oil in a 10-inch skillet on medium heat. Add all ingredients except the broccoli. Heat about 1 minute, stirring frequently, until hot. Pour over broccoli and mix gently. Serves 4.

Glazed Carrots

½   lb. fresh carrots or baby carrots
½   stick margarine
6   Tbsp. brown sugar
1   tsp. cinnamon
1   tsp. ginger (optional)

Clean carrots and cut into bite-size pieces. Steam 10 minutes in a small amount of boiling water just until tender. Melt margarine in a large skillet over low heat. Add brown sugar, cinnamon and ginger. Cook 1-2 minutes. Add hot carrots, stirring well to coat. Remove when shiny and well glazed. Serves 4.

Creamy Carrot Casserole

4   cups carrots, sliced
¾   cup salad dressing (Miracle Whip®)
¼   cup onion, chopped
¼   tsp. salt
¼   tsp. pepper
14   saltine crackers, crushed
1   Tbsp. butter, melted
2   Tbsp. parsley
½   cup shredded American cheese

Put carrots in 1½ quart microwave safe casserole with 2 Tbsp. water. Cover and cook in the microwave on high 6-8 minutes or until tender. Stir once. Drain. Mix salad dressing, onion, salt and pepper. Add carrots. Toss crackers, butter, and parsley. Spoon over carrots. Cook in microwave uncovered 3 minutes. Add cheese. Cook 1-2 minutes longer until cheese is melted. Serves 4.

Flavored Vegetable Butters

Mix one of the following in ¼ cup softened butter or margarine, to flavor your plain vegetables.

+ 1 tsp. basil, fresh chopped or ½ tsp. dried
+ 2 Tbsp. Parmesan cheese, grated
+ 1 Tbsp. chives, chopped and 1 Tbsp. parsley, chopped
+ ½ clove garlic, crushed, or ½ tsp. garlic powder
+ 1 Tbsp. prepared horseradish
+ 1 Tbsp. lemon peel, grated and 2 Tbsp. lemon juice
+ ¼ tsp. dry mustard and 1 tsp. fresh dill or ¼ tsp. dried dill

Cheesy Cauliflower

1   medium head cauliflower

Topping

½   cup mayonnaise
½   tsp. onion salt or 1 tsp. onion, finely chopped
1   tsp. mustard
½   cup Cheddar cheese

Wash cauliflower, don't dry. Place cauliflower in casserole dish. Cover with plastic wrap. Microwave 8-9 minutes until tender. Combine mayonnaise, onion salt or onion and mustard. Spoon on cauliflower and sprinkle cheese on top. Microwave 1-2 minutes to melt cheese. Serves 4.

Cucumbers & Tomatoes

2   medium cucumbers
2   Tbsp. margarine or butter
1   onion, sliced and separated into rings
2   medium tomatoes, cut into wedges
½   tsp. salt
     dash of pepper
1   Tbsp. fresh dill, chopped or 1 tsp. dried dill

Wash and remove seeds from cucumbers. Slice into 1 inch pieces. Heat margarine in a 12-inch skillet over medium heat. Cook cucumbers and onion in margarine about 5 minutes, stirring occasionally (just until cucumbers are tender). Stir in tomatoes. Sprinkle with salt and pepper. Cook just until tomatoes are hot. Sprinkle with dill. Serves 4

Grilled Corn

4   ears corn
2   Tbsp. margarine or butter
1   Tbsp. taco seasoning or lemon pepper
2   Tbsp. water

Husk and clean corn. Mix margarine and taco seasoning.
Spread over corn. Place each ear on a double thickness of
aluminum foil. Sprinkle corn with water. Wrap securely in
aluminum foil and twist the ends tight. Place on medium coals
and grill 15-35 minutes (until tender), turning once. Serves 4.

Egg Rolls

½   lb. beef, pork or chicken, cooked and diced small
2   cups cabbage, chopped
½   cup carrots, shredded
3   green onions or ¼ cup onion, chopped or 1 tsp. onion powder
½   tsp. ginger
½   tsp. salt
2   Tbsp. soy sauce
1   pkg. egg roll wrappers
     vegetable oil
     mustard, ketchup or sweet and sour sauce (p.315)

Add 1 Tbsp. oil in a frying pan. Heat pan very hot and add meat.
Cook 1-2 minutes until lightly browned. Add cabbage, carrots
and onions and cook 2 minutes. Stir in ginger, salt and soy
sauce. Let cool 5 minutes. Follow the directions on the back of
the egg roll wrappers for wrapping. Use 2 Tbsp. filling for each
egg roll. Deep-fry 2-4 egg rolls at a time at 350°, turning
occasionally for 2-3 minutes. Drain on paper towels. Serve warm
with choice of sauces. Makes 20 egg rolls.

Egg roll wrappers can usually be found in the produce department.

Baked Onions

2-4 onions

Place unpeeled onions in a pan to catch the juice. Bake at 350° for about 30 minutes. Time and temperature can be adjusted if you are baking other things. Peel before eating. Baking makes the onions very sweet. Serves 2-4.

Baked Onion Slices

4   large onions, peeled and sliced
¼   cup vinegar
¼   cup sugar
¼   cup margarine, melted
¼   cup boiling water

Arrange onions in a casserole. Combine other ingredients. Pour over onions and bake a 300° for 1 hour. Serves 4.

An optimist is a person who expects the ketchup to come out in 3 shakes

Barbecued Onions

6   medium onions
6   bouillon cubes
3   Tbsp. margarine
     pepper (to taste)

Peel onions. Scoop out a hole in the top of each onion. Fill with bouillon cube, ½ teaspoon margarine and pepper. Wrap onions separately in foil. Place on barbecue grill, turning frequently, for 30 minutes. Serves 6.

Onion Rings

1   egg
½   cup milk
    flour
    cracker crumbs
    vegetable oil, for frying
3-4 onions, sliced

Lightly beat egg in a bowl. Add milk. Put flour in another bowl and cracker crumbs in yet another bowl. Dip several onions rings in flour, then dip in egg mixture and then coat with cracker crumbs. Fry in hot oil, turning once. Drain on paper towels. If you run out of mixture just add more of the ingredient you need. Serves 4.

✦ **To remove onion smell from your hands: Rub a stainless steel spoon between your hands under running water.**

Baked Potato Toppings

✦ basic cheese sauce (p.143)
✦ chili with Cheddar cheese
✦ sour cream and chives
✦ yogurt
✦ onion, bacon, sour cream and chives
✦ broccoli and cheese, melt cheese on top in oven
✦ pizza (pizza sauce, cheese, pepperoni, sausage, olives, mushrooms)
✦ taco salad (hamburger with taco seasoning, lettuce, tomatoes, onion, grated cheese, sour cream, salsa, canned peppers)
✦ chicken Parmesan (margarine, chicken, Parmesan, vegetables)
✦ peppers, onions
✦ bacon bits
✦ ranch dressing

French Fries

potatoes, peeled or unpeeled
vegetable oil for frying
salt (to taste)

Use 1 potato per person. If using unpeeled potatoes, wash thoroughly. Dry. Slice potato into $\frac{1}{4}$-inch thick strips. Store in salted water if unable to use right away. Dry well with paper towel. In a deep saucepan heat vegetable oil to 375°. Fry in vegetable oil until golden brown. Remove with a slotted spoon and drain on paper towels. Fry again for 3-5 minutes for extra crispy french fries.

Fried Potatoes

6   potatoes, peeled and sliced
6   Tbsp. bacon grease or margarine
     salt and pepper

Melt bacon grease or margarine in a frying pan. Add the potatoes in the pan and cook over medium heat. Flip potatoes and cook until golden brown. Remove from pan. Salt and pepper to taste. Serves 4-6.

Lemon Potatoes

10   new potatoes or 5 medium potatoes,
      cut in halves or quarters
2   Tbsp. margarine
½   tsp. lemon peel, grated
1   Tbsp. lemon juice
2   tsp. chives, chopped
½   tsp. salt
⅛   tsp. pepper
      dash of nutmeg

Clean and steam potatoes 20 minutes (until tender). Heat remaining ingredients just to boiling. Pour lemon butter over potatoes and serve. Serves 5-6.

✦ **To keep potatoes from budding, place an apple in the bag with the potatoes.**

Mashed Potatoes

5   large potatoes, peeled and cubed
2   Tbsp. butter
½   cup milk*
2   Tbsp. sugar
1   tsp. salt

In a large saucepan place potatoes and enough water to cover the potatoes. Bring to a boil; reduce heat. Cover and simmer until potatoes are tender (about 10 minutes). Drain. Transfer potatoes to a mixing bowl and mash. Add butter, milk, sugar and salt. Beat until smooth. Serves 5-6.

*Save water after cooking potatoes and just add ¼ cup dry milk.

Garlic Mashed Potatoes

Add 15 cloves garlic, peeled and halved, to the potatoes when boiling.

Oven Fried Potatoes

4   potatoes, thinly sliced
4   Tbsp. vegetable oil
    garlic powder

Rub each potato slice with oil. Spread out on a cookie sheet and sprinkle with garlic powder. Bake at 325° for 30 minutes. Serves 4.

✦ **If homemade mashed potatoes are too moist, add a few instant potato flakes until they are the right consistency.**

Potato Pancakes

2   cups leftover mashed potatoes
2   Tbsp. flour
1   egg
     margarine

Mix first 3 ingredients. Make into patties and fry in margarine until golden brown on each side. Serve warm with butter or margarine. Delicious served with applesauce. Serves 2.

Potato Peels

potatoes
salt
pepper
garlic powder
onion powder
Cheddar cheese, shredded

Grease a cookie sheet and preheat the oven to 400°. Wash and peel potatoes with a knife (trying to get large pieces). Put peels in a bowl and add the spices to taste. Mix well. Bake 8-10 minutes until crisp. Remove from oven and sprinkle cheese on the potato skins. Return to the oven for 2 or 3 minutes until the cheese melts.

✦ **Buy ½ pound of garlic. Chop in your food processor, place in a heavy duty freezer bag and lay flat on a tray. Freeze. The garlic will break into small pieces to be used as needed.**

✦ **Potatoes should be stored in a cool, dry, dark place, but not refrigerated.**

Scalloped Potatoes

6 Tbsp. flour
½ cup dry milk (optional)
1 tsp. onion powder (optional)
 salt and pepper (to taste)
3 cups cold milk
4 cups potatoes, sliced
1 onion, sliced
3 Tbsp. margarine
 ham, bacon or sausage, diced (optional)

Place the flour, dry milk, onion powder (if using instead of onion), salt and pepper into a quart jar. Close and shake thoroughly. Add cold milk. Close and shake again until all the flour is dissolved. In a greased 3-quart casserole dish, layer the potatoes, onions, and meat (if using it), dotting each layer with margarine. Add the flour-milk mixture. Bake in a 325° oven for 1½ hours. Serves 4.

Au Gratin Potatoes

Add 1½ cups of cubed or shredded cheese.

Pierogi Casserole

6-8 lasagna noodles
2 cups diced potatoes
1 onion, diced
1 Tbs. butter
1 cup shredded cheese

Preheat oven to 350 degrees. Cook noodles according to package directions. Drain and set aside. Saute onion in butter until tender. Layer the noodles, potatoes, onion, and shredded cheese in a baking dish. Bake at 350 degrees for 30-40 minutes.

Sweet Potato Casserole

3	cups sweet potatoes, mashed
1/2	cup butter or margarine, melted
1	cup sugar
2	eggs
1	Tbsp. vanilla

Topping

1	cup brown sugar, packed
1	cup pecans
1/2	cup flour
1/3	cup butter, melted

Mix all the ingredients and put in buttered 9x9 casserole dish. Sprinkle on topping. Bake uncovered at 350° for 20 minutes. This is a great dish for holiday dinners and potlucks as it can be made up the day before and then baked the next day. Serves 8-9.

Sweet Potato Chips

2	medium sweet potatoes
2	Tbsp. olive oil
	salt and pepper
	paprika

Preheat the oven to 450° degrees. Peel sweet potatoes and slice as thinly as possible. Toss with 2 tablespoons of olive oil and spread in a thin layer on a cookie sheet. Sprinkle with salt, pepper, and paprika. Bake about 20 minutes or until crispy. Makes 4 servings.

Mexican Summer Squash

4   yellow summer squash
4   ears of corn
3   ripe tomatoes
¼   cup butter
1   small onion, chopped
     salt and pepper (to taste)

Wash squash and cut in small pieces; cut corn from the cob, skin tomato (the skin comes off easily if they are first dipped in boiling water for 1 minute) and cut into cubes. Heat butter in saucepan. Stir in onion, and cook until limp but not brown. Add squash, corn, tomatoes, salt and pepper. Cover and cook over a low heat for 30-40 minutes, stirring occasionally. If desired serve over cooked rice. Serves 4.

Baked Squash

2   squash (any kind of yellow squash)
4   slices of bacon or 2 Tbsp. bacon grease
     salt and pepper (to taste)
     brown sugar

Wash squash and cut them in half. Spoon out seeds and fibers from the center. Put 4 slices of bacon in a shallow baking pan and bake in a preheated oven at 350° until crisp. If using bacon grease just heat in oven until bacon grease is melted. Remove bacon and drain on towels. Sprinkle squash with salt and pepper and place cut side down in bacon grease. Bake at 350° for 1 hour or until tender. Just before serving brush the inside with some bacon grease, sprinkle lightly with brown sugar, and sprinkle the crumbled bacon into the squash cavity. Serves 4.

Fried Mushrooms, Zucchini, Onion Rings and Squash

mushrooms
zucchini
onions
squash
flour
1   egg, beaten
½   cup milk
cracker crumbs
vegetable oil for frying
salt and pepper

Wash all the vegetables. Slice the zucchini, onions and squash into thin slices. Put some flour in a bowl. Put egg and milk in another bowl and mix. Place crackers crumbs into a bowl. Put the vegetable oil in a deep saucepan or fry pan and heat to 375° or until a few crumbs of cracker fry quickly. Dip vegetables into flour, then egg mixture, then cracker crumbs and fry until golden. Drain on paper towels. Salt and pepper to taste and serve hot with ranch dressing.

Tact is the ability to close your mouth before someone else wants you to.

Fried Green Tomatoes

2   qts. water
2   Tbsp. salt
4-6 medium green tomatoes, unpeeled and sliced
1   cup flour
½   cup vegetable oil or bacon grease
     salt (to taste)

In a mixing bowl, mix salt and water. Soak sliced tomatoes in salt water mixture for 30-40 minutes. Drain and drop slices a few at time into a bag in which you have placed the flour. Shake thoroughly to coat. Heat the oil in a large skillet and carefully place the slices into the hot oil. Brown until crisp on both sides. Salt to taste. You can also use squash, zucchini or eggplant in place of or with the green tomatoes. Serves 4-6.

Parmesan Baked Tomatoes

2   (14½ ounce) cans whole tomatoes, drained and quartered
4   Tbsp. seasoned bread crumbs
½   tsp. Italian seasoning
½   tsp. garlic salt
4   Tbsp. Parmesan cheese
2   Tbsp. margarine

Place tomatoes in a greased 1 quart baking dish. Combine bread crumbs, Italian seasoning and garlic salt. Sprinkle over tomatoes. Top with cheese and dot with margarine. Bake uncovered at 325° for 15-20 minutes (until lightly browned). Makes 4-6 servings.

Scalloped Tomatoes

6   ripe tomatoes or 1 (20 ounce) can tomatoes
1   cup coarse dry bread crumbs
1   tsp. sugar
     salt and pepper (to taste)
3-6 Tbsp. butter

Skin tomatoes and cut into slices. The skins will slide right off if you dip them in boiling water for 1 minute first. Combine crumbs, sugar, salt, pepper and butter. Add more butter if you want the mixture less dry. Place a layer of tomatoes in the bottom of a buttered casserole dish and sprinkle with some of the crumb mixture. Repeat layers of tomato and crumb mixture until dish is filled and top with remaining crumb mixture. Bake at 350° for 30 minutes. Serves 6.

Southern Scalloped Tomatoes

Increase sugar to ¾ cup and then mix all the other ingredients together. Bring to a boil in a heavy skillet and add tomatoes. Cook slowly for 1 hour until tomatoes are glazed. If they start to look dry, add more butter.

✦ **Canned beans and other canned ingredients sometimes stick to the bottom of the can and require a spatula to remove. Try opening the bottom of the can instead. Shake and everything should fall out easily.**

✦ **Chop tomatoes in the can. Insert a knife and cut against the sides of can. Why wash a cutting board when you don't have to.**

Stewed Tomatoes

3   large tomatoes, ripe or 1 (28 ounce) can peeled tomatoes
2   slices bread, toasted and cut into ½ inch cubes
1   medium onion, finely chopped
2   Tbsp. green bell pepper, finely chopped
½   tsp. salt
⅛   tsp. pepper
1   Tbsp. sugar

Dip tomatoes into boiling water for 1 minute. Peel; the skin should slip off easily. Cut the tomatoes into small pieces. Mix all ingredients except bread in 2½ quart saucepan. Cover and heat to boiling. Reduce heat. Simmer about 10 minutes (until tomatoes are soft). Stir in bread cubes. Serve warm. Serves 4.

Sun Dried Tomatoes

3   lbs. Italian (Roma) tomatoes
½   tsp. Italian seasoning (optional)
      garlic powder (optional)
      salt
      rosemary sprigs (optional)
      peppercorns (optional)
1¼-1½   cups olive oil

Use only perfect tomatoes without blemishes. Slice lengthwise in half. Gently squeeze out any excess juice. Arrange tomatoes in one layer cut side up on oven-safe wire racks or racks for the dehydrator. Sprinkle with Italian seasoning, garlic powder and salt. Dry at 200° for 8-9 hours. Watch carefully. Do not over dry. Pack tomatoes loosely in a 1-1½ pint jar with rosemary and peppercorns. Fill with olive oil and cover tightly. Let set 2 months in refrigerator before using to develop full flavor. Makes 1-1¼ pints.

Egg Noodles

2 eggs
½ tsp. salt
¼ cup milk
2-3 cups flour

Beat eggs slightly. Add salt and milk. Mix in 2 cups flour. With hands thoroughly mix. Add enough additional flour to make a stiff dough. Turn dough onto well floured counter or board; knead until smooth and elastic. Cover. Let rest 10 minutes. Roll dough very thin. Cut dough into ⅛ inch strips to desired length. Set on side and let dry 2-3 hours* turning once. When ready to use, drop into boiling water or broth. Boil 12 to 15 minutes. Drain thoroughly if cooking in water.

*Noodles may dry longer if you need to make them in the morning for dinner.

Cooked Dry Beans

2 cups beans
5 cups water
  ham bone (optional)
1 onion (optional)
2 tsp. salt

Wash and drain beans. Put beans, water, ham bone and onion if desired in a large pan and bring to a boil. Boil 2 minutes. Remove from heat. Cover and let stand 1 hour. Add salt. Cover and boil gently 1½-2 hours or until tender. Add more water during cooking if needed. Makes 5 cups cooked beans.

Dry Beans Quick Prep Tips

Soak any kind of dry beans overnight. Drain. Freeze beans in 2 to 4 cup portions. To prepare: Cook beans in boiling water for 20 minutes. They will soften very easily if they are frozen first.

Refried Beans

1   (20 ounce) can kidney or pinto beans or
2½ cups cooked kidney or pinto beans
1-2 Tbsp. bacon grease or vegetable oil
1   small onion, grated
1   clove garlic, chopped fine
½   green pepper, chopped fine
1   tsp. chili powder
½   tsp. cumin
4-5 Tbsp. hot beef broth
     salt (to taste)

Drain beans. Reserve the liquid and mash thoroughly. Heat grease in a skillet. Add onion, garlic, and green pepper. Cook over a low heat until tender. Stir in chili powder mixed with hot beef broth, then add the beans. Cook slowly, stirring continuously. Add bean liquid as needed. Beans are cooked when they are completely dry. Salt as desired. Makes 3 cups.

White Sauce

¼   cup dry milk
2   Tbsp. flour
     dash salt
1   cup cold water
1   Tbsp. margarine

In a covered jar, combine dry milk, flour and salt and mix well. Add water. Shake until all the ingredients are dissolved. Melt margarine in a 1-quart saucepan. Stir in flour-milk mixture and cook over low heat until mixture thickens and starts to bubble. Keep stirring until thickened completely. This recipe equals 1 can of cream soup, it can be doubled but add only 1¾ cup water. Makes 1 cup.

Chicken Sauce:

Substitute cold chicken stock for the water. Omit the salt.

Cheese Sauce:

Add ½ cup of processed cheese cubes or shredded Cheddar cheese to white sauce. Heat over low heat, stirring until all the cheese is melted.

✦ **To avoid wasting sour cream, serve with a knife rather than a spoon. You can easily scrape the knife off on the edge of the container or serving dish reducing waste and using every last bit.**

Broccoli and Pasta

1   medium head fresh broccoli
3   Tbsp. butter or margarine
¼   cup olive oil or vegetable oil
1   medium onion, chopped
4   cloves garlic, minced
½   cup chicken broth
      salt and pepper (to taste)
1   (12 ounce) package pasta, cooked
      Parmesan cheese, grated

Wash and cut broccoli into bite-size pieces. Steam until just cooked. Drain well and set aside. In a pan, melt butter and olive oil. Saute onion until translucent. Add garlic and simmer for 1 minute. Add broccoli and broth and simmer 3 minutes. Add salt and pepper. In a large bowl, mix drained pasta with broccoli mixture. Toss well. Top with grated cheese and serve immediately. Serves 4.

Broccoli Pasta Toss

2   cups broccoli florets
4   ounces fettuccine, broken up
1   Tbsp. vegetable oil (optional)
⅛   tsp. garlic powder
3   Tbsp. Parmesan cheese, grated
1   tsp. sesame seed, toasted

In a large saucepan, boil water and add broccoli and pasta. Cook for 6-8 minutes or just until tender, stirring once or twice. Drain. Add oil to pasta mixture and toss. Add garlic, cheese, sesame seeds and pepper to taste. Toss gently to coat. Serve immediately. Serves 2.

Garden Pasta

5	tomatoes, chopped
2	stalks celery, chopped
2	carrots, chopped
1	medium onion, chopped
8	green onions, chopped
1	tsp. sugar
1	tsp. basil
1/4	tsp. garlic powder
1/2	tsp. salt
1/2	tsp. pepper
1/2	tsp. oregano
1	Tbsp. vegetable oil
1	lb. spaghetti

Put the vegetables in a 2-quart saucepan and cover tightly. Cook over medium heat, stirring occasionally, for 10 minutes. Add seasonings. Cover pot, cook over medium-low heat for 5 minutes. Add oil and simmer for 30 min. or until carrots are tender. Cook spaghetti, drain. Toss with the sauce. Serves 6.

Lemon Herb Pasta

1/2	lb. thin spaghetti, cooked
1/4	cup margarine, melted
2	Tbsp. lemon juice
1	Tbsp. parsley flakes
1/2	tsp. marjoram
1/2	tsp. garlic salt

Toss all the ingredients together; mix well. Serves 2.

Quick Pasta

½   lb. spaghetti
1   cup salsa
3   Tbsp. olive oil
1½ cup Monterey Jack cheese, grated

Cook pasta, drain, and toss with the olive oil to coat. Add salsa and cheese. Toss again. Serves 2.

Restaurant Style Pasta Fagioli

1   (15 ounce) can great northern beans, undrained, or
    2 cups northern beans, cooked
1   (28 ounce) can stewed tomatoes, sliced
16 ounce spaghetti sauce (p.192)
    Italian seasoning (to taste)
2   stalks celery, sliced thin
1   small onion, chopped
2   cups small spiral pasta, uncooked
    salt and pepper (to taste)

In a Dutch oven combine everything and bring to a boil on medium high. Turn heat down to low. Cover pan with lid and allow to cook on a slow simmer for 30 minutes or until pasta is tender. Stir occasionally. Serves 6.

✦ **Add ¼ tsp. garlic powder to pasta water when cooking for a wonderful flavor.**

Stewed Tomato Pasta

2   (14½ ounce) cans stewed tomatoes, with juice
1¾ cups chicken broth
2   Tbsp. vegetable oil
1   tsp. Italian seasoning
1   (12 ounce) pkg. spiral pasta

In a Dutch oven, combine everything but the pasta. Bring to a boil and add pasta. Reduce heat; cover and simmer for 16-18 minutes, until pasta is tender. Stir occasionally. Serves 8-10.

Vegetarian Pasta

1   (15½ ounce) can great northern beans, rinsed
    and drained or 2 cups cooked northern beans
2   cups angel hair pasta, cooked
3   Tbsp. butter or margarine
¼   tsp. garlic salt
¼   cup Parmesan cheese
    parsley, fresh and minced

Microwave beans on high for 2 minutes until heated though. Place warm pasta in a serving bowl. Toss with butter and garlic salt until butter is melted. Add beans and cheese; toss to coat. Sprinkle with parsley. Serves 4.

✦ **Add one tablespoon of oil to water for boiling pasta. This keeps the pasta from sticking.**

Rice

Servings	1 cup	4 cups	6 cups
Water	1 cup	3 cups	4 cups
Salt	1/4 tsp.	1 tsp.	1 tsp.
Rice	1/3 cup	1 1/3 cups	2 cups

Use given amounts of water, salt and rice to make the needed servings. To retain vitamins and minerals do not rinse rice. Heat water and salt to boiling. Stir in rice. Cover tightly and cook slowly about 25 minutes until rice is tender. Add a little water during cooking if rice becomes dry. Gently stir only if needed to keep rice from sticking.

Seasoned Rice Mix

1   cup spaghetti, broken into very small pieces
2   cups rice, uncooked
1/4   cup dried parsley flakes
6   Tbsp. instant chicken or beef bouillon powder
2   tsp. onion powder
1/2   tsp. garlic powder
1/4   tsp. dried thyme

Mix all the ingredients and store in an airtight container. To use, put 1 cup mix, 2 tablespoons margarine, and 2 cups water in a saucepan. Bring to a boil, cover, reduce heat and simmer for 15 minutes or until the rice is tender. Makes 3 cups uncooked.

✦ **Use left over rice for soups, casseroles, Spanish rice, fried rice, rice and beans on tortillas for burritos.**

Cheesy Rice and Tomatoes

3	cups cooked rice
3	Tbsp. oil
1	medium onion, chopped
3	stalks celery, chopped
1	green pepper, chopped
2	cups cooked tomatoes or stewed tomatoes
2	cups cheese, shredded
1	tsp. salt
	dash pepper

Cook rice if uncooked. Saute in a pan with oil, onion, celery, and green pepper. Add tomatoes, rice, cheese, salt and pepper. Cover and simmer until cheese is melted. Serves 8.

Fried Rice

1/2	green pepper, finely chopped
1	tsp. margarine
2	eggs
4	cups rice, cooked
2	Tbsp. soy sauce

Saute green pepper in a skillet with a tiny bit of margarine. Add eggs and stir until scrambled and set. Add rice and soy sauce, heat though. Serves 8.

Spanish Rice

1   chicken bouillon cube
½   cup water
1   cup rice, cooked
1   Tbsp. (or less) taco seasoning
1   clove garlic, minced
1   cup tomato sauce

Dissolve bouillon in water. Mix all the ingredients and bake uncovered at 375° for 30 minutes. Serves 4.

Red Beans and Rice

1   cup white rice
1   small onion, chopped
2   (15 ounce) cans dark red kidney beans, or
      4 cups cooked kidney beans
2   (15 ounce) cans diced tomatoes
      garlic salt (to taste)
      oregano (to taste)
      basil (to taste)

Prepare rice. In a skillet with a cover, saute the onion until translucent. Add remaining ingredients and cook over medium heat until bubbly, stirring occasionally. Cover, lower heat, and simmer about 15 minutes. Serve over rice. Top with grated Cheddar cheese (if desired). Serves 8.

✦ **Leftover beans? add to Jambalaya, Spanish rice, red beans and rice instead of meat.**
✦ **Leftover rice? Saute onion in butter. Add rice and chopped up leftover meat. Season with garlic powder, salt and pepper.**

Japanese Goulash

2-3 cups cooked rice
2   pieces bacon, fried and crumbled or ½ cup hamburger,
    browned, or ½ cup ham, diced
1   egg
1   carrot, finely diced

Fry meat in a skillet. Remove meat and drain on paper towels.
Scramble egg. Add meat, rice and carrot to skillet with the egg.
Cook until warmed. Serve with soy sauce.

Rice Casserole

1   lb. hamburger
½   cup onion, diced
1   cup celery, diced
½   cup uncooked rice
1   (10¾ ounce) can cream of chicken soup
1   (10¾ ounce) can cream of mushroom soup
1   soup can water
1   cup crushed potato chips

Brown hamburger, onion and celery. Add rice, soups and water.
Place in a 9x13 inch baking pan. Bake 90 minutes at 325
degrees. Add water if casserole becomes dry during baking.

Stuffing Mix

6   cups cubed bread
1   Tbsp. parsley flakes
3   Tbsp. chicken bouillon powder
¼   cup dried minced onion
½   cup dried minced celery, or fresh celery
     may be sauteed and added just before cooking
1   tsp. thyme
1   tsp. pepper
½   tsp. sage
½   tsp. salt

Preheat oven 350°. Spread the bread cubes on a cookie sheet and bake for 8 to 10 minutes, turning to brown evenly. Cool. In a plastic bag or bowl, toss the cubes with the rest of the ingredients until well-coated. Store in a tightly closed container in the pantry for up to 4 months, or in the freezer for up to a year.

To use: Combine 2 cups stuffing mix with ½ cup water and 2 tablespoons melted butter. Stir to combine thoroughly. Warm on the stove top or in a microwave. Stir again just before serving. Serves 8-12.

For stuffing, use any day old-bread such as French bread, dinner rolls, hamburger and hot dog buns.

Recipes reprinted with permission from The Complete Tightwad Gazette by Amy Dacyczyn.

Salads, Dressings, Pickles & Dips

Life is too short to stuff a cherry tomato

Salads, Dressings & Pickles Tips

✦ **Flavored Oil:** Nearly any type of quality oil, from olive to truffle and walnut oils, can be enhanced with a little help from some herbs and spices. This, in turn, enlivens the flavor of breads, salads or virtually whatever you are cooking that requires the use of oil. A 750-millimeter bottle with cork (wine bottle) is a good way to store flavored oils. Allow oils over time to marinate to your desired taste, or serve them right away. (*Refrigerate all oil containing garlic** and use un-baked garlic oil within 1 week.)

✦ Keep several cans of fruit in the refrigerator. If you need to make a quick fruit salad, the fruit is already chilled.

✦ When you **run out of pickles** but still have juice left, slice a cucumber and pack it in the juice. Let it sit in the refrigerator at least 1 week before using.

✦ **If your cheese slicer sticks** when cutting through soft cheeses, spritz the roller bar with a nonstick cooking spray.

✦ **Use kitchen shears to cut green onions** or chives for salads and to use in recipes. It is much safer and faster than using a knife.

✦ **To save time when preparing potato salad,** put the peeled cooked potatoes and peeled hard-cooked eggs into a bowl and use a pastry blender to chop them.

To Make Sprouts

Place ¼ cup of mung beans in a quart jar and cover with tepid water. Cover with cloth (such as cheesecloth) and tie securely around jar. Soak overnight. Drain water off. Set in a warm dark place. Every day, rinse with tepid water and drain. Place in a warm dark place again. Repeat for four or five days until sprouts are as big as you want.

Bean Salad

1   can each, whole corn, green beans and wax beans
1   cup green and red peppers, diced
½   cup celery, chopped
1   onion, chopped (or to taste)

Mix together and cover with dressing. Refrigerate at least 1 hour.
This gets better the longer it sits. Serves 6.

Dressing

1   cup sugar
1   cup vinegar
½   cup vegetable oil
½   tsp. salt
Combine and shake well.

Carrot Salad

2   cups carrots, cooked but not mushy
1   cup chopped onion
½   cup chopped green peppers
1   stalk celery, chopped (optional)
1   cup sugar
½   cup oil
¼   cup vinegar
¼   tsp. Worcestershire sauce
½   tsp. mustard
1   cup tomato sauce

Mix all ingredients and refrigerate overnight before serving.
Serves 4.

Cole Slaw

½   cup mayonnaise or salad dressing
¼   cup sugar
3   carrots, shredded
1   small head cabbage, shredded

Mix mayonnaise or salad dressing in a bowl with the sugar. Mix cabbage and carrots together. Add sauce to cabbage and carrots just before serving. The dressing can be made in advance and stored in a separate container in the refrigerator. Serves 8.

Cucumber Salad

3   medium cucumbers, peeled and diced
½   medium onion, diced
1   Tbsp. white vinegar
⅓   cup sugar
¼   cup water

Mix all the ingredients in a bowl. Cover and refrigerate several hours or overnight. Serves 4.

Cottage Cheese Salad

2   cups cottage cheese
½   green pepper, chopped
½   onion, chopped or ½ tsp. onion powder
½   tomato, chopped
½   Tbsp. chives and/or parsley
     salt and pepper (to taste)

Mix all ingredients in a bowl and refrigerate at least 1 hour before serving (overnight is better). Serves 4.

Other stir-ins for cottage cheese

+ peaches
+ apricots
+ pineapple
+ pears
+ salsa

+ cucumbers
+ marshmallows and sugar
+ salt and pepper
+ nuts

+ **To soften marshmallows that have become hard, place them in a resealable plastic bag with a few slices of fresh bread for a few days. To prevent drying out, store in your freezer.**

+ **If you find a good deal on cottage cheese, turn the container upside down in the fridge. It will last several weeks to a couple of months!**

Garden Salad

⅓   cup zucchini, sliced
⅓   cup fresh mushrooms, sliced
1   small tomato, sliced
⅓   cup green pepper, sliced
⅓   cup celery, sliced
⅓   cup green onions with tops
½   tsp. fresh basil, chopped

Combine all of the vegetables in a bowl. In a small bowl, whisk together dressing ingredients. Pour over salad and toss to coat. Makes 2 servings. This recipe can be easily doubled or tripled. Serves 4.

Dressing

¼   cup olive or vegetable oil
2   Tbsp. red wine vinegar
¼   tsp. dried oregano
⅛   tsp. garlic powder
⅛   tsp. salt
⅛   tsp. pepper

Salad Topping

2   cups old-fashioned oats
½   cup butter or margarine, melted
⅓   cup Parmesan cheese, grated
⅓   cup wheat germ
1   tsp. oregano, dried
½   tsp. thyme, dried
¼   tsp. seasoned salt

Mix all the ingredients in a bowl. Spread onto an ungreased 15x10x1-inch baking pan. Bake at 350° for 15-18 minutes until lightly browned. Cool. Store in an airtight container for up to 3 months. Makes 3 cups.

Garlic Salad

4   stalks celery
4   carrots
1   pint Hellmann's™ or Best Foods™ mayonnaise
     (no substitutes)
¼   tsp. garlic powder
¼   Tbsp. garlic salt

Place celery and carrots in a blender with a little water. Chop finely, drain and dry between two paper towels. Add garlic powder, garlic salt and mayonnaise. Mix well and chill overnight. Serves 4.

Macaroni Salad

6   cups macaroni, cooked
1   dill pickle, chopped (optional)
½   cup mayonnaise
2   hard boiled eggs, chopped (optional)
½   onion, finely chopped or 1 tsp. onion powder
2   stalks celery, diced
2   carrots, diced
1   tsp. garlic powder
     salt (to taste)
½   lb. chicken, turkey, or ham (optional)

Mix all the ingredients together and chill before serving. Simple but delicious. Serves 6-8.

Minty Peas and Onions

2   large onions, cut into ½ inch wedges
½   cup sweet red pepper, chopped
2   Tbsp. cooking oil
2   (16 ounce) pkgs. frozen peas
2   Tbsp. fresh mint, minced or 2 tsp. dried mint

In a large skillet, saute onions and red pepper in oil just until onions begin to soften. Add peas. Cook, uncovered, stirring occasionally, for 10 minutes or until heated through. Stir in mint and cook for 1 minute. Serves 4.

Potato Salad

¼   cup mayonnaise
1   tsp. garlic powder (or more to taste)
1   tsp. onion powder or
½   onion, finely chopped (more to taste)
1   dill pickle, diced into small pieces
2   carrots, peeled and chopped
2   slices bacon, fried and crumbled (optional)
3   eggs, hard-boiled and chopped
6   potatoes, peeled, cubed into small pieces and boiled
     salt

Mix the mayonnaise, garlic powder, onion powder, and pickle in a large bowl. Add eggs and warm potatoes, carrots and bacon, if desired, and mix well. Add salt to taste. Mix well. Chill 1-2 hours before serving. If the potato salad seems dry, add a couple of tablespoons of milk. Serves 10.

✦ **When making potato salad, add the dressing to warm potatoes for the best taste. Warm potatoes will absorb the flavor from the dressing while cool ones will not.**

Tomato Basil Salad

4   large tomatoes
1   Tbsp. wine vinegar
⅓   cup fresh basil leaves, chopped into small pieces
       salt and pepper (to taste)
2   Tbsp. oil

Dice tomatoes and combine with salt, pepper, vinegar, oil and basil. Serve.

Variation:

Add cubes of mozzarella cheese

Croutons

1½   tsp. garlic, minced
¼   tsp. salt and pepper (to taste)
¼   cup olive oil or vegetable oil
3   cups bread cubes*
2   tsp. Parmesan cheese
½   tsp. onion powder (or less to taste)
½   tsp. Italian seasoning (optional)

Preheat oven to 350°. In a small bowl, mix garlic, salt and pepper, and olive oil. Put bread cubes into a bowl and sprinkle with Parmesan cheese, onion powder and Italian seasoning, if desired. Pour oil mixture over bread crumbs and toss. Spread out on a baking sheet. Bake, turning once, until golden brown, about 15-20 minutes. Store in an airtight container. These taste best if they are allowed to sit for one day before using.
Makes 3 cups.

*Any thick pieces of leftover bread will work.

Deviled Eggs

6   hard-boiled eggs
1/8   tsp. salt
1/4   tsp. prepared mustard
1/3   cup mayonnaise
1   tsp. vinegar (optional)
       paprika
       parsley, chopped

Shell hard boiled eggs and cut in half. Remove yolks and mash; add salt, mustard, mayonnaise and vinegar if using and mix until smooth. Heap yolk mixture into whites and sprinkle with paprika or chopped parsley. Serves 6.

Garlic Deviled Eggs

Add 1 clove garlic, pressed, to egg yolk mixture in preceding recipe.

✦ **To stuff deviled eggs, put the filling in a resealable plastic bag, cut off a small corner of the bag and squeeze filling into egg halves.**

Bleu Cheese Dressing

1 qt. (4 cups) mayonnaise
1 cup buttermilk
1 cup small-curd cottage cheese (optional)
1 tsp. garlic powder
1 tsp. salt (more to taste)
1 tsp. Worcestershire sauce
3 ounce bleu cheese, crumbled

Combine all ingredients in a bowl except bleu cheese. Mix with a blender if using cottage cheese. Stir in bleu cheese with a fork, and refrigerate. Makes 1½ quarts.

Cucumber-Buttermilk Dressing

1 cup buttermilk
¼ cup cucumber, peeled and grated
1 Tbsp. Dijon-style mustard
2 Tbsp. green onions, white and green parts, or chives, minced
2 tsp. fresh parsley, minced or 1 tsp. dried parsley
¼ tsp. dill, dried
¼ tsp. black pepper, freshly ground
1 tsp. lemon juice or vinegar

Combine all ingredients in a jar with a tight lid. Shake well. Refrigerate. Makes 1¼ cups.

Chile Garlic Oil

6   dried chilies of choice
4   cups 10% olive oil and 90% vegetable oil, or 100% olive oil
4   cloves garlic

Preheat oven to 350°. Split chilies lengthwise. Peel and slice the garlic into halves. Pour 2 tablespoons oil into a pie tin. Add the garlic and chilies and roast in an oven for 20 minutes, turning the chilies and garlic every 5 minutes. Remove pie tin from oven and allow to cool. Place chilies, garlic and oil into a bottle, then add remaining oil. Cork. Makes 4 cups.

*Refrigerate **all** oil containing garlic and use within 1 month. Baking kills the spores that cause botulism.

Herbed Vinegar

2   cup white vinegar
1   cup fresh herbs: basil, mint, dill, rosemary, chives or oregano (choose one)

Decide which herb you'd like to flavor your vinegar. Place the vinegar in a glass jar or bottle. Add herbs, seal and let steep for 2-4 weeks. The longer you let it steep, the stronger the vinegar. Remove herbs and put in 2 or 3 sprigs of the herb for decoration. Seal bottle with cork and then pour melted paraffin around the top and tie with a ribbon for gift giving. Makes 2 cups.

Garlic Vinegar

Substitute 6 cloves garlic for herbs.

Berry Vinegar

Substitute 2 cups crushed berries for herbs.

Italian Vinaigrette

½ cup red wine vinegar
1 cup olive oil or vegetable oil, or a combination
2 Tbsp. onion, finely chopped, or ¼ tsp. onion powder
2 large cloves of garlic, crushed
¾ tsp. of salt
¼ tsp. black pepper
1 Tbsp. parsley, minced
1 tsp. dry mustard
½ tsp. dried basil or oregano
1 tsp. sugar

Combine ingredients in a large jar with tight lid. Shake well. Makes 1½ cups.

For **Creamy Italian Dressing** beat ½ cup mayonnaise into Italian Vinaigrette.

For **Low-Calorie Vinaigrette** substitute apple juice for the oil and reduce vinegar to ⅓ cup.

Zesty Vinaigrette

¾ cup vegetable oil
¼ cup white wine vinegar
1 tsp. salt
1 tsp. dry mustard
½ tsp sugar
½ tsp garlic powder
3-4 drops Tabasco sauce

In a jar with a tight-fitting lid, combine ingredients and shake well.

Lemon Garlic Dressing

½   cup olive oil or vegetable oil
¼   cup lemon juice
½   tsp. salt
⅛   tsp. pepper
2   cloves of garlic, split

Combine all ingredients in a jar with a tight lid and shake. Let stand at room temperature for 1 hour. Remove garlic before serving. Makes ¾ cup.

Lemon Pepper Dressing

1   cup plain or non-fat yogurt
1   Tbsp. parsley, chopped or 1½ tsp. dried parsley
1   Tbsp. lemon juice
¼   tsp. pepper
1   clove garlic, crushed or ¼ tsp. garlic powder

For herbed dressing add:

1   tsp. fresh herbs or ¼ tsp. dried herbs (dill, oregano, basil, rosemary or tarragon)

Mix all ingredients and stir well. Refrigerate before serving. For a low-fat dressing, use low-fat yogurt. Makes 1 cup.

Old-Fashioned Salad Dressing

2   cups sugar
2   Tbsp. flour
1   tsp. salt
½   tsp. ground mustard
3   eggs, slightly beaten
1   cup vinegar
1   cup water
     mayonnaise

In a saucepan, combine sugar, flour, salt and mustard. Stir in eggs. Gradually stir in vinegar and water until smooth. Bring to a boil over medium heat, stirring constantly; cook and stir for 2 minutes. Cover and refrigerate. Just before serving, combine desired amount of dressing base with an equal amount of mayonnaise. Refrigerate leftovers. Tastes great on potato salad, coleslaw or salad greens. Makes 4 cups.

Orange Mint Vinegar

     orange peel
½   cup fresh mint leaves
     apple cider vinegar or
     distilled white vinegar

Remove peel (colored portion only) from one small orange in a thin spiral and place in a sterilized pint jar. Lightly crush mint leaves and add to jar. Heat apple cider or distilled white vinegar to just below the boiling point. Fill jar with vinegar and cap tightly. Allow to stand 3 to 4 weeks. Strain vinegar, discarding peel and mint. Pour vinegar into a clean, sterilized jar, adding fresh mint and peel for garnish, if desired. Seal tightly. Use in dressing for tossed green salads with orange and grapefruit sections or to marinade chicken or lamb chops.

Poppy Seed Dressing

¾ cup sugar
1 tsp. dry mustard
1½ tsp. onion salt
⅓ cup vinegar
1 cup vegetable oil
1 Tbsp. poppy seeds

Mix sugar, mustard and onion salt. Add vinegar and mix well. Add oil slowly, beating with a mixer or blender constantly until thick. Add poppy seeds and beat until well blended. Great on fruit salad. Makes 1½ cups.

Ranch Dressing

1 cup mayonnaise (low-fat may be used)
1 cup buttermilk
1 Tbsp. onion flakes
½ tsp. oregano
¼ tsp. onion powder or 1 Tbsp. fresh onions, minced
1 tsp. dried parsley
¼ tsp. garlic powder or ½ to 1 clove garlic, finely minced
¼ tsp. paprika
⅛ tsp. cayenne pepper
¼ tsp. salt
¼ tsp. black pepper

Combine ingredients in a container with a lid and refrigerate before serving. Makes 2 cups.

For Ranch Dip, use sour cream or yogurt in place of buttermilk.

Sweet Tomato French Dressing

Taste like Catalina Dressing

²/₃   cup ketchup
½   cup sugar (or to taste)
²/₃   cup vegetable oil
½   cup lemon juice or vinegar
     salt (to taste)
1- 2   cloves garlic, pressed
½   tsp. onion powder

Combine all ingredients in a jar with tight lid and shake. Refrigerate. Makes 2 cups.

Thousand Island Dressing

¾   cup mayonnaise
1   Tbsp. sweet pickle relish or sweet pickle, minced
2   Tbsp. chili sauce or ketchup
2   Tbsp. green bell peppers, minced
1   Tbsp. fresh or 1½ tsp. dried parsley
½   tsp. onion powder or 2 Tbsp. onion, minced
½   tsp. granulated sugar
¼   tsp. Worcestershire sauce
1   Tbsp. lemon juice
1   hard-boiled egg, chopped

Combine all the ingredients in a bowl except egg. Mix well. Stir in the egg. Refrigerate. Makes 1⅓ cups.

Dilled Onions

½   cup sugar
2   tsp. salt
¾   tsp. dill seed
½   cup white vinegar
¼   cup water
6   white onions, sliced

In a saucepan, heat all the ingredients except the onions. Bring to a rolling boil. Add onions and let stand until cool. Store in jars covered in the refrigerator. Makes 2 cups.

Dilled Veggies

6-8 carrots, cut into sticks
     cauliflower
     bell peppers
     leftover brine from dill pickles

Simmer carrots in salted water until not quite tender. Drain. Pour leftover pickle brine over the carrots and heat just until boiling. Cool and put into a jar. Store in the refrigerator up to several weeks. You may use also cauliflower and peppers in place of or with carrots.

✦ **Store toothpicks in an empty spice bottle with a shaker top and screw-on lid. It's easy to remove the lid and gently shake out a toothpick through the holes when you need one.**

Easy Pickles

5   lbs. cucumbers, 3-5 inches long
½   gallon water
1½   cups pickling salt, divided
2   Tbsp. pickling spices
4-5 cloves garlic, unpeeled
4-5 sprigs fresh dill
6¼   cups water
½   cup salt
2½   cups apple cider vinegar
3   Tbsp. sugar

Wash cucumbers well. Place in a large glass container. Combine ½ gallon water with 1 cup salt. Stir until salt is dissolved. Pour over cucumbers. Place a plate on cucumbers to keep them submerged in liquid. Cover and refrigerate overnight. Drain and rinse the cucumbers, discarding brine. Place into 4 or 5 sterilized wide-mouthed quart jars. Divide pickling spices, garlic and dill between the jars. Combine 6¼ cups water, ½ cup salt, vinegar and sugar in a medium saucepan. Bring to a boil and pour into jars. Cool at room temperature. Cover and refrigerate at least 2 weeks before using. Use within 2 months. Makes 4-5 quarts.

Sometimes an unanswered prayer
is
a blessing.

Garlic Pickles

4 (1 pint) jars
8 heads of dill
4 clove garlic
8 Tbsp. pickling spices
1 hot pepper, cut into 4-5 pieces
12 cucumbers, sliced (4-5 inches long)
1 cup water
4 cups vinegar
1/2 cup salt, non-iodized

Place 2 heads of dill, 1 clove of garlic and 2 Tbsp. of pickling spice in each jar. Add 1 piece of pepper to each jar. Pack sliced cucumbers into jars. Boil last three ingredients and pour over cucumbers. Refrigerate several weeks before serving.
Makes 4-5 pints.

Refrigerator Bread and Butter Pickles

4 cups sugar
4 cups vinegar
1/2 cup pickling salt
1 1/3 tsp. turmeric
1 1/3 tsp. celery seed
1 1/3 tsp. mustard
cucumbers, sliced thin
4 medium onions, sliced

Mix sugar, vinegar, and spices in a bowl. Wash and sterilize 4 quart-sized jars. Slice cucumbers to fill jars and add onions. Stir syrup and pour over cucumbers and onions. Screw on lids and refrigerate 5 days before using. Makes 4 quarts.

Watermelon Pickles

3   pounds white portion watermelon rind, cubed
5   cups sugar
2   cups cider vinegar
1   cup water
1   Tbsp. whole cloves
1   Tbsp. whole allspice
3   cinnamon sticks, 3 inches each
1   lemon, sliced

Put watermelon cubes in a large pot with enough salted water to cover. Soak overnight. Drain. Cover with fresh, cold water and bring to a boil. Cook over low heat until tender. Drain. In another large pot, combine sugar, vinegar and water. Tie cloves, allspice, cinnamon and lemon in a cheesecloth bag. Add to sugar mixture and stir over medium heat until mixture boils. Boil 5 minutes. Add watermelon cubes and simmer until translucent, about 15 minutes. Remove spice bag and pack pickles in hot, sterilized jars. Refrigerate 2 weeks before using. Makes 4 quarts.

Herb Dip

1   clove garlic
2   pkgs. (8 ounce each) cream cheese
1/4   tsp. each dried basil, dill, marjoram, thyme and pepper
1   cup butter or margarine
1   tsp. dried oregano

Crush garlic and blend all ingredients together. You can store this in the refrigerator for up to a week or in the freezer for 3 months. Makes 2 cups.

Vegetable Dip

1   cup mayonnaise
1   tsp. horseradish
1   tsp. dry mustard
1   tsp. curry powder
     dash of lemon juice
2   Tbsp. sour cream

Mix well and chill before serving. Serve with raw vegetables. Yogurt or cottage cheese may be added in place of or with sour cream. Makes 1 cup.

Yogurt Dip

1   cup vanilla yogurt
2   Tbsp. brown sugar
1   (8 oz.) can crushed pineapple, drained
1/4   cup coconut

Mix and refrigerate 1 hour or overnight. Great with fruit or cheese cubes. Makes 2 cups.

Meats

&

Main Dishes

Romance is cooking up a gourmet meal…
Reality is washing all the dishes afterwards.

Meats and
Main Dishes Tips

✦ **Cut the amount of meat in recipes by a half,** a quarter or a third. If a recipe calls for a pound of ground beef, use only half a pound.

✦ **Add 5 or 6 drops of lemon juice when boiling tough meat.** It will make it tender.

✦ **To make 3 meals out of 1 chicken:** use the breast, thighs and drumsticks for fried chicken. Then boil the wings and the neck and make a broth. Remove the wings and the neck. Cool. Pick off any meat and return to the broth. Divide the broth in half and make Chicken and Dumplings and Chicken Soup.

✦ **Leftover pineapple juice?** Add some oil, soy sauce and garlic. Mix well. Marinate chicken for several hours. Bake chicken in marinade until juices run clear.

✦ **Buy several hams at Easter** when they are on sale. Freeze and use all year.

✦ **Cook chicken breasts** with skin and remove skin just before eating. This helps the chicken stay juicy.

✦ **Finely chop any leftover meat** and use in spaghetti or pizza sauce.

✦ **Ask the butcher to cut your round steak** for you when it's on sale. Use for stews, fajitas, etc.

✦ **Cut your meat into smaller pieces.** It will go much further in stews and other recipes.

✦ **Save livers and gizzards** in a bag in the freezer and add to them each time you cook a chicken or turkey. Then when you have enough, fry them. You can also use livers and gizzards for giblet gravy.

✦ **When using canned corned beef,** place the can in a saucepan with hot water for about 30 seconds. When open it the corned beef will slip right out.

Barbecued Beef

leftover roast beef
3   Tbsp. water
barbecue sauce

Put leftover beef in a saucepan and add water. Cook over medium heat until warmed through. Add enough barbecue sauce to coat beef and simmer for 3 minutes. Serve on buns, bread or toast.

Barbecued Meatballs

3   lbs. ground beef
2   cups oatmeal
2   eggs
1   tsp. onion powder or 1 Tbsp. onion, finely chopped
1   cup evaporated milk
2   tsp. salt
2   tsp. chili powder
$^1/_2$ tsp. pepper

Mix all the ingredients in a bowl and blend well. Form hamburger mixture into balls. Put in a 9x13 inch pan and an 8x8 inch pan, pour barbecue sauce over them. Bake at 350° for 1 hour. Makes 30 medium meatballs.

Barbecue Sauce

1$^1/_2$ cups brown sugar
2   cups ketchup
$^1/_2$ tsp. garlic powder
2   Tbsp. liquid smoke

Combine all the ingredients in a bowl. Mix well. Sauce may be refrigerated several weeks.

Barbecued Ribs

Place as many ribs as will fit into your crockpot and cover with barbecue sauce. Let simmer all day on low, basting every few hours. These will be the best ribs you have ever eaten. Serve with corn bread and cole slaw.

Beef and Bacon Over Pasta

6	slices bacon
1	clove garlic, minced
1/2	onion, chopped
1/2	green pepper, chopped
2	Tbsp. flour
1-1 1/2	cups beef stock
	sage, salt, pepper (to taste)
1	tsp. parsley, chopped
	leftover rare beef (bite-size pieces)
1	(15 ounce) can black-eyed peas
	cooked pasta

Fry bacon in a skillet on medium until crisp. Remove, cool and crumble into pieces. To the bacon grease, add garlic, onion and green pepper; lightly saute. Stir in flour; stir until smooth. Slowly stir in beef stock. Add sage, salt, pepper and chopped parsley. Add beef, black-eyed peas and bacon. Simmer and serve over warm pasta with Parmesan cheese. Good with chipped beef. Serves 6.

Beef Jerky

1   lb. flank or round steak
1   tsp. seasoned salt
½   tsp. garlic powder
½   tsp. onion powder
¼   tsp. pepper
⅓   cup soy sauce
⅓   cup Worcestershire sauce
2   Tbsp. liquid smoke

Pat steak dry with paper towel. Slice thinly across grain. In a bowl, combine the rest of the ingredients. Place meat in bowl, making sure each slice is coated with marinade. Place in refrigerator overnight. Drain meat on paper towels, blotting well. Place meat on oven rack and cook at 140° for 3 hours, or in a food dehydrator for 8 hours. Store in a jar in the refrigerator.

Beef and Noodles

1   lb. leftover roast
1   cup water
¼   cup flour
     salt and pepper (to taste)
1   tsp. garlic powder
1   lb. egg noodles, cooked

Mix water and flour in a jar and shake well. Pour into saucepan and boil until it starts to thicken. Add roast. Cook until roast is heated though. Add garlic powder, salt and pepper. Serve over cooked noodles or on toast. Serves 6.

Beef Marinade

3   Tbsp. olive oil or salad oil
¼   cup soy sauce
¼   cup red wine vinegar
1   Tbsp. crushed rosemary
4   cloves garlic, minced (more or less to your taste)
    salt and pepper

Combine ingredients in a bowl. Place beef in a shallow pan. Pour marinade over beef. Marinate beef for 1 hour or overnight for best flavor. When cooking the meat (whatever method you choose), put the excess marinade in a pan and simmer. If you want a thicker sauce, dissolve 1 Tbsp. cornstarch in 1½ Tbsp. water and add to simmering marinade. Use this as a sauce on the side.

Variations

✦ Substitute balsamic vinegar for the soy and red wine vinegar.
✦ Substitute ginger for the rosemary for a teriyaki flavor.
✦ Substitute rice wine vinegar or lemon juice for red wine vinegar.
✦ Add some sugar or honey for sweetness.
✦ Add Worcestershire sauce or chili powder for a different flavor.

Beef Stroganoff

½-1 lb. round steak
1 cup sour cream or yogurt
1 (10¾ ounce) can cream of mushroom soup
1 Tbsp. ketchup
1 tsp. onion salt
½ tsp. garlic powder
1 Tbsp. Worcestershire sauce
2-3 cups rice or egg noodles, cooked

Cut round steak into small bite-sized pieces. In a large skillet, brown on medium high for 5-10 minutes (until cooked through). Add the rest of the ingredients and blend well. Cook only until heated through. Serve over rice or egg noodles. Serves 4.

Beef Taco Bake

½ lb. ground beef
1 (10¾ ounce) can tomato soup
1 cup salsa
½ cup milk
8 corn tortillas or 6 flour, cut into 1-inch pieces
1 cup Cheddar cheese, shredded

In a large skillet, brown beef on medium heat until thoroughly cooked. Drain off fat. Add soup, salsa, milk, tortillas and half the cheese. Spoon into a 2-quart baking dish and cover. Bake at 400° for 30 minutes until hot. Sprinkle remaining cheese on top. Serves 4.

Burritos

Refried beans (p.142)
tortillas, warmed
sour cream (optional)
ground beef, browned and seasoned with taco
      seasoning (optional)
olives (optional)
salsa (optional)
cheese, grated

Spoon beans onto tortillas. Add other ingredients if desired. Top with grated cheese. Roll and tuck ends. Serve warm.

Cheeseburger Rolls

1	batch Ninety-minute roll dough (p.75)
1/4	lb. ground beef
1/2	tsp. onion salt
1/2	tsp. garlic salt
	salt and pepper (to taste)
	Cheddar cheese, grated

Make up Ninety-minute roll dough. Roll into twelve 3-inch circles. In a saucepan, brown ground beef; drain. Add onion salt, garlic salt, salt and pepper. Put 1 tablespoon ground beef mixture and 1 tablespoon of cheese in the center of the 6 circles. Then press another circle on top and seal the edges. Bake at 350° for 10-15 minutes (until golden brown). Serves 6.

Chicken-Fried Steak

1   cup flour
      salt and pepper (to taste)
1   tsp. onion powder
1   lb. ground beef
2   cloves garlic, crushed and chopped
1   egg, lightly beaten
½   cup milk
      cracker crumbs
      vegetable oil for frying

Put some flour in a bowl with salt, pepper and onion powder. Put cracker crumbs in another bowl. Stir garlic into ground beef, form into patties and smash flat. Combine milk and egg in a bowl. Dip each patty into flour, then into the egg/milk mixture and then into the cracker crumbs. Fry in hot oil until golden brown on each side. Serve with white gravy. Serves 4.

White Gravy

2-4 Tbsp. drippings from chicken fried steak
4   Tbsp. flour
2   cups milk
      salt and pepper (to taste)

After frying the chicken fried-steak leave 2-4 Tbsp. of drippings and crumbs in the pan. Add the flour quickly, stirring constantly until all the crumbs are loosened and mixture is thick. Then add milk and boil until thickened. Add more or less milk depending on the consistency you like. Salt and pepper to taste and pour over chicken-fried steak.

Fajitas

1½ lbs. round steak or beef chuck
½ cup lime juice
2 jalapeno peppers, seeded and finely chopped
1 clove garlic, minced
6 flour tortillas, warmed (p. 99)
1 tsp. vegetable oil

Salsa:
1 Tbsp. fresh cilantro
1 large tomato, chopped
1 small onion, chopped

Cut meat crosswise into ½ inch thick strips. Pound each piece to ¼ inch thickness. Slice into ½ inch slices. Combine lime juice, jalapenos and garlic. Place beef in a plastic bag; add lime juice mixture, turning to coat beef. Close bag securely; marinate in refrigerator 4-6 hours, turning occasionally. Combine tomato, onion and cilantro for salsa. Cover tightly; refrigerate. Remove beef from marinade; discard marinade. Pat beef dry with paper towels. Heat oil in a large skillet on high. Cook beef pieces 2 at a time, in hot oil for 2-3 minutes, turning once. Season with salt and pepper. Serve beef slices in warm tortillas with salsa. Top with Cheddar cheese if desired. Serves 6.

✦ **Eat by candlelight with tablecloths and placemats. It makes even plain meals look special.**

Hamburger Casserole

½	lb. ground beef, browned
6	cups macaroni, cooked
2	cups American cheese
1	(15 ounce) can tomato sauce
½	tsp. garlic powder
½	tsp. onion powder
	salt (to taste)

In a casserole mix browned ground beef with macaroni and add cheese; stir until melted. Add tomato sauce, garlic powder, onion powder, and salt. Heat in oven at 350° for 20 minutes. Serves 4.

Bean Goulash

½	lb. ground beef
½	lb. bacon
1	stalk celery
1	small onion
1	(15 ounce) can kidney beans or 2 cups cooked beans
1	(15 ounce) can butter beans
1	(15 ounce) can pork and beans
1	Tbsp. vinegar
½	tsp. dry mustard
½	cup barbecue sauce or ketchup
½	cup sugar
½	cup brown sugar

Brown ground beef, bacon, celery and onion. If using canned beans, drain them. Mix the rest of the ingredients together with ground beef mixture. Bake at 350° for 30 minutes or put in the crockpot on low for 1-2 hours. Serves 8-10.

Hash

½   lb. ground beef
1   large onion, chopped
1   large green pepper, chopped
1   (16 ounce) can tomatoes, chopped
½   cup white rice, uncooked
2   tsp. chili powder
2   tsp. salt
⅛   tsp. pepper

In a large skillet, brown beef, onion, and green pepper. Drain fat. Add tomatoes, rice, chili powder, salt and pepper. Heat through. Pour into 2-quart casserole. Cover and bake 1 hour at 350°. Serves 4.

Liver and Onions

2-4 slices bacon
1   lb. liver
¼   cup flour
1   tsp. salt
    dash of pepper
    oil
1   onion, sliced

Fry bacon in a large skillet. When crisp, remove and set aside, leaving grease in skillet. In a shallow dish combine flour, salt and pepper. Mix well. Coat liver on both side with flour mixture. Place in skillet and fry in hot bacon grease over medium heat. Turn when browned. Fry 5-8 minutes until crisp and golden. Remove to platter. Add a small amount of oil to the skillet if necessary. Add onions and fry briefly just until lightly browned. Sprinkle with salt and pepper. When onion rings begin to wilt, remove and spread over liver. Arrange crisp bacon on top and serve with ketchup. Serves 4-6.

Maidrites

6　lbs. ground beef
8　slices bread, cubed
3　cups milk
1½　cup tomato juice
4　eggs
　　onion powder (to taste) or 1 cup chopped onion
　　salt (to taste)

Mix ingredients together. Pour into three 9x13 pans. Bake at 300° for 1½ to 2½ hours (until done). Stir frequently. Serve with pickles on hamburger buns or bread as with Sloppy Joes. You can halve the recipe, and it freezes very well. Serves 30.

Mexican Hamburger Casserole

½　lb. ground beef, browned
1　(10¾ ounce) can cream of chicken soup
½　lb. Cheddar cheese
1　(15 ounce) can tomato sauce
1　sm. can green chilies, diced
1　(10 count) pkg. corn tortillas

Mix browned ground beef, chicken soup, tomato sauce and green chilies in a bowl. Put a layer of tortillas on the bottom of a 9x13 pan, then a layer of meat, a layer of tortillas, and sprinkle cheese on top. Bake 300° 30-45 minutes. Serves 6-8.

Pasties

Filling

1	Tbsp. water
4	Tbsp. butter or margarine
2	chicken bouillon cubes
1½	cups carrots, chopped
4	medium potatoes, peeled and diced
½	onion, chopped
½ -1	lb. ground beef, browned
	salt and pepper (to taste)

Dough

1	cup shortening
3	cups flour
¼	tsp. salt
6	Tbsp. water

In a saucepan, simmer the carrots in the water, butter, and chicken bouillon cubes. Add potatoes, onion, ground beef and salt and pepper. Divide into fourths. Mix dough ingredients and roll into four 10-inch circles. Put the meat mixture on one side of the dough. Fold the other half of the dough over and seal with fingers or a fork. Bake 1 hour at 375°. Serves 4-6.

✦ **These are also great with leftover turkey, chicken, roast beef and pork. You could also add other vegetables. This is a good way to use those leftovers.**

Slow Cook Roast

1   beef roast, 3-5 lbs.
1   (10¾ ounce) can cream of mushroom soup
1   onion, sliced

Place roast in pan. Pour cream of mushroom soup and onion on top. Cover tightly. Bake at 250° for 1 hour. Then turn down to 225° and cook for 15 or more hours. 10 hours for roasts smaller than 3 pounds.

✦ **This is excellent for inexpensive roasts.** It makes them so tender they fall off the bone and are almost impossible to lift out of the pan. Excellent for Sunday after church or for guests, because it can cook for 2 or 3 hours longer without overcooking. Serves 4.

✦ Use a **meat thermometer** to make sure internal temperature reaches 145°

Brown Gravy

     meat broth
2   Tbsp. flour or 1 Tbsp. cornstarch
1   cup cold water
     salt and pepper

Add at least one or two cups of water to the roasting pan of your roast, pork or chicken while the meat is cooking. Remove the meat when done and skim off the fat. Put the pan on a stove-top burner on medium heat. Put flour or cornstarch in a jar. Add cold water (¼ cup dry milk could also be added), cap and shake until all the lumps are gone. Pour the flour mixture slowly into the simmering broth and stir constantly until thickened. If there is a lot of liquid you may need to use more flour. Salt and pepper to taste. Serves 4.

Pepper Steak

1   lb. round steak
2   Tbsp. Worcestershire sauce
½   cup celery, chopped (optional)
¼   lb. mushrooms, sliced (optional)
1   medium onion, chopped (optional)
1   medium green pepper, cut into slivers
2   tomatoes, cut into wedges
1   Tbsp. lemon juice
1   Tbsp. soy sauce
     dash of pepper
1   Tbsp. flour
1   Tbsp. oil
½   cup water
1-2 cups cooked rice

Cut round steak into 1x3 inch strips. Make sauce by combining Worcestershire sauce, lemon juice, soy sauce and dash of pepper. Add meat, flour, celery, mushrooms, and onions to sauce. Stir to coat. Saute in hot oil until meat is browned. Add water. Cover and simmer about 1 to 1½ hours. Add green peppers and simmer until tender. Add tomatoes, mix and cook 5 more minutes. Serve over rice or noodles . Serves 4.

+ **Don't serve the entire roast. Save some for barbecue beef, beef and noodles, etc. Use only a small amount of meat on buns for barbecue beef.**
+ **A Dutch oven is the same as a 6 or 8 quart saucepan in recipes.**
+ **To add garlic to meat: slice garlic clove thin. Make some slits in the top on the meat and place garlic slivers in the slits. Roast, broil or bake as usual.**

Spanish Pot Roast

3-4 lb. pot roast
1 cup sweet tomato dressing (p.169)
¾ cup water
8 small onions
8 small potatoes
2 Tbsp. flour

Cook meat in a Dutch oven on medium high heat in ¼ cup dressing; add remaining dressing and ½ cup water. Cover and simmer 3 hours on medium-low heat. Add onions and potatoes. Continue simmering 45 minutes or until vegetables and meat are tender. Remove meat and vegetables. Gradually add remaining water to flour, stir until blended. Add flour mixture to hot liquid in pan. Cook, stirring constantly until mixture boils and thickens. Simmer 3 minutes. Serve gravy over hot meat and vegetables. Serves 4.

Meat Loaf

1½ lb. ground beef
1 cup milk
½ tsp. salt
½ tsp. dry mustard
¼ tsp. pepper
¾ cup quick cooking oatmeal or ½ cup dry bread crumbs
1 egg
¼ tsp. garlic powder
1 tsp. onion powder
1 Tbsp. Worcestershire sauce
½ cup ketchup or BBQ Sauce

Mix everything together except catsup. Put into a loaf pan. Spread catsup over the top. Bake at 350 for 1 hour or until done. Serves 6.

Shepherd's Pie

½   lb. ground beef
1   onion, chopped
2   carrots, diced
1   can peas, drained or 1 can mixed vegetables for carrots and peas
1   (15 ounce) can tomato sauce
     salt and pepper (to taste)
1   tsp. sugar
2   tsp. onion powder
1   tsp. garlic powder
1   tsp. chili powder
4   cups mashed potatoes
¾   cup grated Cheddar cheese

Brown ground beef and onion. Add carrots and cook until tender. Drain grease and add peas. In a casserole dish, combine tomato sauce, salt, pepper, sugar, onion powder, garlic powder and chili powder. Mix well and add the beef mixture. Mix again thoroughly. Top with mashed potatoes and then grated cheese. Bake in the oven uncovered at 350° for 15 minutes or until the cheese melts. Serves 4.

✦ **To freeze 1 lb. portions of browned ground beef or one or two chicken parts, place in a bread bag. Tie a with a twist tie or knot above each section into 1/2 lb. or 1 lb. portions. Freeze. Then as needed cut off each section above the knot.**

✦ **When shaping hamburger patties, poke a hole through the center of each one with your index finger. The burgers cook faster this way, and the outside doesn't get overcooked before the center is done. The hole disappears as the burgers cook.**

Stacked Enchiladas

½   lb. ground beef
1   onion, chopped, or 1 tsp. onion powder
2½ cups enchilada sauce (p.216)
8   corn tortillas
    vegetable oil for frying
1   cup Cheddar cheese, grated
1   tomato, chopped
2   cups lettuce, chopped
    sour cream (optional)
    olives (optional)

In a skillet, brown ground beef and onions. Drain on paper towels and set aside. Soften tortillas by heating ½ inch oil in a small skillet. (Oil is hot when tortilla sizzles when dropped in skillet.) Dip one tortilla in hot oil for 5 seconds, turn and then remove softened tortilla to paper towel. Soften all tortillas, draining on paper towel before stacking. Place one tortilla on serving plate. Place ¼ cup beef mixture on top of tortilla. Add another tortilla and repeat stacking, ending with beef mixture on top. Add tomato, lettuce, sour cream, olives and shredded cheese. Serve warm. Serves 4.

✦ **Ever cook a dish and found it too spicy for your taste? Add sugar 1 tablespoon at a time, tasting after each addition. This helps cut the 'fire" in spicy foods.**

Steak and Mushroom Gravy

1   Tbsp. margarine
½   onion, chopped
5   Tbsp. flour
    salt and pepper (to taste)
5   Tbsp. dry milk
2   cups water
1-2 cups leftover beef
1   small can mushroom pieces
1   tsp. beef bouillon powder

Melt margarine in a large skillet and saute onion. Mix flour, salt and pepper and dry milk in a jar. Add water and shake. Stir into onions until simmering and thickened. Add beef, bouillon powder and drained mushrooms. Reduce the heat. Simmer, stirring constantly, until heated through. Serve over noodles, rice or mashed potatoes or toast. Serves 4.

Tacos

½   lb. ground beef
    salt and pepper (to taste)
1-3 Tbsp. taco seasoning (p.305)
8   corn or flour tortillas
    hot oil
    lettuce, chopped
    tomatoes, chopped
    cheese, grated
    onion, chopped

Brown ground beef with salt, pepper and taco seasoning, drain well. Fry tortillas in hot oil. Drain on paper towels, either flat or folded. Fill with meat mixture. Add lettuce and tomatoes. Top with grated cheese and onions. Serve immediately. Serves 4.

Swiss Steak

2	lbs. round steak
2	Tbsp. flour
½	tsp. salt
	dash of pepper
1	Tbsp. oil
1	medium onion, chopped
2-3	stalks celery, chopped
¼	cup green pepper, chopped
1	cup tomatoes, peeled
2	carrots, sliced (optional)
2	cups water
8	potatoes, boiled or mashed (optional)

Mix flour salt and pepper in small bowl. Rub into round steak. Cut into serving-sized pieces. Brown meat in oil in a skillet over medium heat. Pour all vegetables except potatoes over steak and add water. Cover and reduce heat to low. Simmer 1 to 1½ hours or all day on low in the crockpot. Serve over potatoes, if desired. Serves 4.

✦ **To make a great taco filling, that won't fall out of the shells, add ⅓ cup quick cooking oats to each pound of ground beef as you brown it. Season as usual.**

Roast Turkey

1   turkey, 20-22 lbs.
1   stick margarine or butter

Defrost frozen turkey for several days in the refrigerator according to the directions on the package. Line a roasting pan with aluminum foil. Remove the insides of the turkey and save for liver gravy or for fried livers and gizzards. Lay turkey, breast side down, in the pan and place the stick of butter on the inside. Cover tightly with aluminum foil. Bake at 250° for 1 hour. Reduce heat to 200° and roast for 20-22 hours or more hours. Cooking time can be longer to fit your schedule. Test with a meat thermometer to make sure the temperature in the thigh is 180 °. This is the best turkey you will ever eat. The meat will just fall off the bones so you will have to serve it already carved. It will be very juicy and moist.

Giblet Gravy

      turkey drippings or broth
2   Tbsp. flour or 1 Tbsp. cornstarch
1   cup cold water
      salt and pepper
1   hard boiled egg, chopped
      livers and gizzards from turkey, chopped

Boil liver and gizzards until cooked through. Pour 2-3 cups turkey broth into a saucepan. Add 1 cup additional water if more gravy is needed. Skim off the fat. Put the pan on a stove-top burner on medium heat. Simmer. Put flour or cornstarch in a jar. Add cold water; cap and shake until all the lumps are gone. Pour the flour mixture slowly into the simmering broth and stir constantly until thickened. If there is a lot of liquid you may need to use more flour. Stir in egg, livers and gizzards. Salt and pepper to taste.

Chicken and Dumplings

4	cups chicken broth
1/2-1 1/2	cups chicken or turkey, cooked
1/2	cup celery, sliced
1/2	cup carrots, sliced
1	bay leaf
1	tsp. parsley flakes

Dumplings

2	cups baking mix (p.50)
1/4	tsp. thyme, dried
1/2	tsp. parsley flakes
2/3	cup milk

In a Dutch oven, combine broth, chicken, celery, carrots, bay leaf and parsley. Bring to a boil. In a bowl, combine baking mix, thyme, and parsley. Stir in milk just until moistened. Drop by tablespoonfuls into the boiling broth. Cook uncovered for 10 minutes and then cover and cook an additional 10 minutes. DO NOT PEEK or your dumplings will be soggy. Remove dumplings with a slotted spoon and serve in bowls. Remove bay leaf and spoon broth over the top of the dumplings. Serves 4.

✦ **Have the butcher cut your turkey in half for you when it's on sale. Then you don't have to cook the whole thing at once and waste it. Most butchers will do it for free.**

✦ **Save the bones from a turkey or chicken for soup.**

✦ **Don't buy a turkey with added ingredients, such as butter. Simply add your own.**

Chicken and Pasta

1   lb. fresh spinach, rinsed well
1   cup chicken broth
1   (6 ounce) pkg. pasta shells
1   tsp. olive oil or vegetable spray
½   lb. chicken breast, boned, skinned, grilled, and cut
     1 inch pieces
½   cup Parmesan cheese, grated
4   cloves garlic, minced
½   tsp. nutmeg or mace
     salt and pepper

Cook the spinach in the broth until tender. Drain and reserve broth. Remove excess liquid by mashing. Cook pasta. In heavy skillet over medium heat, add the oil or vegetable spray and saute the garlic, stirring constantly, until it is white (about 1 minute). Don't allow it to brown. Add the spinach and nutmeg or mace, salt and pepper. Add the chicken pieces to the spinach, stir and add a small amount of the reserved cooking broth. Stir the spinach until it is hot. If the spinach starts to get dry, add broth as necessary. Add the cooked pasta to the spinach mixture and blend well. Serve immediately with Parmesan cheese sprinkled on top. Serves 4.

If you would like your house to be clean, invite someone over to dinner.

Chicken Pot Pie

1⅔   cups frozen mixed vegetables, thawed
1½   cup chicken or turkey, cooked and cubed
1   (10¾ ounce) can cream of chicken soup
¼   tsp. dried thyme
1   cup biscuit mix
½   cup milk
1   egg

In a bowl, combine vegetables, chicken, soup and thyme. Pour into an ungreased 9-inch pie plate. Combine biscuit mix, milk and egg. Pour over chicken mixture. Bake at 400° for 25-30 minutes until golden brown. Serves 4-6.

Chicken Wings and Easy Barbecue Sauce

1   lb. chicken wings
¼   cup grape or other jelly
¼   cup ketchup
      garlic to taste

Mix jelly, ketchup and garlic. Spread chicken wings on a cookie sheet and spoon half or a little more of the barbecue sauce over the chicken wings. Bake in a 350° oven for 20 minutes. Turn and baste with remaining sauce. Bake for another 20 minutes. Save the wings from your fryer packs until you have a good amount, then make this recipe. Serves 4.

Fried Chicken

	water
1/4	cup salt
8	chicken fryer pieces
2	eggs, slightly beaten
1/2	cup buttermilk
2	cups flour
1/4	cup cornmeal
1	tsp. salt
	pepper (to taste)
	spices of your choice:
	paprika
	thyme
	oregano
	vegetable oil for frying

Mix water and salt in a bowl. Place chicken in salt water and soak 2-4 hours. Rinse salt water from chicken. Pat dry. Mix buttermilk and eggs in a bowl. In a separate container, combine flour, cornmeal, salt, pepper and the spices of your choice. Roll cut chicken in the buttermilk mixture. Coat in flour mixture. Cover and let sit in the refrigerator 2 hours. Fill skillet 1/2 inch deep with vegetable oil. Heat to 375°. Fry covered 5 minutes. Uncover, fry 5 minutes. Turn chicken over and fry 10 minutes uncovered or until juices run clear. Serves 6-8.

Hawaiian Chicken Wings

2	lbs. chicken wings
2	Tbsp. water
1/4	cup soy sauce
1/4	tsp. garlic powder
1/4	cup green onions, finely chopped or 1 sm. onion, finely chopped
2	Tbsp. sugar
1/2	tsp. dry mustard
1/2	tsp. ground ginger
2	Tbsp. margarine
1	cup chicken broth rice, cooked
1	tsp. cornstarch
1	Tbsp. water

Arrange chicken in a shallow baking dish. Combine the rest of the ingredients except the chicken broth, rice, cornstarch and water in a saucepan. Bring to a boil and cool. Pour over chicken and refrigerate for several hours. Turn pieces over and bake uncovered at 350° for 45 minutes, turning after 30 minutes. Place rice on a platter and arrange chicken wings. Save fat from remaining sauce and quickly heat with chicken broth. Thicken with cornstarch and water. Put sauce in a dish and serve. Serves 4-6.

It must have taken a lot of courage
to discover that frog legs
are edible.

Herbed Chicken

1   chicken, cut with skin removed
2   medium tomatoes, chopped
1   medium onion, chopped
2   cloves garlic, chopped or 1 tsp. garlic powder
½   cup plus 2 Tbsp. chicken broth
1   bay leaf
1½   tsp. salt
1   tsp. thyme, dried
¼   tsp. pepper
2   cups broccoli florets
     rice, cooked

Place chicken in crockpot. Top with tomatoes, onion and garlic. Combine broth, bay leaf, salt, thyme and pepper. Pour over chicken. Cover and cook on low for 8 hours. Add broccoli; cook 45-60 minutes longer (until the juices run clear). Discard bay leaf. Juices may be thickened with a little cornstarch if desired. Serve over hot rice. Serve 4-6.

Honey-Baked Chicken

6   chicken fryer pieces
⅓   cup margarine, melted
⅓   cup honey
2   Tbsp. prepared mustard
1   tsp. salt

Arrange chicken in a baking dish with the skin side up. Combine the rest of the ingredients and pour over chicken. Bake at 350° for 1 hour and 15 minutes, basting every 15 minutes (until chicken is tender and brown). Serve with rice. Serves 4-6.

Hot Wings

12 chicken wings
½ cup butter, melted
1 cup hot sauce
  oil for frying
  Ranch or Blue Cheese dressing

Cut the tips off the chicken wings. In a large saucepan heat oil to 350°. Place wings in pot, do not crowd. Fry until golden and crispy about 10 minutes. Combine butter and hot sauce. Toss wings in ½ butter sauce. Serve with dressing and extra butter sauce for dipping. Makes 12 wings. Recipe may be doubled or tripled.

Italian Chicken

4-8 pieces chicken
  lemon pepper
1 onion, sliced
2 cups Italian dressing

Place the chicken in a greased baking dish. Sprinkle with lemon pepper, add onion and cover with Italian salad dressing. Bake at 350° about 1 hour or until chicken is done. Serves 4-6.

Grilled Italian Chicken

Marinate chicken in dressing for several hours, then place on a hot grill. Cook until juices run clear.

Lemony Chicken Breast

2	bell peppers, chopped
1	whole chicken breast, boneless and skinless
1	Tbsp. flour
½	tsp. salt
½	tsp. pepper
2	tsp. olive oil
⅓	cup chicken broth
2	Tbsp. lemon juice
1	Tbsp. parsley, chopped
2	cups pasta, cooked

In a skillet, saute bell peppers over medium heat in a small amount of oil. Cut chicken into strips. Mix flour, salt and pepper in a bowl. Coat chicken with flour mixture. Remove peppers. Heat oil in the skillet, still on medium heat. Add chicken and cook 6-8 minutes until brown. Add peppers and warm. Put pasta on a serving dish. Place chicken and peppers on pasta. Add chicken broth and lemon juice to skillet. Stir over medium heat 2-3 minutes. Scrape brown bits on the bottom of the pan and cook until reduced. Stir in parsley. Pour over chicken. Serves 2.

Maple-Glazed Chicken

¼	cup maple syrup
4	tsp. lemon juice
1	Tbsp. butter or margarine
	salt and pepper (to taste)
4	pieces chicken

Preheat oven to 450°. Mix maple syrup, lemon juice and butter together in small saucepan. Simmer for 5 minutes. Spray a baking dish and place chicken in it. Salt and pepper the chicken. Bake for 10 minutes. Remove from oven and pour on glaze. Bake for 15 minutes more or until juices run clear. Serves 4.

Mexican Chicken

4-6 pieces chicken (remove skin)
1   cup salsa

Place chicken in a baking dish and top with salsa. Cover. Bake
at 350° for about 45 minutes or until done. Sprinkle grated
Cheddar cheese on top and serve. Great over rice. Serves 4-6.

Oven Fried Chicken

6   pieces chicken
1-1½ cups baking mix (p.52)
½   stick margarine or butter
        salt and pepper to taste

Preheat oven to 375°. Melt margarine in a 9x13 pan. Dip chicken
pieces in melted margarine, then roll or shake in baking mix until
coated. Return to 9x13 pan. Bake uncovered 50 minutes, turn
chicken, bake 15 minutes until chicken is done. Serves 4-6.

✦ **To prevent salt and peper shakers from leaking while
   filling, place a piece of tape over the hole. Once they're
   filled, turn upright and remove the tape.**

Roast Chicken

1	chicken
1-2	cloves garlic
1	tsp. thyme (to taste)
1	tsp. rosemary (to taste)
1	tsp. oregano (to taste)
	olive oil
	salt and pepper

Rub the inside of the chicken with garlic cloves. Put thyme, rosemary and oregano to taste inside the bird. Rub the outside of the bird with olive oil and salt and pepper. Bake at 450° to 500° for 15 minutes then turn the oven down to 400° and roast for 35-45 minutes (for a 2½ pound bird) or 1 hour (for a 3-5 pound bird) or until the temperature of the thigh reaches 180°. Allow to rest 10 minutes before serving. Serves 6-8.

Recipe for a Happy Marriage

1	cup consideration
2	cups flattery, carefully concealed
2	cups milk of human kindness
1	gallon faith in God and in each other
1	reasonable budget, mixed with a generous dash of cooperation
1	cup each confidence and encouragement
2	cups praise
1	small pinch in-laws
3	teaspoons pure extract of "I'm sorry"
1	cup contentment
1	large or 2 small hobbies
1	cup of blindness to the other's faults

For extra flavor, add recreation and a dash of happy memories. Stir well and remove any specks of jealousy, temper or criticism. If you like a sweeter product, add a generous portion of Love. Keep warm with a steady flame of devotion. Never serve with a cold shoulder or a hot tongue. Add to the recipe the presence and love of God and you will have quite a home.

Roast Sticky Chicken or Turkey

This recipe is a great way to roast a large chicken. It is very easy to make and makes a great deli style chicken. The meat comes out very moist and flavorful. This is the only way I will roast a chicken now. It also makes wonderful leftovers!

4	tsp. salt
2	tsp. paprika
1	tsp. cayenne pepper
1	tsp. onion powder
1	tsp. thyme
1	tsp. white pepper
½	tsp. garlic powder
½	tsp. black pepper
1	large (10 lbs.) whole chicken, chicken parts or 20 lb. Turkey*
1	cup chopped onion or
	1 sliced orange

Combine all the spices. Remove giblets from chicken. Rinse chicken. Rub the spice mixture into the chicken, both inside and out, making sure it is evenly distributed and down deep into the skin. Place in a 9x13 inch pan, seal with foil and refrigerate overnight. If using chicken parts just rub over both sides of parts. When ready to roast chicken, stuff cavity with onions or oranges. If using chicken parts place pieces on top of onions or oranges. Roast, uncovered, at 250 degrees for 5 hours. Roast chicken parts 3-5 hours. Roast a Turkey 8-10 hours. After the first hour, baste chicken with pan juices every half hour to 45 minutes. If you don't have enough juices after 3 hours to baste add 1 cup of water to the pan. The chicken will be golden to dark brown with caramelized juices on the bottom. Let chicken rest about 10 minutes before carving. Notes:

*Double spices if using on a turkey. You can put the spice rub on the chicken and freeze until you want to cook it.

It's **not recommended** to make this in the crockpot.

Stir Fry

½-1 cup of leftover beef, turkey or chicken
3-4 slices ginger root, peeled and minced
2 Tbsp. soy sauce
½ tsp. hot sauce
3 Tbsp. peanut butter
1 Tbsp. cornstarch or 2 Tbsp. flour
1 cup water
2 stalks celery, sliced
2 onions, sliced
2 green peppers, sliced
2 cups cabbage, shredded
2 cloves garlic, mashed or 1 tsp. garlic powder
1 Tbsp. oil
2 Tbsp. of water

In a bowl, mix peanut butter, soy sauce, hot sauce. Stir cornstarch in 1 cup water. Add to bowl. In a deep skillet, simmer the oil with ginger and garlic over medium heat. Add vegetables, starting with the firmest as you dice the others. Stir after each addition and sprinkle on water as needed. Make sure you do not overcook the vegetables. Add cooked meat last. Push vegetables to the side and add sauce to the pot while stirring. Add additional water if needed. As the sauce clears, mix in vegetables. Serve over rice. Serves 4.

✦ **Peel the whole fresh ginger root and freeze. Then grate as needed and return to the freezer. Stays fresh for several months this way.**

Spiced Honey Ham

1	ham
½	cup mustard
½	cup brown sugar
¼	cup honey
¼	cup orange juice
1	tsp. cloves

Mix ingredients. Score the top of 1 Slow-Cook Ham. Pour mixture over ham and begin basting the ham 3 hours before serving. Baste every half hour or so with ham juices. Serves 4-6.

Sweet Pork Chops

1	onion, sliced, or a sprinkle of onion powder
4	Tbsp. ketchup
½	cup sweet pickle juice
4	pork chops

Arrange pork chops in a baking pan. Sprinkle with salt and top with 1 slice onion and 1 tablespoon ketchup. Pour the pickle juice around the pork chops. Cover and bake at 350° for 1 hour. Serves 4.

Ham and Beans

2   cups dried lima or
     great northern beans, washed well
1   tsp. salt
1/8 tsp. pepper
2   cups ham, cubed in pieces

Soak beans overnight in 6 cups of water. Drain and put in pot with 6 cups fresh water. Season with salt and pepper. Add ham and simmer over low heat for 2-3 hours or until beans are tender. Serves 6-8.

Great with corn bread

Ham and Potatoes

6   potatoes, peeled and thinly sliced
2   cups Cheddar cheese, shredded
1   (10¾ ounce) can cream of mushroom soup
1   onion, chopped
½-1 lb. ham, thinly sliced

Layer the potatoes, then some cheese, then some ham and chopped onion. Continue to layer to 3 inches from top of crockpot and then pour cream of mushroom soup on top. Let simmer for several hours on low until potatoes are cooked through. Serves 4-6.

Ham and Vegetable Pot

1   (1 lb.) ham bone
6-8 cups water
4   potatoes, diced
1   lb. frozen green beans or corn
    salt and pepper (to taste)

Bring 6 cups of water to a boil. Add salt, pepper and ham bone. Reduce the heat to a simmer. Cook for several hours, until the meat comes off the bone. If necessary, add water during the cooking. Add vegetables during the last half hour of cooking. Scoop meat and vegetables out to serve. Salt and pepper. Serves 4-6.

Ham Casserole

1   lb. noodles, cooked
1-1½   cups ham, cooked and cubed
1   tsp. salt
¾   cup peas, drained and cooked
2   cups white sauce (p.191)
1   bouillon cube

Add ham and peas to cooked noodles. Dissolve bouillon into ¼ cup boiling water. Mix the bouillon and salt in the white sauce. Bake covered at 300° for 20-30 minutes. Serves 4-6.

12 ounces of tuna may be used in place of ham.

Maple Ham

1	ham
¾	cup maple syrup, divided
4	tsp. ground mustard
2	cups apple juice
4	Tbsp. cornstarch
3	Tbsp. water
2	Tbsp. margarine
6	tart apples, cored and sliced

Combine ½ cup maple syrup and mustard. Pour over ham before baking. Pour apple juice in the bottom of the roasting pan. Bake as directed for Slow-Cooked Ham. Remove ham and keep warm. Transfer juice to a saucepan. Combine cornstarch and water in a bowl and stir until smooth. Add to saucepan. Bring to a boil over medium heat and boil for 1 minute until thickened. In a skillet, melt margarine over medium heat. Add apples and ¼ cup maple syrup. Cover and cook for 10-15 minutes, stirring occasionally. Slice ham and serve with apples and gravy. Serves 4-6.

Peachy Pork Chops

4	pork chops
½	cup peach jam
1	Tbsp. vinegar
1½	tsp. mustard
½	tsp. Worcestershire sauce
	dash Tabasco® sauce

In a frying pan brown meat and cook until done. Combine rest of ingredients, heat in a saucepan and serve over meat. Serves 4.

Sheala's Ham and Noodles

1   (8 ounce) pkg. egg noodles, cooked
1   (10¾ ounce) can cream of chicken soup
½   lb. ham, chopped
1   cup Cheddar cheese, grated

Mix first three ingredients together in a casserole dish and bake at 350° for 20 minutes until warmed. Top with cheese and bake an additional 5 minutes or until cheese melts. Serves 4.

1 package of any vegetable may be added.

Slow-Cooked Ham

1   ham

Cover the bottom of a roasting pan with aluminum foil. Bake ham at 250° for 1 hour. Reduce the heat to 200° and roast another 12-15 hours. This is great because you can put in the oven overnight and it will be ready the next day for the noon meal. The cooking time can go for longer if needed to fit your schedule, since it is at such a low temperature. Serves 4-6.

Navajo Tacos

Navajo Fry Bread

4½   cups flour
½   tsp. salt
2   tsp. baking powder
1½   cups water
½   cup milk
     oil for frying

Mix dry ingredients in a bowl. Stir in the water and milk. Knead several times. Roll out into 5-inch circles. Make a small hole in the center with your fingers. In a skillet, fry in several inches of hot oil at 375°. Dough will puff and bubble. Turn when golden brown. Drain on paper towels and serve hot for tacos or with honey. Serves 6.

For Tacos

navajo fry bread
refried beans (p.142)
cheese, shredded
lettuce, shredded
tomatoes, chopped

Place refried beans on navajo fry bread. Then top with cheese, lettuce and tomatoes. Serve warm.

Green Chile

½-1   lb. pork roast, or chops,
      meat removed, cubed into small pieces
10½   ounce chicken broth
1   onion, finely chopped
¼-½   tsp. garlic powder
1   (7 ounce) can green chilies, diced
¼   jalapeno, finely chopped
1   tsp. salt
2   Tbsp. flour, dissolved in water
      white flour tortillas (p.99)

Toppings

Cheddar cheese, grated
lettuce, shredded
tomato
sour cream

Simmer pork in broth on low for 10 minutes. Add all other ingredients except flour and simmer 45 minutes. Thicken with flour so it is like a thick soup. Spoon about ¼ cup into the center of a flour tortilla. Roll up tortilla and top with more green chile. Sprinkle with cheese, lettuce and tomato. Top with sour cream if desired. This green chile freezes really well. Serves 4.

Cheese Enchiladas

6-8 tortillas warm
1 cup Cheddar cheese
1 cup Monterey Jack cheese
½ onion, chopped
1 clove garlic, crushed
1 can of enchilada sauce or homemade (see below)

Heat oven to 350°. Mix Cheddar cheese, Monterey Jack cheese, onion and garlic. Place enchilada sauce in a bowl. Dip 1 tortilla into sauce. Place in a greased 9x9 inch pan. Spoon about ¼ cup cheese mixture down the center of each tortilla. Roll up and tuck in ends; place seam sides down. Repeat with rest of tortillas. Top with remaining enchilada sauce and sprinkle the rest of the cheese on top. Bake covered until cheese is melted and bubbly (about 40 minutes). Serves 4.

Enchilada Sauce

1 (15 oz.) can tomato sauce
1 Tbsp. chili powder
5 Tbsp. green pepper, chopped (optional)
1 tsp. onion powder
½ tsp. dried oregano
½ tsp. salt (more to taste)
1 tsp. garlic powder
¼ tsp. cumin

Combine all ingredients in saucepan, mixing well. Cook and stir over medium heat until thickened. Makes 2 cups.

Quesadillas

1   (7 ounce) can green chiles (optional)
     salsa (optional)
½-1 lb. Jack cheese
12   flour or corn tortillas
     margarine

Place half a chile pepper or 1 Tbsp. salsa on a stick of Jack cheese in the center of each tortilla. Fold tortilla over cheese and pin shut with a toothpick. Melt margarine in a skillet and fry until crisp, turning occasionally. Drain on paper towels. Serves 6.

Pizza/Spaghetti Sauce

1   onion, chopped
½   lb. Italian sausage
2   (16 oz.) cans stewed tomatoes, chopped, with juice
1   (8 oz.) can tomato paste
     salt to taste
1   clove garlic, pressed, or garlic powder (to taste)
1   bay leaf
2   tsp. Italian Seasoning (p.304)

Crumble sausage in a 2-quart saucepan. Brown with onion. Drain fat. Add other ingredients and simmer for 1 hour. Remove bay leaf before serving. Serves 4.

Pizza

Dough

1	cup warm water (120°)
1	pkg. or 1 Tbsp. yeast
1	Tbsp. sugar
1	tsp. salt
2	Tbsp. oil (olive oil is best)
2½-3	cups flour
2	tsp. crushed garlic (optional)
1	tsp. basil (optional)
1	tsp. thyme (optional)
1	tsp. oregano (optional)

Dissolve yeast in a bowl with warm water. Add sugar, salt and oil and spices as desired. Mix well. Gradually add flour to form a stiff dough. Knead on floured surface until smooth. Place in greased bowl. Turn dough over so as to grease both sides in the bowl. Cover and let rise until doubled. Makes 2 medium pizzas.

Toppings

	Pizza sauce (p.217)
½	lb. mozzarella cheese, grated
	pepperoni
	onions
	olives
	green peppers
	mushrooms
	sausage
	ground beef, browned

Divide dough in half for 2 medium pizzas or roll out entire dough for a 9x13 pan ¼-½ inch thick. Bake for 5 minutes in an oven at 400° so the dough does not become soggy. Cover with pizza sauce. Add your choice of toppings and cheese. Bake at 400° for about 15 minutes.

Garden Vegetable Pizza

Thinly sliced zucchini, diced tomato, mushrooms, onions, bell pepper.

Greek Pizza

Black olives, artichoke hearts, red onion, and feta cheese.

Hawaiian Pizza

Ham or Canadian bacon and pineapple.

Meat Pizza

Sausage, salami, Italian sausage, Canadian bacon. Choose any or all meats you enjoy.

Barbequed Chicken Pizza

Spread with Barbeque Sauce. Top with Barbeque chicken, gouda, mozzarella, red onion and cilantro.

✦ **Instead of a traditional tomato sauce, brush crust with a mixture of olive oil and minced garlic. Then top as usual.**

Garden Pizza/Spaghetti Sauce

6   onions, finely chopped
3   green peppers, finely chopped
¾   cup vegetable or olive, oil
½   tsp. black pepper
18   tomatoes, skinned or stewed tomatoes, chopped
2   cloves garlic, minced
1½   Tbsp. salt
2   Tbsp. sugar
1   Tbsp. each, oregano,
        basil, thyme
6   bay leaves
3   (12 oz.) cans tomato paste
1   cup beef stock or bouillon (optional)

Saute onions and green pepper in vegetable oil in a Dutch oven. Add black pepper. Add tomatoes, garlic, salt, sugar, and herbs to the pot. Bring to a boil. Add tomato paste one can at a time and beef stock, if using. Simmer on low for 1 hour to reduce. Freeze in 1-quart bags. Makes 4 quarts.

✦ **How to cut down on meat:**
    1. Have meat two nights per week
    2. Eat soup and a sandwich once a week
    3. Have a pasta or rice night twice a week
    4. Have a "leftovers" day
    5. Have a baked potato night

Veggie Burgers

2   cups lentils, drained and cooked*
1   egg
½   cup cracker crumbs
1   small onion, minced or 1 tsp. onion powder
1   Tbsp. parsley, chopped
1   carrot, grated
     salt and pepper (to taste)
     tomato juice
     oil or bacon grease for frying

Combine all ingredients in a bowl using just enough tomato juice to hold the mixture together. Form patties and fry or grill as you would hamburgers in oil or bacon grease. Serve on buns. Serves 4.

*Boil lentils about 20 minutes until tender.

Hot Doggie Roll-Ups

hot dogs
refrigerated biscuits or refrigerated croissants

Roll each biscuit or croissant flat, then wrap around hot dog. Bake on a cookie sheet at 450° for 10-12 minutes.

Polish Sausage

2   lb. pork butt, coarsely ground
¾   beef, finely ground
1½   tsp. coarse salt
1½   tsp. peppercorns, crushed
1½   tsp. marjoram
1   Tbsp. paprika
1   tsp. garlic powder
1½   tsp. sugar (optional)
½   tsp. ground nutmeg

Sprinkle the seasoning over the ground meat. Knead until thoroughly blended. Make into patties. Refrigerate in airtight containers for 2 to 3 days to allow flavors to blend. Fry until golden brown. Freeze any unused sausage. Serves 4-6.

Breakfast Sausage

1   lb. ground pork or beef
¼-1   tsp. sage (to taste)
¼-½   tsp. marjoram
¼-½   tsp. thyme (optional)
1   tsp. salt
⅛   tsp. pepper
1-3   Tbsp. water

Prepare per instructions for Polish Sausage

✦ **When you finish grinding meat, run a piece of bread though the meat grinder. This will make it easier to clean.**

Italian Sausage

1   lb. ground pork or ½ lb. ground pork and ½ lb. ground beef
1   onion, minced
1½ tsp. salt
1   clove garlic, minced
1   tsp. basil
½   tsp. pepper
½   tsp. dried oregano
¼   tsp. paprika
⅛   tsp. thyme
1   tsp. cayenne pepper
1   tsp. fennel seeds

Prepare per instruction for Polish Sausage

Salami

2-2½ lbs. ground beef
½   tsp. onion powder
½   tsp. garlic powder
2   Tbsp. curing salt
1   Tbsp. mustard seed
1½ tsp. liquid smoke
¾   cup water
     pinch of crushed red pepper

Mix all the ingredients together. Shape into three rolls on foil and wrap securely. Refrigerate 24 hours. Open foil and bake at 300° for 1 hour and 15 minutes. Makes 3 rolls.

Baked Fish and Vegetables

4	fish fillets
4	medium potatoes, cut into 1-inch cubes
4	medium carrots, cut into 1-inch pieces
	salt, pepper, garlic powder, celery seed (to taste)
4	small onions, quartered
4	Tbsp. margarine

On each of four square 9-inch pieces of aluminum foil, place a fish fillet and a portion of potato, carrot, and onion. Add 1 tablespoon margarine to each square. Sprinkle with seasonings. Fold foil over and seal edges well. Bake on a cookie sheet at 350° for 45 minutes. This can also be put on the grill. Serves 4.

Fish Patties with Salsa

1	pound fish, cooked and flaked
$\frac{1}{2}$	cup onion, chopped finely, or 1 tsp. onion powder
2	Tbsp. lemon juice
1	tsp. fresh or $\frac{1}{2}$ tsp. dried marjoram
$\frac{1}{2}$	tsp. salt
$\frac{1}{2}$	tsp. dry mustard
2	slices bread, torn into crumbs
2	eggs, beaten
1	Tbsp. vegetable oil
	salsa

Mix all the ingredients except the oil and the salsa. Shape into 8 patties. Heat oil in a skillet over medium heat. Add patties and cook about 8 minutes until golden brown. Serve with salsa. Serves 2.

Cakes, Pies, Candy, Cookies & Desserts

The problem - how to get 2 pounds of chocolate home from the store in a hot car. The solution - eat it in the parking lot.

Cake, Frosting and Filling Tips

To frost a cake:

+ Brush loose crumbs from the sides of the cake and spread on a thin base coat of frosting.
+ Dip your knife into water from time to time to spread frosting easily.
+ Let cake set. Then apply a finishing coat.
+ If you want a flat cake, cut the rounded top off, turn it over and use the flat side as the top.
+ Place 2 pieces of waxed paper under cake. Frost. Then gently pull the waxed paper out from under the cake. Your cake plate will stay clean!

+ **Reuse squeezable mustard bottles** by washing and filling with icing for cakes.

+ **Dust cakes with powdered sugar.** Place a doily on top of the cake. Sprinkle with powdered sugar and then gently lift the doily off.

+ **When a cake recipe calls for flouring the baking pan,** use a bit of the dry cake mix instead. This eliminates white mess on the outside of the cake.

+ **Use cake or brownie crumbs** for ice cream topping.

+ **Put flour in an old spice bottle** to dust pans for cakes.

+ **To make sour milk sweet again:** Add ½ tsp. baking soda per cup of sour milk. Reduce baking powder in recipes by 2 tsp. when using sweet milk.

+ **When cooking in glass pans,** reduce the temperature by 25°.

+ **To prevent dried fruits and nuts from sinking to the bottom** of a dessert or cake, mix with flour before adding to the batter.

Applesauce Cake

½	cup shortening
1½	cups sugar
2	eggs, beaten
½	tsp. salt
1	tsp. cinnamon
½	tsp. cloves
2½	cups flour
1½	cups applesauce
1	tsp. soda in 2 Tbsp. hot water
1	cup raisins
½	cups nuts (optional)

Cream together shortening and sugar until fluffy. Add eggs, salt, cinnamon and cloves. Mix well. Add alternately flour and applesauce. Dissolve soda in hot water and pour into mixture. Stir. Fold in nuts and raisins. Bake in a well-greased loaf pan at 350° for 1 hour. Makes 1 loaf.

✦ **When you have a partially eaten apple, save the good part and chop into pieces. Place in a microwave safe dish. Blend together 1 teaspoon each brown sugar, flour, oatmeal and margarine and a dash of cinnamon. Place mixture over apple and microwave until apple is tender.**

Banana Cake

½   cup shortening
¾   cup brown sugar, packed
½   cup sugar
2   eggs
1   cup ripe bananas, (2-3 medium) mashed
1   tsp. vanilla
2   cups flour or whole wheat flour
1   tsp. baking soda
1   tsp. salt
½   cup buttermilk
½   cup nuts, chopped (optional)

In a bowl, cream shortening and sugars. Add eggs, one at a time, beating well after each addition. Beat in bananas and vanilla. Combine flour, baking soda and salt. Add to creamed mixture alternately with buttermilk. Stir in nuts. Pour into a greased 9x13 inch pan. Bake at 350° for 25-30 minutes or until a toothpick put in the center of the cake tests clean. Cool and frost with Caramel Frosting (p.241). Serves 18.

If you fatten up
everyone else around you,
you will look thinner.

Chocolate Oatmeal Cake

1	cup oatmeal
1½	cups hot water
¾	cup white sugar
¾	cup brown sugar
⅓	cup vegetable oil
4	egg whites
1½	cups flour
½	cup cocoa
1	tsp. baking soda
½	tsp. salt
1	tsp. vanilla

Pour water into oatmeal and let it thicken about 5 minutes. Mix sugars and oil in a bowl. Beat egg whites in another bowl and pour into sugar mixture. Mix well. Add flour, cocoa, baking soda and salt, blend. Add oatmeal and vanilla and mix well. Bake in greased 9x13 inch pan at 350° for 30-35 minutes. Serves 18.

Devils Food Cake

⅓	cup cocoa, packed
½	cup plus 2 Tbsp. shortening
1	cup boiling water
2	cups flour
2	cups sugar
2	eggs, beaten
½	cup sour milk or buttermilk
1½	tsp. baking soda
½	tsp. salt

Dissolve cocoa and shortening in boiling water. Mix all ingredients. Beat for 2 minutes. Pour into a well-greased and floured 9x13 in. or two 9 inch pans. Bake at 350° for 30-35 minutes or until a toothpick inserted into the center comes clean. This tastes just like the package mix. Serves 9 or makes 20 cupcakes.

Eggless Crazy Cake

3	cups flour
2	cups sugar
2	tsp. soda
1/4	cup cocoa, packed
1	tsp. salt
1	tsp. vanilla
1	Tbsp. vinegar
3/4	cup vegetable oil
2	cups water

DO NOT GREASE PAN. Sift dry ingredients into a 9x13 inch pan. Make 3 holes in the mixture. Put vanilla in one hole, vinegar in another and vegetable oil in the last hole. Pour water over all the mixture and blend gently with a fork. Do not beat. Bake 25-30 minutes at 350°. Cool and top with filling and then frosting. Serves 18.

Filling

2½	Tbsp. flour
½	cup milk
½	cup margarine
½	cup sugar
½	tsp. vanilla

Mix milk and flour in a saucepan and cook over medium heat to a thick paste, stirring constantly. Cool. Cream together margarine and sugar. Add lukewarm milk mixture and beat until fluffy. Fold in vanilla. Spread on top of cake.

Eggless Crazy Cake Frosting

2   Tbsp. cocoa
1/4 cup margarine
1/4 cup milk
1   cup sugar
2   Tbsp. light corn syrup
1/2 tsp. vanilla

Bring all the ingredients except vanilla to a boil and boil for 1 minute. Add vanilla and beat until thick. Drizzle over cake.

Gingerbread

1/2 cup butter
1/2 cup sugar
1   cup molasses
1   cup sour milk or buttermilk
1 3/4 tsp. soda
2 1/4 cup flour
2   tsp. ginger
1   tsp. cinnamon
1/4 tsp. ground cloves
1/2 tsp. salt

Mix everything in a bowl until smooth. Pour in a greased 9x9 inch pan. Bake at 350° for 30-35 minutes. Serves 9.

Hot Fudge Cake

1	cup flour
¾	cup sugar
2	Tbsp. cocoa
2	tsp. baking powder
¼	tsp. salt
½	cup milk
2	Tbsp. butter or margarine, melted
1	tsp. vanilla
½	cup nuts

Topping

3	Tbsp. cocoa
½	cup sugar
1	cup hot water

Mix all the ingredients and pour into a buttered deep casserole dish. Mix cocoa and sugar for topping and sprinkle on top of batter. Pour hot water over top and bake at 350° for 30-35 minutes. This has a delicious fudge sauce in the center when baked. Serves 9.

✦ **To send a piece of frosted cake in a lunch pail . . . slice the cake in half horizontally and then make a "sandwich" with the frosting in the middle. It won't stick to the plastic wrap.**

Pound Cake

2¾ cups sugar
1¼ cups margarine or butter, softened
1   tsp. vanilla
5   eggs
3   cups flour
1   tsp. baking powder
¼   tsp. salt
1   cup milk

In a large bowl, combine sugar, margarine, vanilla and eggs. Beat on low until mixed, about 1 minute scraping bowl constantly. Beat on high speed for 5 minutes, occasionally scraping the bowl. Mix flour, baking powder and salt. Beat in alternately with milk on low speed. Spread in a well-greased 10x4 tube pan. Bake at 350° for 70 minutes to 80 minutes or until a toothpick inserted in the center comes out clean. Cool 20 minutes in the pan, then remove onto a wire rack and cool completely. Serves 8-10.

✦ **To cut a layer cake in half horizontally to frost or fill use a length of dental floss or sewing thread. Just wrap the thread around the sides of the cake, making sure it is centered and even. Cross the ends of the thread over each other and pull to slice the cake into two layerrs. The floss makes a neater cut.**

✦ **To chop nuts, place them in a plastic bag and roll them with a rolling pin.**

Red Velvet Cake

3/4   cup butter
2   eggs
1 1/2   cups sugar
1 1/2   tsp. cocoa
1/4   tsp. salt
1   tsp. soda
2   tsp. vinegar
2   tsp. vanilla
1-2   ounce red food coloring
2 1/2   cups flour
1   cup buttermilk

Cream together butter, eggs and sugar in a bowl. Add the rest of the ingredients except the flour and buttermilk. Mix well. Add flour and buttermilk alternately. Beat until all the lumps are out. Pour into a greased and floured 9x13 inch pan. Bake at 350° for 30 minutes or until a tooth pick inserted in the center comes clean. Frost with Red Velvet Frosting. Serves 18.

Red Velvet Frosting

2/3   cup milk
1/2   cup flour
1/2   cup butter
1/2   cup sugar
1   tsp. vanilla

In a saucepan heat milk and flour until thick, stirring constantly. Cool thoroughly. Beat milk and flour for 1 minute until fluffy. Beat butter and sugar until creamy. Add to milk and flour, then add vanilla. Mix well. Frosts 1 Red Velvet Cake.

Sinful Double Chocolate Cake

2 cups flour
1 cup sugar
1½ tsp. baking powder
1½ tsp. baking soda
4 Tbsp. cocoa
1 cup cold water
1 cup mayonnaise
2 tsp. vanilla

Mix ingredients together until smooth. Place in a greased 9x13 inch pan. Bake at 350° for 30-40 minutes or until a toothpick inserted into the center comes clean. Serves 18.

Frosting

1 cup sugar
¼ cup cocoa
¼ cup milk
½ cup margarine

Combine all ingredients in saucepan; bring to a boil. Boil for 1 minute. Poke holes in hot cake with a fork. Pour hot frosting over cake.

Spice Cake

1   cup butter
2¼   cups sugar
5   eggs
3   cups flour
1   Tbsp. ground cloves
1   Tbsp. cinnamon
     pinch of salt
1   cup buttermilk
1   tsp. baking soda
     powdered sugar

Cream butter until soft. Gradually add sugar until mixture is very light and fluffy. In a separate bowl, beat the eggs thoroughly and add to creamed mixture. Mix well. Sift flour with cloves, cinnamon and salt. Beat about third of the flour combination into the batter, then stir in half the buttermilk. Add another third of the flour-spice combination and mix thoroughly. Stir baking soda into remaining half cup of buttermilk and mix into batter along with the remaining flour. Pour into a greased 10-inch tube pan. Bake in a 350° oven for 45-55 minutes or until a toothpick inserted in the center of the cake comes clean. Cool 10 minutes before removing from pan. When cool, sift powdered sugar over the top, or frost with Caramel Frosting (p. 242). Serves 15

✦ **To keep your place in a recipe, place all ingredients on the right side of the bowl. As they are used, move them to the left side.**

What Cake

1	cup oatmeal
½	cup margarine, cut into pieces
1½	cups boiling water
1	tsp. soda
1½	tsp. cinnamon
½	tsp. salt
1½	cup flour
1	cup plus 2 Tbsp. sugar
1	cup brown sugar, packed
2	eggs, beaten

Mix oatmeal and margarine together; pour boiling water over them to soften. Add soda, cinnamon, salt, flour, sugar, brown sugar, and eggs. Mix well and pour into a greased 9x13 inch pan. Bake at 375° for 25 minutes. Spread topping over cake. Serves 18.

Topping

¾	cup brown sugar
2	Tbsp. milk
6	Tbsp. butter
1	cup coconut
	nuts (optional)

Combine brown sugar, milk and butter in a saucepan and bring to a boil. Boil for 1 minute. Add coconut and nuts and stir. Spread onto cake. Put under broiler until lightly browned.

White Cake

2⅔ cups flour
1½ cups sugar
3   tsp. baking powder
½   tsp. salt
1   cup milk
½   cup shortening
1   tsp. vanilla
4   egg whites

Mix all the ingredients together in a bowl except the egg whites. Beat on low for 30 seconds, scraping the bowl. Beat on high for 2 minutes until smooth. Add egg whites and beat on high for 2 additional minutes, scraping the bowl occasionally. Pour into 1 greased and floured 9x13 pan or three 8-inch or two 9-inch pans.

Bake at 350° for the times listed below:

8-inch pan	23-28 minutes
9-inch pan	30-35 minutes
9x13-inch	40-45 minutes
30 cupcakes	20-25 minutes

Cake is done when a toothpick inserted into the center comes out clean. Cool completely. Frost with chocolate frosting. Serves 18.

✦ **Use leftover margarine wrappers to grease your pans. Store them in a plastic bag in the refrigerator until you need them.**

Yellow Cake

¾ cup butter or maragrine, softened
1½ cups sugar
2½ tsp. vanilla
3 eggs
1⅓ cups buttermilk or
    sour milk
3 cups flour
3 tsp. baking powder

Beat butter and sugar together in a bowl until fluffy. Add vanilla and eggs one at a time beating well after each addition, scraping the sides constantly. Add buttermilk, and beat well. Sift dry ingredients together in a bowl. Add to butter mixture slowly mixing well. Pour into 1 well greased and floured 9x13 inch pan or three 8-inch or two 9-inch pans. Serves 18.

Bake at 350° for the times listed below:

8-inch pan	23-28 minutes
9-inch pan	30-35 minutes
9x13-inch	40-45 minutes
30 cupcakes	20-25 minutes

Cake is done when a toothpick inserted into the center comes out clean. Cool completely. Frost with chocolate frosting.

✦ **For better accuracy when decorating a picture on a cake, take a cookie cutter and put an imprint on the top of the cake. Then follow the lines as you are piping the frosting on the cake.**

Zucchini Cake

2	cups flour
2	cups zucchini, grated
1¼	cups sugar
½	cup vegetable oil
⅓	cup water
1¼	tsp. baking soda
1	tsp. salt
1	tsp. ground cinnamon
1	tsp. ground cloves
1	tsp. ground nutmeg
1	tsp. vanilla
3	eggs

Preheat oven to 350°. Mix all the ingredients in a bowl and beat on low for 1 minute, scraping bowl constantly. Beat on medium for 2 minutes, scraping bowl occasionally. Pour into a greased 9x13 inch pan. Bake for about 45 minutes. Serves 18.

It would be easier to lose weight
if replacement parts
weren't so handy in the
refrigerator.

Baker's Frosting

1   lb. (4 cups) powdered sugar
½   cup shortening
¼   tsp. salt
½   tsp. vanilla
4   Tbsp. water
     food coloring

Mix ingredients in a bowl and beat on high with a hand mixer for 10 minutes. Add food coloring as desired. Use to decorate wedding and birthday cakes. Frosts one 9x13 inch cake.

Butter Creme Frosting

3   cups powdered sugar
⅓   cup margarine or butter, softened
1½ tsp. vanilla
1-2 Tbsp. milk

Mix powdered sugar and margarine. Stir in vanilla and 1 Tbsp. milk. Beat until smooth. If the frosting is too stiff, add 1 more tablespoon of milk and beat again until smooth. Frosts one 9x13 inch cake or two 8-inch cakes. This can easily be halved. Frosting can also be refrigerated several weeks.

Peppermint Frosting

Use peppermint flavoring instead of vanilla.

Caramel Frosting

½   cup margarine or butter
1   cup brown sugar, packed
¼   cup milk
2   cups powdered sugar

Heat margarine over medium heat in a 2-quart saucepan. When margarine is melted, stir in brown sugar. Heat to boiling, stirring constantly. Reduce heat to low and boil 2 minutes longer, still stirring. Stir in milk and heat to boiling. Remove from heat and cool. Slowly stir in powdered sugar. Place saucepan of frosting in bowl of very cold water and beat frosting until smooth. If frosting is too stiff, add an additional 1 teaspoon of milk at a time until frosting is smooth. Frosts one 9x13 inch cake.

Chocolate Frosting

¼   cup margarine, melted
¼   tsp. salt
½   cup cocoa
¼   cup milk
1½   tsp. vanilla
3½   cup powdered sugar

Put all the ingredients in a bowl and beat until smooth. Frosts one 9x13 inch cake.

Fluffy White Frosting

1½ cups sugar
2   egg whites
⅓   cup water
¼   tsp. cream of tartar
1   tsp. vanilla

In a saucepan, combine sugar, egg whites, water and cream of tartar. With a hand mixer, beat mixture on low for 1 minute. Continue to beat on low speed over low heat until frosting reaches 160° (about 8-10 minutes). Pour into a large mixing bowl and add vanilla. Beat on high until frosting forms stiff peaks (about 7 minutes). Makes 7 cups.

Milk Chocolate Frosting

⅓   cup butter, unsalted
½   cup baking cocoa
3   cups powdered sugar
½   cup milk, scalded
1   tsp. vanilla

Melt butter and cocoa together. Stir in powdered sugar, milk and vanilla. Place pan in ice water and beat until spreadable. Use a hand-held electric mixer for lighter color and fluffier texture. Beat by hand for darker color. Frost one 9x13 inch cake.

Vanilla Glaze

⅓   cup margarine or butter
2   cups powdered sugar
1½   tsp. vanilla
2-4   Tbsp. hot water

Heat margarine in a saucepan until melted. Stir in powdered sugar, vanilla and 1 tablespoon water. Mix well. Add the rest of the water, 1 tablespoon at a time, until the frosting is smooth. Glazes one bundt cake or one 10-inch angel food cake.

Lemon Glaze

Use the Vanilla Glaze recipe and substitute 1⅓ tsp. lemon juice for the vanilla and add ½ tsp. grated lemon peel to the margarine.

Fondant

1   (14 ounce) can sweetened condensed milk
3   Tbsp. light corn syrup
2   tsp. vanilla
2   lb. powdered sugar

Beat condensed milk, corn syrup and vanilla in a large bowl until well mixed. Stir in powdered sugar. There will be a large mass of crumbs. Turn onto a board and knead until smooth. Roll out as needed for cakes. To color: knead paste food coloring into fondant until desired shade is reached. Stores well in a sealed container in the refrigerator or freezer for several months.

Cupcake Filling #1

¼   lb. butter
½   cup shortening
1   cup sugar
⅔   cup evaporated milk
2   tsp. vanilla

Mix all ingredients in a bowl and beat with an electric mixer without stopping for 30 minutes. With a long pastry tip, poke a hole in the center of each cupcake and fill. Fills one cupcake recipe or makes a good center filling for layer cakes. This is just like the filling in the cupcakes at the store. Kids love to take them in lunches and they freeze well. Eat right from the freezer either thawed or frozen. Frost cupcakes as desired.
Fills 20-24 cupcakes.

Cupcake Filling #2

5   Tbsp. flour
1   cup milk
½   cup butter (1 stick)
½   cup shortening
¾   cup sugar
I   tsp. vanilla

Mix flour and milk in saucepan. Cook on medium heat, stirring constantly until a paste forms. Cool. In a bowl, cream together butter, shortening, sugar and vanilla. Beat 5 minutes. Add flour paste and mix 5 more minutes. With a long pastry tip, poke a hole in the center of each cupcake and fill. Fills one cupcake recipe or makes a good center filling for layer cakes. Fills 20-24 cupcakes.

✦ **To make cupcakes all the same size, use an ice cream scoop to measure the batter**.

Pie Tips

✦ **For Pies:** Berry pies can be frozen unbaked.

Mass produce several pie crusts at a time and freeze in 1-crust-size balls in the freezer.

Freeze pumpkin puree for pies in 1-pint sizes.

✦ For an extra treat: **Place leftover pieces of rolled-out pie crust** on a baking sheet. Sprinkle with cinnamon and sugar. Bake 10-15 minutes at 425 degrees while baking pies.

✦ **Use leftover pie crust** to make one or two pasties (p.188) or a couple of mini pot pies.

✦ **If you have trouble learning to make pies,** make 10 in a row during 1 week. Practice makes perfect. Even if you have a couple of failures with the first few pies, in the long run it will save you money.

✦ **Brush beaten egg white over pie crust** before baking. This will give your pie crust a beautiful glossy finish.

✦ **Substitute oatmeal** browned in a bit of butter for nuts in cookies, cakes, and pies. The oatmeal adds a nice flavor and crunch.

✦ **If you don't have enough dough to make a top crust,** simply use a lattice top instead.

✦ Sundae Pie. Crumble leftover **cookies, angel food cake, pound cake or brownies** in a pie pan. Spoon vanilla ice cream on top. Spread on a thin layer of strawberry jam and cover that with chocolate and butterscotch ice cream topping. Freeze and serve for dessert.

Pie Crust

3 cups flour
½ tsp. salt
2 Tbsp. sugar
1¼ cups shortening, cold
1 egg, cold
1 Tbsp. vinegar, cold
5 Tbsp. cold water
sugar

Mix flour, salt and sugar in a bowl. Cut in shortening with a pastry blender or 2 knives. Add egg, vinegar and 3 tablespoons water. Mix lightly. If dough is too dry, add more water. Mix with hands. Don't overmix. Mix just until the dough sticks together. Divide into thirds. Roll out to make 3 pies crusts. When using the crust for the top of the pie sprinkle sugar on top. Crust can be frozen in balls and then defrosted and rolled out when ready to use. Makes 3 crusts.

Graham Cracker Crust

2 cups graham cracker crumbs
3 Tbsp. sugar
1 stick margarine, melted

Mix all ingredients together and press into a 9-inch pie plate. Bake at 350° for 10 minutes. Cool and fill with favorite pudding filling. Makes 1 crust.

Apple Crumb Pie

8	apples, peeled and sliced
	or 1 (20 oz) can sliced apples (NOT pie filling)
½	cup sugar
¼	cup brown sugar
¼	tsp. salt
¾	tsp. cinnamon
¼	tsp. nutmeg
2	Tbsp. flour
2	Tbsp. butter

Stir all the ingredients in a bowl except butter. Pour into a 9 inch pie crust, dot with butter. Top with another piecrust or with Topping. Bake at 450° for 15 minutes then turn down heat to 350° and bake for 45 minutes. If using canned apples bake at 425° for 10 minutes, turn heat down to 350° and bake for 25-35 minutes. Make 19 inch apple pie

Topping

½	cup butter
½	cup brown sugar
1	cup flour

Mix together and sprinkle on top.

Apple Pie Filling

9   cups baking apples, peeled, cored and sliced
1½   Tbsp. lemon juice
2¼   cup sugar
½   cup cornstarch
5   cups water
1   tsp. ground cinnamon
½   tsp. salt
⅛   tsp. nutmeg

Toss apples with lemon juice and set aside. Combine the rest of the ingredients in Dutch oven and bring to a boil for 2 minutes, stirring constantly. Add apples and return to boil. Reduce heat, cover and simmer until apples are tender (6-10 minutes). Cool for 30 minutes. Then ladle into freezer containers or bake immediately. Makes two 9-inch pies.

Cherry Pie

1¼   cups sugar
2½   Tbsp. flour
¼   tsp. salt
1   qt. tart red cherries, pitted
2   Tbsp. margarine or butter
1   pie crust

Mix sugar, flour, salt and cherries together. Line pie pan with pie crust; add cherry mixture. Dot with margarine and cover with top crust. Bake at 425° for 10 minutes. Then reduce heat to 350° and bake 25 minutes longer. Makes one pie.

Chocolate Pie

1½ cups sugar
⅓   cup cornstarch
½   tsp. salt
⅓   cup cocoa
2   Tbsp. butter or margarine
3   cups milk
4   egg yolks
2   tsp. vanilla
1   9-inch, baked pie crust
    whipped topping (p.294)

In a saucepan, combine sugar, cornstarch, salt, cocoa and butter. Blend milk and eggs yolks and add to cornstarch mixture. Cook over medium heat to boiling, stirring constantly. Boil 1 minute. Add vanilla. Pour into baked pie shell. Top with whipped topping. Makes one pie.

Ultimate Chocolate Pie

1   (8 oz). Hershey's with Almonds candy bar
    (Use only Hershey's)
1½ cups whipping cream
1   (10 oz). bag marshmallows
1   graham cracker crust
    whipped cream

Break candy bar into a saucepan. Add 1 cup whipping cream and marshmallows. Cook on medium heat until melted stirring constantly. Remove from heat. Add the rest of the whipping cream. Mix well. Pour into pie shell. Refrigerate for 24 hours before serving. Serve topped with whipped cream

Coconut Pie

1½   cups milk
¼   cup sugar
¼   tsp. salt
3   Tbsp. flour
1   egg yolk
1   Tbsp. butter
½   tsp. vanilla
1½   cups coconut
1   baked pie shell
     whipped cream

Scald 1 cup milk in a double boiler. Mix sugar, salt, flour, and remaining milk together. Stir into hot milk and cook slowly until thickened, stirring constantly. Cover and cook over boiling water for 5 minutes. Add mixture slowly to egg yolk and cook 1 minute longer. Add butter and vanilla. Stir in coconut. Cool. Pour into baked pie shell and top with whipped cream if desired. Makes one pie.

Banana Pie

Substitute 4 sliced ripe bananas for coconut. Alternate layers of bananas and cooled filling.

Lemon Meringue Pie

5 Tbsp. cornstarch
1½ cups sugar
½ tsp. salt
2 cups boiling water
3 egg yolks (save whites for Meringue)
4 Tbsp. lemon juice
2 Tbsp. butter
2 Tbsp. grated lemon rind
1 pie shell, baked

Combine dry ingredients. Add water. Cook until thick stirring constantly. Add egg yolks in a small bowl, beat slightly. Add a 1/4 cup of hot cornstarch mixture 1 Tbsp. at a time mixing after each addition to the eggs. (This keeps the eggs from scrambling when added to the saucepan.) Add egg mixture to the saucepan. Simmer 2 minutes stirring occasionally. Add rest of ingredients. Stir until mixed. Pour into pie shell. Cover with Meringue. Makes 9 inch pie.

Meringue

1 Tbsp. cornstarch
½ Tbsp. cold water
½ cup boiling water
3 egg whites
6 Tbsp. sugar
1 tsp. vanilla

In a saucepan, mix cornstarch with water. Add boiling water and cook until thick on medium heat. Set aside to cool. Beat egg whites to soft peak. Add cornstarch mixture, beat until stiff. Add sugar 1 Tbsp at a time until all is incorporated and then add vanilla. Cover top of pie with Meringue. Bake at 325 for 15 minutes. Turn off oven and leave pie in oven and let cool with door open. DO NOT cut until completely cooled.

Pineapple Millionaire Pie

2   cups powdered sugar
1   stick margarine
2   large eggs (pasteurized eggs may be used)
1/8   tsp. salt
1/4   tsp. vanilla

Cream ingredients and pour into a baked pie shell. Chill 1 hour.

1/4   cup powdered sugar
1   cup crushed pineapple (drained)
1/2   cup pecans
2   cups whipped topping

Mix first three ingredients, fold in whipped topping. Spread onto chilled base mixture. Chill well before serving. Makes 9 inch pie.

Pineapple Sour Cream Pie

1   pkg. (5 oz.) instant vanilla pudding
1   (8 oz) can crushed pineapple with juice
2   cups sour cream
1   Tbsp. sugar
1   baked pie shell

Combine all except pie crust. Slowly beat one minute. Chill 3 hours, top with whipped cream. Makes 9 inch pie.

Peach Pie

2 pie crusts (p.247)
2/3 cup sugar
1/3 cup flour
1/4 tsp. cinnamon
1 Tbsp. margarine or butter
6 cups sliced peaches (fresh, frozen or canned, drained)
1 tsp. lemon juice

Prepare pie crust. Mix the rest of the ingredients in a large bowl. Place pie crust in a 9-inch pie plate. Add peach mixture and dot with margarine. Cover with top crust and cut a few slits in it (I cut my initial). Seal and flute the edges. Cover edges with a 2-inch strip of aluminum foil to prevent them from burning. Bake at 425° for 30 minutes. Remove foil and continue to bake for an additional 15 minutes. Remove from oven and cool slightly before serving. Makes one pie.

Pecan Pie

1 stick butter
1 cup light corn syrup
1 cup sugar
3 large eggs
1/2 tsp. lemon juice
1 tsp. vanilla
   dash of salt
1 1/4 cups pecans, chopped

Brown butter in a pan until golden brown. Do not burn. Cool. Add other ingredients in order given in a separate bowl. Mix well. Blend in cooled butter well. Pour into pie crust. Bake 10 minutes at 425° and then 40 minutes at 325°. Makes one pie.

Pumpkin Pie

1	pie crust
2	eggs
1	(15 ounce) can pumpkin
¾	cup sugar
½	tsp. salt
1	tsp. cinnamon
½	tsp. ground ginger
¼	tsp. ground cloves
1	(12 ounce) can evaporated milk

Bake pie crust at 350° for 1-2 minutes until crust starts to puff with small bubbles. Watch carefully. Blend all ingredients together in a bowl. Pour into pie crust and bake at 425° for 15 minutes. Then turn the oven down to 350° for 45 minutes. When a knife is inserted into the center of the pie and comes out clean it is done. Makes one pie.

Candy Tips

+ Be very careful when making homemade candies. It you don't get **everything on sale** for a really good price then it can be more expensive than buying the candy pre-made.

+ Use the **leftover syrup from the candied orange** peels on your pancakes, waffles or French toast for a gourmet taste.

+ If you **overcook chocolate**, it becomes dull looking. To save it, put the pan on low heat and beat in 1 teaspoon shortening or oil at a time until you have restored the shiny, smooth consistency.

+ When you are **melting chocolate** make sure that **all utensils are completely dry.** Even a little water will make chocolate grainy and lumpy.

Candy Cooking Tests

When placed in a cold cup of water, candy will:

Soft Ball	234°-240°	form a soft ball that can be flattened
Firm Ball	242°-248°	form a firm ball that holds its shape until pressed
Hard Ball	250°-268°	form a ball that is pliable and holds its shape
Soft Crack	270°-290°	separates into hard but not brittle threads
Hard Crack	300°-310°	cracks easily
Caramel	320°-350°	mixture coats metal spoon and forms light caramel-colored mass when poured onto a plate
For High Altitude		lower candy temperature 2° for each 1,000 feet of elevation.

+ **Check the accuracy of your thermometer by placing in boiling water. It should read 212°**

Applesauce Candy

1	cup applesauce*
1	cup sugar
1	pkg. fruit gelatin
1/2	cup nuts, finely chopped
	extra sugar for coating

Combine applesauce and sugar in a saucepan. Bring to a boil and cook 2 minutes. Dissolve the gelatin in the applesauce mixture. Add the nuts and pour into an 8x8 inch pan. After 24 hours cut into 1 inch squares and roll in sugar. Roll in the sugar a second time 24 hours later. Makes 64 pieces.

*Puree fruit cocktail, peaches or pears instead of applesauce

If swimming is so good for your figure then why do whales look the way they do?

Black Forest Chocolate Cups

1   (12 ounce) pkg. semi-sweet chocolate chips
2   Tbsp. black cherry preserves
½   cup milk chocolate chips
¼   cup powdered sugar
½-1 tsp. of water
      red food coloring

Stir the semi-sweet chocolate in a medium-size saucepan or double boiler over low heat until melted. Spoon about ½ tsp. of the melted chocolate into each of twenty-four 1-inch paper or foil bonbon cups. You can put these in mini muffin tins. Drop about ¼ teaspoon preserves into each cup. Spoon enough of the remaining melted chocolate into each cup to fill to the top and cover preserves. Set the cups aside to harden.

Stir the milk chocolate chips in a small saucepan or double boiler over low heat until melted. Remove from the heat and set aside. Stir the powdered sugar and water in a small bowl until blended and smooth; add a drop of food color. Stir until it is a light pink color. Spoon the melted milk chocolate and the icing into separate heavy-duty sandwich bags. Seal or twist the bags shut. Cut a tiny hole in one corner of each. Pipe icing in lines across the tops of the chocolate cups. Pipe chocolate in lines crosswise to the icing. Refrigerate at least 30 minutes until set. Store in an airtight container in the refrigerator for up to 1 week. Makes 2 dozen cups.

Candied Orange Peel

Peels from 3 large oranges or grapefruits
³/₄   cup water
2   Tbsp. corn syrup
2 ³/₄ cups sugar

Cut the peel on each fruit into quarters. Pull the peel off in these quarter sections. Slice peel into ¼ inch-wide strips. Put them in a 3 quart saucepan (not aluminum) and add water. Bring to a boil, reduce heat, and simmer 15 minutes. Drain. Boil the water, syrup, and 2 cups of sugar until the sugar dissolves. Add the peels. Simmer 40 minutes, stirring occasionally. Remove the peels with a slotted spoon. Then put on a rack over a baking pan. Drain for 5 minutes, separate peels, and dry for another hour. Toss the peels into a plastic bag with the remaining sugar. Allow to air dry 3 more hours, then store in an airtight container. Keeps one month or can be frozen. Makes 30-40 pieces.

Recipes reprinted with permission from The Complete Tightwad Gazette by Amy Dacyczyn.

Caramels

2   cups brown sugar, packed
1   cup white corn syrup
1 ½   cups evaporated milk
½   cup butter
½   tsp. salt
1   tsp. vanilla
1   cup nuts

Combine sugar, corn syrup, evaporated milk, butter and salt in a saucepan. Heat gradually to boiling stirring constantly. Boil to 240°. Add vanilla and nuts. Pour into well buttered 8 inch pan. Cool several hours or overnight. Cut into small squares. Makes 64 pieces.

Chocolate Covered Pretzels

1 pkg. pretzels*
1 pkg. melting white, dark, milk chocolate or almond bark

Melt chocolate or almond bark in the top of a double boiler. Remove from heat when melted and dip pretzels in to cover. Set on waxed paper until cool.

*Fortune cookies and Oreo's® can be used instead of pretzels.

Chocolate Marbled Fudge

2 cups sugar
²/₃ cup heavy cream
1 cup milk
¼ cup light corn syrup
¼ tsp. salt
1 tsp. vanilla
½ cup semi-sweet chocolate, chopped

Combine sugar, cream, milk, corn syrup, and salt in large heavy saucepan. Bring slowly to boiling, stirring constantly, until sugar is dissolved. Boil gently, stirring occasionally, until mixture reaches 238° on a candy thermometer. Remove from heat. Cool 5 minutes. Add vanilla. Beat vigorously until mixture begins to thicken and lose it's glossy look (about 5 minutes). Pour the fudge into well buttered 8x8 inch baking pan. Sprinkle evenly with the chocolate chips. When chocolate chips are melted, run a knife though them to create a marbled effect. Cool completely on wire rack. Cut into 1 inch squares. Makes 64 pieces.

Easy Fudge

½ cup butter
⅓ cup water
1 (16 ounce) pkg. powdered sugar
½ cup dry milk
½ cup cocoa, packed
¼ tsp. salt
   nuts

Heat butter and water to a boil. In a bowl mix dry ingredients. Add butter and water mixture to the dry ingredients. Put into a greased 8x8 inch pan. Chill several hours then cut into squares. Makes 16 pieces.

Fudge

2 cups sugar
¾ cup milk
½ cup cocoa, packed
2 Tbsp. shortening
2 Tbsp. light corn syrup
¼ tsp. salt
2 Tbsp. butter
1 tsp. vanilla

Combine sugar, milk, cocoa, shortening, corn syrup and salt in a 2 quart saucepan. Cook over medium heat, stirring constantly until mixture boils. Cook, stirring occasionally to 234°. Remove from heat, add butter and vanilla. Do not stir. Allow fudge to cool at room temperature without stirring until it reaches 110°. Beat until fudge thickens and loses some of it's gloss. Quickly pour fudge into a lightly buttered 8x8 inch square pan. Makes 32 pieces.

Chocolate Truffles

1	Tbsp. sugar
1/4	cup whipping cream
2	Tbsp. unsalted butter
6	ounce semi-sweet chocolate, chopped
2	Tbsp. desired liquor (optional)
	(brandy, amaretto, kahlua, rum etc.)
	or any flavoring (orange, mint, raspberry, coffee)
1/2	cup nuts, finely chopped
1/2	cup unsweetened cocoa powder*

In a 1-quart saucepan combine the sugar, whipping cream and butter. Cook and stir until butter is melted and mixture is very hot. Remove from heat. Stir in semi-sweet chocolate until melted and well blended. Stir in liquor. (If desired, halve the batch at this point and stir 1 Tbsp. of 2 different liquors into each portion.) Cover and chill 1 hour or until mixture is completely cool, stirring often. Drop mixture from a rounded teaspoon onto a baking sheet lined with waxed paper. Chill 30 minutes or until firm. Roll balls into nuts or unsweetened cocoa powder. Store in a cool, dry location. Makes 15-20 pieces.

You may roll truffles in coconut, sprinkles, powdered sugar or dip in melted white, dark or milk chocolate.

If you have melted chocolate
all over your hands,
you're eating it too slowly

Glazed Nuts

1½ cups sugar
1   lb. mixed unsalted nuts
½   cup honey
½   cup water
½   tsp. vanilla

Mix sugar, honey and water in saucepan. Bring to boil and cook, without stirring to 252° on a candy thermometer. Remove from heat and stir in nuts and vanilla. Let cool slightly. Stir again until creamy. Place on waxed paper and separate nuts with fingers. When cool put in small jars and decorate. You can use just one kind of nuts if you like. Can be stored in airtight container for up to 2 weeks. Makes one pound.

Honey Roasted Nuts

3   cups nuts
2   Tbsp. margarine
½   tsp. cinnamon
½   cup honey
½   tsp. orange peel, grated
     salt

Microwave all ingredients in bowl 4 to 7 minutes at high power, stirring halfway through cooking time. Spread nuts on foil to cool. Lightly salt. Makes 3 cups.

✦ **Save the greeting cards you receive. Cut out the fronts and use them to decorate the front of tissue wrapped packages.**

Microwave Candy

1   cup chocolate chips
1   cup peanuts, walnuts, raisins or chopped dried apricots

Place the chocolate chips in a microwave-safe bowl and microwave on high 1 to 2 minutes, stirring halfway through cooking, until melted. Stir in the nuts or dried fruit (or a combination of both). Drop the mixture by the teaspoonful onto a waxed paper-lined baking sheet and refrigerate until firm. Store at a cool room temperature. Makes 15 candies.

Molded Mints

2½   cups powdered sugar
1   (3 ounce) pkg. cream cheese, softened
1   tsp. peppermint flavoring
    food coloring
    sugar

Mix ingredients and knead several times. When dough is smooth, roll into a ball and wrap in plastic wrap. Chill 2 hours. For mints, roll into small balls, dip in sugar and press into mold. Remove from mold and let dry ½ hour. Store in airtight container. Can be frozen or refrigerated. This is a great mint for weddings. It is very classy when molded into leaves or shells. You can use color to match the bride's wedding colors. If mints stick to mold, knead in more powdered sugar. Makes approximately 100 one inch mints.

Mounds

22   graham crackers, crushed
½   cup butter, melted
3   Tbsp. sugar
12   ounce coconut
1   can (14 ounce) sweetened condensed milk (p.302)
1   pkg. (12 ounce) chocolate chips

Mix graham crackers, butter, and sugar and spread evenly into a 9x13 cake pan. Bake 5 minutes and cool. In a saucepan heat sweetened condensed milk and coconut for 10 minutes. Do not scorch. Spread on crust. Put chocolate chips on top. Place in a preheated 325° oven until chips melt. Chill before serving. Makes 18 pieces

Party Mints

2½   cups powdered sugar
1   egg white (meringue powder may be substituted)
2   Tbsp. butter, melted
4   small lids peppermint flavoring
¼   cup paraffin, shaved
1   (12 ounce) pkg. chocolate chips

Mix powdered sugar, egg white or meringue, butter and peppermint flavoring. Make into small balls about the size of a quarter and then flatten on a cookie sheet. Put in the freezer. Melt chocolate and paraffin over a double boiler. When melted take mints out of freezer. Put a toothpick though the center of the mint and dip into chocolate. If mints on the cookie sheet begin to soften and thaw, refreeze because they are easier to dip. Put back on cookie sheet and let chocolate harden in the freezer. Wrap each mint in a piece of 5x5 inch foil. Makes twenty 2 inch mints.

Peanut Brittle

¾ cup corn syrup
2 cups sugar
¾ cup hot water
2 cups raw peanuts
1 tsp. soda
1½ tsp. salt

Grease 2 jelly roll pans. In a saucepan add corn syrup, sugar, and water. Bring to a boil and cook to a hard ball stage 260°. Add peanuts and cook to hard crack at 290°. Add soda and salt. Stir well and pour into pans and spread thin. Cool quickly. I usually make this for Christmas and don't have room left in my refrigerator so I just set it outside in the snow for a few minutes until it has cooled. Makes 3-4 dozen pieces.

Peanut Butter Cups

2 cups powdered sugar
½ cup butter
1 cup peanut butter
1 tsp. vanilla
1 (12 ounce) pkg. chocolate chips
¼ cup paraffin, shaved

Cream butter. Add peanut butter, sugar and vanilla. In a microwave safe dish, place chocolate chips and paraffin. Microwave until melted, stirring frequently. Pour a small amount of melted chocolate in bottom of paper holders. Put in filling and pour more chocolate on top until filling is covered. Let chocolate harden before serving. Makes 2 dozen.

Peanut Butter Balls

Shape into small 1½ inch balls. Dip peanut butter balls into chocolate and place on wax paper to harden.

Roasted Chestnuts

With a sharp knife make a slit in each chestnut. Place in boiling water and boil for 4 minutes. Remove and dry. In a saucepan, melt 3 Tbsp. of butter. Add chestnuts and heat, stirring thoroughly, until very hot. With a sharp-pointed knife, both skins can then be peeled, leaving the nut whole.

Sponge Candy

1   cup sugar
1   cup dark corn syrup
1   Tbsp. white vinegar
1   Tbsp. baking soda
1/2   cup chocolate chips, melted (optional)

Combine sugar, corn syrup and vinegar and cook over medium heat, stirring until sugar melts. Cook, without stirring to 300°. Remove from heat and add soda. Pour into a well greased jellyroll or 9x13 inch pan. Sprinkle chocolate chips on top of candy and spread when melted. When hard, break into pieces. Very good coated with chocolate! Makes 24 pieces.

Sugared Nuts

3   cups walnut halves
1½   cups pecan halves
2   cups sugar
1   cup water
¼   tsp. cinnamon

Mix ingredients in a heavy skillet. Cook until water disappears and nuts have a sugary appearance. Remove from heat and pour nuts onto a baking sheet. Separate quickly with 2 forks. Makes 5 cups.

Toffee

1   cup nuts, chopped pecans or walnuts are best
¾   cup brown sugar, packed
½   cup butter
½   cup chocolate chips

Butter an 8x8 inch pan. Spread nuts in the bottom of pan. On medium heat bring to a boil sugar and butter 7 minutes. Spread into pan. Sprinkle chocolate chips on top. Let sit a few minutes. When melted, spread evenly. Let cool before cracking into pieces. Makes 24 pieces.

Turtles

72   pecan halves (about 4 ounces)
24   caramels
4   ounce semi-sweet chocolate

Heat oven to 300°. Cover baking sheet with foil- shiny side up, and grease. For each candy place 3 pecan halves into a "Y" shape on the foil. Place 1 caramel on the center of each "Y". Bake just until candy is melted. If they looked deformed after baking, reshape while the caramel is warm. Heat chocolate over low heat, stirring constantly, just until melted. Spoon mixture over candies, leaving the ends uncovered. Refrigerate until firm (about 30 minutes). Makes about 24 turtles.

✦ **Leftover melted chocolate from making candies? Pour it into a small non-stick cake pan, smooth it into an even layer and refrigerate until hardened. Then "pop" it out onto a cutting board, chop it into small chunks and store it in the fridge to be used later in any recipe that calls for chocolate chips.**

Vinegar Candy

2   cups sugar
½   cup cider vinegar
2   tsp. butter

Combine ingredients in a saucepan and cook to 275°. Pour into well buttered jelly roll pan, let cool, and break. Makes 24 pieces.

Vinegar Taffy

2   cups dark corn syrup
1   cup sugar
2   Tbsp. butter
     food coloring
1   Tbsp. vinegar
1   tsp. baking soda
1   tsp. vanilla

Combine first four ingredients in a saucepan. Bring to a boil over medium heat, stirring constantly until sugar dissolves. Continue cooking to 260°. Remove from heat and stir in soda, vanilla and a few drops of food coloring. Beat until smooth and creamy. Pour into a buttered pan. When cool enough to handle butter hands and pull until light in color. Pull into long strips and cut into 1 inch pieces. Makes 8 dozen.

✦ **If you can't eat all of your chocolate, it will keep in the freezer. But, if you can't each all of your chocolate, what's wrong with you?**

Cookie Baking Tips

+ **Roll cookie dough into logs** and wrap in double-thick plastic wrap. Write the temperature to bake and the amount of time on the plastic wrap with a permanent marker. Freeze. To prepare: Defrost, slice and bake at recommended temperature.

+ **Buy the little chocolate sprinkles** from a restaurant that has an ice cream bar. They will usually sell them to you for much less than the little bottles in the store.

+ **Use a grater** for scraping off the burned bottoms of cookies.

+ **To freshen homemade cookies,** place a few in the microwave for 20-30 seconds.

+ **Use either the cut end of a clean empty 10¾ ounce soup can** or the ring from a canning jar if you don't have a cookie or biscuit cutter.

About Cookies and Mothers

A house should have a cookie jar for when it's half past three

And children hurry home from school as hungry as can be,

There's nothing quite so splendid as spicy ginger cakes,

With a glass of milk a great BIG smile, from loving hands that bake.

A house should have a mother just waiting with a hug,

No matter what a boy brings home a puppy or a bug!

For children only loiter when the bell rings to dismiss, If no one's

Home to greet them with a cookie and a kiss!!!!!!!!!!!!!!

Caramel Cream Sandwich Cookies

1   cup butter
¾   cup brown sugar
1   egg yolk
2¼ cups flour

Cream butter and brown sugar. Add egg yolk and flour. Mix well; shape into walnut-sized balls and flatten with a fork. Bake on ungreased cookie sheet for 9-12 minutes at 325°. Cool. Frost 1 cookie with frosting and put another cookie on top to form a sandwich. Makes 1 dozen.

Frosting

2   Tbsp. butter
1¼   cup powdered sugar
½   tsp. vanilla
4-5 tsp. milk

Melt butter and blend in powdered sugar. Add vanilla and 4 tsp. milk. Stir until woll blondcd. Onc morc teaspoon of milk may be added if needed to make smooth.

Carrot Cookies

¾   cup sugar
¾   cup shortening
1   egg
1   cup (3-4 med.) raw carrots, grated
     pinch of salt
1   tsp. vanilla
2   tsp. baking powder
2   cups flour

Mix all ingredients and place by spoonfuls on ungreased cookie sheet. Bake 350° for 10-12 minutes. Frost with Orange Frosting. Makes 2 dozen.

Orange Frosting

juice of half an orange
rind of 1 orange
powdered sugar

Mix rind and orange juice in a bowl. Add enough powdered sugar to make a creamy frosting.

Chocolate Sandwich Cookies

1¼ cup margarine, softened
2 cups sugar
2 eggs
2 tsp. vanilla
2 cups flour
¾ cup cocoa, packed
1 tsp. baking soda
½ tsp. salt

Cream margarine, sugar and eggs. Add vanilla. Combine flour, cocoa, soda and salt. Add to creamed mixture. Drop by teaspoonsful onto a cookie sheet and bake at 350° for 8-9 minutes. Cool, then spread Butter Cream Frosting between cookies to make sandwiches. Makes 1 dozen.

Butter Creme Frosting

3 cups powdered sugar
⅓ cup margarine or butter, softened
1½ tsp. vanilla
1-2 Tbsp. milk

Mix powdered sugar and margarine. Stir in vanilla and 1 Tbsp. milk. Beat until smooth. If the frosting is too stiff, add 1 more tablespoon of milk and beat again until smooth. Frosts one 9x13 inch cake or two 8-inch cakes. This can easily be halved. Frosting can also be refrigerated several weeks.

No-Bake Fudge Cookies

½   cup milk
2   cups sugar
½   cup cocoa
1   stick margarine
½   cup nuts (optional)
½   cup peanut butter (smooth or chunky)
1   tsp. vanilla
3   cups oatmeal

Mix milk, sugar, cocoa and margarine in a saucepan. Bring to a rolling boil and boil 1 minute. Remove from heat; add peanut butter and vanilla and stir well. Add oatmeal and mix until well coated. Drop by teaspoonsful on waxed paper and let cool until hardened. If the humidity is very high or you didn't let them boil long enough they won't set. If this happens, scoop the cookies off the wax paper and use as an ice cream topping. Makes 2 dozen.

Ginger Cremes

¼   cup shortening
½   cup sugar
1   egg
½   cup molasses
2   cups flour
½   tsp. salt
1   tsp. ginger
½   tsp. nutmeg
½   tsp. cloves
½   tsp. cinnamon
1   tsp. soda dissolved in ¼ cup hot water

Mix all ingredients. Drop by teaspoonsful and place on a greased cookie sheet. Bake at 400° until brown, about 5-10 minutes. Cool and frost with Butter Creme Frosting (p.269). Makes 3 dozen.

Ginger Snaps

$\frac{1}{2}$	cup molasses
$\frac{1}{4}$	cup sugar
3	Tbsp. margarine
1	Tbsp. milk
2	cups flour
$\frac{1}{2}$	tsp. soda
$\frac{1}{2}$	tsp. salt
$\frac{1}{2}$	tsp. cloves
$\frac{1}{2}$	tsp. cinnamon
	granulated sugar

In a saucepan bring first 4 ingredients to a boil. Place dry ingredients in a bowl and stir until blended. Add wet ingredients and stir until blended. Shape into a ball and wrap in wax paper. Chill 1 hour. Roll out and cut with a 2-inch cookie cutter. Sprinkle top of cookie with sugar. Place on greased cookie sheets. Bake at 375° for 8 minutes. Let stand 2 minutes before transferring. Makes 2 dozen.

Ice Box Cookies

1	cup butter
2	cups brown sugar, packed
3	eggs, well beaten
$3\frac{1}{2}$	cups flour
1	tsp. soda
$\frac{1}{2}$	tsp. salt
	nuts (optional)

Cream butter and brown sugar. Add eggs and blend until smooth. Add flour, soda, and salt and mix well. Blend in nuts. Roll into a log shape and wrap in wax paper. Chill in the refrigerator several hours. Cut into $\frac{1}{4}$ inch slices and put on a greased cookie sheet. Bake at 325° for 5-10 minutes until done. Makes 4 dozen.

Honey Spice Snaps

1 cup brown sugar, packed
¾ cup shortening
1 egg
¼ cup honey or dark corn syrup
1 tsp. ginger
½ tsp. salt
½ tsp. cinnamon
¼ tsp. cloves
1½ tsp. soda
2¼ cups flour

In a mixing bowl, cream brown sugar and shortening. Add the egg and honey or corn syrup and mix well. Mix all the dry ingredients in bowl. Stir into sugar mixture until well blended. Shape into balls. Dip half the ball in water, then in sugar. Place sugar side up. Bake on ungreased cookie sheet at 350° for 12-15 minutes. Makes 2 dozen.

Shortbread

½ cup butter, softened
¼ cup plus 1 Tbsp. sugar
1 cup plus 1 Tbsp. flour (do not use self-rising flour)

Whip butter. Add sugar and flour and beat until light and fluffy. Pat dough ½ inch thick into a 9x9 inch pan. Prick with a fork and sprinkle a little sugar on top. Bake at 375° for 15-20 minutes until light brown. Cool before serving. Makes 9 pieces.

Joto Chocolate Drop Cookies

½   cup sugar
¼   cup shortening
½   cup dark corn syrup
1   egg
½   cup cocoa
½   cup sour milk
½   tsp. soda
1   tsp. salt
1   tsp. vanilla
2   cups flour
    nuts (optional)

Preheat oven to 350°. Mix all the ingredients together in a bowl. Drop by teaspoonful onto a greased cookie sheet. Bake for 5-10 minutes. When cool, frost with Chocolate Frosting (p.242). Makes 4 dozen.

✦ **When using a recipe card, slip the card between the tines of a fork and stand the fork in a glass. The card will be held at just the right angle for reading and will be safe from spills.**

Nan's Sugar Cookies

1 cup shortening
2 cups sugar
3 eggs
1 cup buttermilk
3 tsp. baking powder
1 tsp. soda
6 cups flour
1 tsp. vanilla

Cream together the sugar, shortening, eggs and vanilla. Add buttermilk. Stir well and add the dry ingredients. Mix until smooth. Roll into balls and drop about 3 inches apart on a greased cookie sheet. Lay a clean dish towel flat on the counter. Place a clean glass upright in the center of the towel. Gather the towel at the top of the glass and twist so that the towel is drawn tight against the bottom and the sides of the glass. Dip bottom of towel-covered glass into flour and press cookies flat. Place a drop or two of water on the top of each cookie and spread around. Then sprinkle sugar on top. Bake at 350° for 5-10 minutes. Makes 4 dozen.

Walnut Butter Cookies

1 cup butter
6 Tbsp. sugar
2 cups flour
1 tsp. vanilla
1 cup walnuts
   powdered sugar

Cream butter and sugar together. Add flour, vanilla and nuts. Roll into walnut-sized balls onto a greased cookie sheet and lightly flatten. Bake at 400° for 10 minutes. Remove from oven, place on waxed paper and sprinkle with or roll in powdered sugar. Makes 3 dozen.

Oatmeal Cookies

¾	cup shortening, softened
1	cup brown sugar, packed
½	cup granulated sugar
1	egg
¼	cup water
1	tsp. vanilla
1	cup flour
1	tsp. salt
½	tsp. soda
3	cups quick oatmeal

Beat shortening, sugars, egg, water and vanilla together until creamy. Sift together flour, salt and soda. Add to creamed mixture. Blend well. Stir in oats. Drop by teaspoonsful onto greased cookie sheets. Bake in an oven preheated to 350° for 12-15 minutes. Chocolate chips, coconut, raisins or nuts may be added. Makes 3 dozen.

Peanut Butter Cookies

1	cup shortening
1	cup sugar
1	cup brown sugar, packed
1	cup peanut butter
2	eggs
3	cups flour
1	tsp. soda
½	tsp. salt
1	tsp. vanilla

Cream shortening and sugars. Add peanut butter, eggs and dry ingredients. Stir until well blended. Roll into balls and place on a cookie sheet; flatten with a fork dipped in flour. Turn fork 90° and make another fork print for the design. Bake at 375° for 10 minutes or until brown. Makes 6-8 dozen.

Pumpkin Cookies

½   cup shortening
1   cup sugar
1   cup pumpkin
1   cup raisins
½   cup nuts
1   tsp. vanilla
1   tsp. soda
1   tsp. brown sugar
1   tsp. cinnamon
2   cups flour

Cream shortening, sugar and pumpkin in a bowl. Add the rest of the ingredients and mix well. Drop by small spoonfuls onto a ungreased cookie sheet. Brush tops with milk. Bake at 375° for 8 minutes. Top with Butter Creme Frosting (p.241). Makes 2 dozen.

Vanilla Wafers

⅔   cup margarine
½   cup sugar
1   egg
2   Tbsp. milk
1   tsp. vanilla
1¼ cups flour
1   tsp. baking powder

Cream margarine, sugar, egg, milk and vanilla. Beat in flour and baking powder until well blended. Drop by teaspoonsful on well-greased cookie sheet. Bake at 350° for 10 minutes. This makes a soft cookie. For a cracker type cookie, add ½-1 cup additional flour. Knead 3-4 times. Roll out thin on well floured surface and cut with a round cookie cutter. Bake as above. Makes 2 dozen.

Apple Oatmeal Bars

1   cup oatmeal
½   tsp. salt
½   cup butter
1   cup flour
½   tsp. cinnamon
2½ cups apples, chopped or ¾ cup apple butter
     (omit cinnamon)
½   cup sugar

Combine the first five ingredients, and pat half into an 8x8 inch pan. Layer on apples and sugar. Crumble remaining mixture on top. Bake 35 minutes at 350°. Makes 9 bars.

Recipes reprinted with permission from The Complete Tightwad Gazette by Amy Dacyczyn.

Fudge Brownies

1   cup margarine, melted
2   cups sugar
½   cup cocoa
4   eggs
1   cup flour
1   cup chopped nuts (optional)

In a bowl, mix margarine, sugar and cocoa. Add eggs and mix well. Stir flour into egg mixture and mix well. Add nuts if desired. Grease a 9x13 inch pan and pour batter into pan. Bake at 350° for 30 minutes or until brownies test done with a wooden pick. Cool in pan. Frost if desired. Makes 18 brownies.

Brownies

¼   cup cocoa
1   cup flour
1   cup sugar
    pinch of salt
1   tsp. baking powder
1   stick butter or margarine, melted
1   tsp. vanilla
1   egg

Mix dry ingredients in a bowl. Add butter and vanilla. Stir, then add egg. Spread into a greased 8x8 inch pan and bake at 350° for 20 minutes. Makes 9 brownies.

Romance Cookies

1   cup butter
2   cups flour
¼   cup sugar
1   tsp. salt
2   eggs, beaten
1½   cups packed brown sugar
¾   tsp. baking powder
1   tsp. vanilla
½   cup flaked coconut
½-1   cup chopped walnuts (to taste)
    powdered sugar

Preheat oven to 350 degrees. Cream butter. Add flour, sugar and salt. Spread in an ungreased 9x13 inch pan. Combine eggs, brown sugar, baking powder, vanilla, coconut and nuts. Pour over flour mixture. Bake for 20 minutes. Dust with powdered sugar. Cut into bars. Makes 24 cookies.

Lemon Bars

Crust

2   cups flour
1   cup butter or margarine, melted
½   cup powdered sugar

Filling

4   eggs, well beaten
2   cups granulated sugar
⅓   cup lemon juice (1 lemon)
¼   cup flour
½   tsp. baking powder

Preheat oven to 350°. Mix all the crust ingredients in a bowl. Press into greased 9x13 pan. Make sure the edges are higher than the center to contain the filling. Bake crust for 20 minutes or until it begins to brown. Combine, eggs, sugar and lemon juice and mix well. Stir in flour and baking powder. Pour into baked crust and bake 20-30 minutes at 350°. Bars are done when they are firm to the touch. Cut into small squares and dust with powdered sugar. These bars are extremely rich so cut into small pieces. Makes 18 bars.

✦ **A pizza cutter makes cutting brownies a breeze. You can cut the pieces more evenly, and the brownies won't stick to the cutter.**

Dessert Tips

✦ Try cutting the amount of sugar in cookie and cake recipes. Depending on the recipe, you may **cut the amount of sugar by one quarter, one third, one half.** This does not usually alter the quality of the product.

✦ Try adding ¼ **to ½ tsp. baking soda** and half the amount of sugar when making sweets desserts. The soda brings out the sweetness of the sugar so you can use less.

✦ **Use brownie crumbs** for ice cream topping.

✦ Stuff a **miniature marshmallow in the bottom of a sugar cone** to prevent ice cream drips.

✦ **Pour boiling water** over pecans in the shell and let them sit 30 minutes. When you shell them, they should come out whole.

✦ Dried-out **coconut can be revitalized by sprinkling with milk.** Let it stand until it regains its freshness.

✦ Dried-out **raisins or other fruit may be plumped** by soaking in juice or water.

✦ **Desserts are not needed every night.** Serve them only one or two times a week or only on weekends. This not only saves money, but calories too.

✦ **To dress up desserts:** Place chocolate syrup, lemon curd or other sauces into squirt bottles. This makes it easier to decorate cakes, fruit dishes or other desserts.

✦ **Buy the chocolate bunnies and hearts on clearance** after each holiday. Break them into chunks, melt them down in a double boiler or microwave and use them for anything that needs to be dipped in chocolate.

✦ **To soften brown sugar,** place a slice of bread or an apple slice in the bag and seal.

Apple Crisp

6	apples, peeled and sliced
1	cup brown sugar
½	cup oatmeal
½	cup flour
½	cup butter or margarine, softened
1	tsp. cinnamon and/or nutmeg
¼	cup water

Preheat oven to 350°. Arrange apples in well-greased baking dish. Blend all remaining ingredients except water. Spread evenly over top of apples. Pour water over the topping. Bake 45 minutes until apples are tender and top is crisp. Serves 6.

Peach Crisp

Use peaches in place of apples.

Baked Apples

1	apple, cored

Filling:

1	Tbsp. honey or brown sugar
1	tsp. margarine
	dash of cinnamon
	dash of nutmeg
	raisins (optional)

Use 1 apple for each person. Fill the center of the apple with all the ingredients. Bake at 350° until tender or put in a Dutch oven on top of stove and simmer on very low until tender. Serves 1.

Fried Apples

3   Tbsp. butter or margarine
4   large apples, cored and sliced (tart works best)
⅓   cup brown sugar
½   tsp. ground cinnamon

Cut apples into ¼ inch slices. Heat butter in a large skillet. Put
the apples, brown sugar, and cinnamon in the skillet and cover.
Over medium-low heat, cook apple slices 7-10 minutes or until
they begin to soften and the syrup thickens. Serve coated with
excess syrup on top. Serves 4.

Bread Pudding

8   slices bread, cubed (about 6 cups)
⅔   cup sugar
2   eggs
2   cups milk
1   tsp. vanilla
1   tsp. nutmeg
2   Tbsp. lemon juice
½   tsp. salt
1   cup raisins (optional)

Mix all the ingredients in a bowl and pour into a greased 8x8
inch pan. Bake at 350° for 45 minutes and top with lemon glaze
(p. 244). Serves 9.

Custard

2	eggs, slightly beaten
$\frac{1}{2}$	cup sugar
$\frac{1}{8}$	tsp. salt
$\frac{1}{2}$	tsp. vanilla
2	cups milk
	nutmeg

Preheat over to 350°. In a bowl mix all the ingredients together until well blended. Pour into four 6 ounce custard cups. Sprinkle a dash of nutmeg on top. Place custard cups on a rack in a 9x13 baking pan. Pour water into the baking pan 1-1½ inches deep. Bake about 1-1½ hours or until a knife inserted in the center comes out clean. Remove from water and serve warm or chilled. Makes 4 servings.

Dipped Fruits in Chocolate

1 bag of white, dark semi-sweet or milk chocolate chips

Fruit suggestions:
strawberries
kiwi
banana
grapes
melon (use a small scoop, towel dry)
pineapple
mango
orange and grapefruit slices, whole and skinned
papaya

Melt the chocolate chips in a bowl in the microwave or on a double boiler. Put the dry fruit on the end of a toothpick or skewer. Dip the fruits in the chocolate and then briefly let the excess chocolate drip off. Place the fruits on a sheet of waxed paper to harden.

Frozen Peach Dessert

1   can peach halves
      strawberries, frozen or fresh
      whipped topping (p.294)

Place a strawberry in the center of each peach half. Top with whipped topping and freeze. Thaw 20-30 minutes before serving. This is a great after school snack. Serves 3-4.

Fruit Gelatin

1   cup fruit juice
1   pkg. unflavored gelatin
1   cup cold fruit juice or water
1   Tbsp. lemon juice
1   Tbsp. orange juice*

Combine and dissolve fruit juice and gelatin in a saucepan. Heat to almost boiling. Remove and add the remaining ingredients. Stir well. Chill until set. Serves 4-6.

When partially set, fresh or canned fruit may be added.

1 cup chilled yogurt may be substituted for the second cup of fruit juice or water.

✦ **For great gelatin-substitute canned fruit juices for water. For example, if using peaches in a gelatin salad, reserve the juice and use in place of some of the water.**

Funnel Cakes

1   cup sifted flour
1   tsp. baking powder
¼   tsp. salt
½   tsp. cinnamon
1   egg
1   cup milk
    vegetable oil

Mix dry ingredients. Add egg and milk. Stir until smooth. Pour oil into a skillet and heat to 375°. Holding finger over the end of a funnel, pour in ¼ cup batter. Holding over the hot oil, remove finger and let drizzle over the hot oil. As batter flows, move funnel in a circle to form a spiral cake. Fry about 2 minutes or each side, turning once, until golden brown. Remove from oil and drain. Sprinkle with powdered sugar, glaze, or nuts. Makes 6 cakes.

"If at first you don't suceed,
destroy all evidence that you ever tried"

Granola Bars

¾ cup brown sugar
½ cup sugar
½ cup margarine, softened
2 Tbsp. honey or corn syrup
½ tsp. vanilla
1 egg
1 cup flour
1 tsp. cinnamon
¼ tsp. salt
½ tsp. baking soda
1½ cups oatmeal
1¼ cups crispy rice cereal, crushed bran flakes, corn flakes
    or crushed graham crackers
1 cup chocolate chips*

In a large bowl, cream sugars and margarine until fluffy. Add honey, vanilla and egg. Mix well. Blend in flour, cinnamon, baking soda and salt. Stir in remaining ingredients. Press firmly into the bottom of a greased 9x13 pan. Bake at 350° for 20-25 minutes. To microwave: Press ingredients into a microwave-safe dish. Microwave on medium power for 7-9 minutes. Rotate dish every three minutes. Bars will firm as they stand. Cool and cut into bars. Save the crumbs for yogurt or ice cream topping.
Makes 24 bars.

The following may be used in addition to or to replace chocolate chips:

1 cup coconut
½ cup creamy or chunky peanut butter
½ cup nuts
½-1 cup raisins, dried apples, apricots
½ cup fruit preserves

Ice Cream Sandwiches

½   cup margarine
1   cup brown sugar
2   eggs
1   tsp. vanilla
¼   tsp. salt
½   cup cocoa powder
2   cups flour
1   tsp. baking powder
1   half gallon brick ice cream

Beat margarine and brown sugar until fluffy. Beat in eggs one at a time and add vanilla. Add baking powder, salt, cocoa and flour. Mix well. Place dough on plastic wrap and wrap tightly. Chill 1 hour. Roll dough into a rectangle on a lightly floured board. Cut into rectangles 2 x 5 inches each. Place rectangles on ungreased baking sheet. Prick surfaces of cookies lightly with fork. Bake 8-10 minutes or until edges look set (centers of cookies will be slightly puffed). Cool; remove from baking sheet. Cut ice cream into 2x5 inch rectangles about ¾ inch thick. Place each ice cream rectangle between aluminum foil or plastic wrap and freeze at least 24 hours. Store up to one week. Cookies should be frozen separately if you want to freeze them longer than 1 week. Makes 6 sandwiches.

Popcorn Balls

40   large marshmallows
¼   cup butter
     food coloring (optional)
8-10 cups popped popcorn, old maids and hulls removed

Melt marshmallows and butter over low heat. Add food coloring and mix well. Pour popped corn in a large bowl. Place marshmallow mixture over popcorn while stirring. Mix well to coat all of the popped corn. Butter your hands to form the popcorn mixture into balls. Makes 8-10 popcorn balls.

Peanut Caramel Popcorn

(just like Cracker Jacks™)

1   cup margarine
2   cups brown sugar
½   cup light or dark corn syrup
1   tsp. salt
1   tsp. baking soda
1   tsp. vanilla
6   qts. popped corn
½-1 cup peanuts

Melt margarine in large saucepan. Stir in brown sugar, corn syrup and salt. Bring to a boil, stirring constantly. Boil without stirring for 5 minutes. Remove from heat. Stir in baking soda and vanilla. Gradually pour over popped corn and peanuts. Mix until coated. Makes 6 quarts.

Poppycock

2   qts. popped corn, kernals and hulls removed
2   cups nuts (optional)
1⅓ cups sugar
1   cup butter
½   cup white corn syrup
1   tsp. vanilla

Mix popcorn and nuts. Mix sugar, butter and syrup. Bring to a boil and boil until it turns a light caramel color. Add vanilla. Pour over popped corn and stir. Makes 2 quarts.

Pineapple-Orange Gelatin

1   pkg. unflavored gelatin
1   cup cold water
3   Tbsp. sugar
2   Tbsp. frozen orange juice concentrate
     drained juice from pineapple chunks plus water to
     make 1¼ cups
1   cup pineapple chunks, drained
1   banana, sliced (optional)

Combine gelatin, cold water and sugar in a saucepan. Heat to dissolve gelatin. Add the orange juice concentrate, pineapple juice and water. Stir until blended. Fold in fruit. Chill until set. Serves 6.

Rice Pudding

½   cup rice, uncooked
4   cups milk
½   tsp. cinnamon
½   tsp. nutmeg
¼   cup sugar
½   tsp. salt
½   cup raisins (optional)

Combine all the ingredients except raisins and pour into a greased baking dish. Bake at 275° for 3 hours. Stir frequently during the first hour. The mixture should not boil. Add raisins during last ½ hour. Serve either hot or cold. Serves 6.

Whipped Topping

1   tsp. unflavored gelatin
2   tsp. cold water
3   Tbsp. boiling water
½   cup ice water
½   cup dry milk powder
3   Tbsp. sugar
3   Tbsp. oil

Chill a small bowl. Soften gelatin in the cold water. Add the boiling water, stirring until the gelatin is dissolved. Cool until tepid. Place the sugar in a small bowl or cup and the oil in a bowl or cup. This will aid in mixing if you are using a hand mixer. Place the ice water and milk powder in the chilled bowl. Using a mixer, beat the milk and water on high. After soft peaks form and while you are still beating, add the sugar, then the oil and the gelatin. Place in the freezer for about 15 minutes, then transfer to the refrigerator. This does not store well so it is best to use it the same day. Stir before using. Makes 2 cups.

Recipes reprinted with permission from The Complete Tightwad Gazette by Amy Dacyczyn.

Vanilla Pudding

⅓	cup sugar
2	Tbsp. cornstarch
⅛	tsp. salt
2	eggs, slightly beaten
2	cups milk
2	Tbsp. butter or margarine, softened (not soft type)
2	tsp. vanilla

Mix sugar, cornstarch and salt in a 2 quart saucepan. Add eggs to sugar mixture and slowly stir in milk until combined. Cook over medium heat, stirring constantly, until mixture thickens and boils. Boil and stir 1 minute. Remove from heat; stir in margarine and vanilla. Cool slightly, pour into dessert dishes and chill. You can also top with nuts or whipped topping. Serves 4-6.

Chocolate Pudding

Stir 3 tablespoons cocoa into sugar-cornstarch mixture.

Chocolate Peanut Butter Pudding

Stir into chocolate pudding ¼ cup peanut butter. Omit margarine.

Butterscotch Pudding

Substitute ⅔ cup packed brown sugar for the sugar and decrease vanilla to 1 teaspoon.

Yogurt

½   cup dry milk
4   cups 2% or whole milk
¼   cup yogurt
2   Tbsp. honey (optional)

In a saucepan combine dry milk, milk and honey. Mix well. Place over medium heat and bring to 120º. Remove from heat. Remove ½ cup of milk, place it in a bowl and add yogurt. Whisk well. Pour yogurt mixture back into pan. Whisk well, again. Pour into a clean quart jar. Cover with plastic wrap or lid. Set on heating pad covered with a dish towel. Turn heating pad on low and incubate for 8 hours. Refrigerate when done. Makes 1 quart.

Custard Style Yogurt

1   package (2.75 oz.) fruit flavored gelatin
1   cup boiling water
3   cups yogurt
⅓   cup sugar (optional)
up to 1 cup fruit, chopped (optional)

In a bowl combine gelatin and water. Stir until completely dissolved. Stir in yogurt, sugar and fruit. Place in individual containers for lunches or a bowl and chill until set. Makes 3 cups.

Butterscotch Sauce

1   stick butter
1   cup evaporated milk
2   cups brown sugar, packed

Melt butter in a saucepan. Add brown sugar and evaporated milk. Cook on medium heat, stirring constantly until blended. Keep refrigerated. Great on top of ice cream. Makes 2 cups.

Peanut Butterscotch Sauce

Add ½ cup peanut butter with brown sugar and evaporated milk.

Caramel Sauce

2   egg yolks, beaten
¼   cup margarine or butter
½   cup brown sugar, packed
½   cup water
¼   cup granulated sugar
1   tsp. vanilla

In a saucepan, heat all ingredients to boiling, stirring constantly. Boil 1 minute. Serve warm or cold. Makes 1 cups.

Chocolate Syrup

½ cup cocoa, packed
1   cup water
2   cups sugar
⅛ tsp. salt
¼ tsp. vanilla

Mix cocoa and water in a saucepan. Heat and stir to dissolve the cocoa. Add the sugar and stir to dissolve. Boil 3 minutes. Add the salt and the vanilla. Pour into a sterilized jar. Store covered in the refrigerator. Keeps for several months. Makes 2 cups.

Recipes reprinted with permission from The Complete Tightwad Gazette by Amy Dacyczyn.

Hot Fudge Sauce

½ cup packed plus 1 Tbsp. cocoa
¼ tsp salt
¾ cup margarine or butter
1   (12 oz.) can evaporated milk
2   cups sugar
1   tsp. vanilla

Mix all ingredients except vanilla in a saucepan and heat to a rolling boil. Boil for 1 minute. Remove from heat and add vanilla. Serve warm or chilled. Makes 3 cups.

Miscellaneous Recipes

Ever notice that immediately after you buy an item, you find a coupon for it.

Miscellaneous Tips

✦ **If honey becomes crystallized** or cloudy, it is still good. Just warm it up in the microwave or in a pan of boiling water for a few minutes. Stir until it becomes clear again.

✦ **If jelly or jam doesn't set up well,** use for popsicles or add more water, boil and make syrup.

✦ **Put seasoned salt, taco seasonings,** etc. in old spice bottles to make them more convenient to use. Make sure to re-label bottles.

✦ **To make chopped garlic:** Peel and dice garlic and put in a small glass jar. Press down on the garlic with the back of a spoon and place 2 tablespoons olive oil on top. Seal and refrigerate. Keep for one to two weeks.

✦ **Store garlic in a jar or bottle of vegetable oil.** This will keep the garlic from drying out and then you will have garlic flavored oil for salads. Use within one week.

✦ **To make an all-in-one salt and pepper shaker:** Place 1 part pepper to 6 parts salt in an old spice jar or salt shaker.

✦ **To prevent milk or cheese from curdling,** add a dash of baking soda.

✦ **When you find a gift item on sale, buy it. Keep a box going all year for good finds on gifts. The end of January and February are a great time to find good bargains on everything from clothing to toys.**

✦ **Raw potatoes will take food stains off of your fingers. Just slice the potato and rub on the stains, then rinse your fingers with water.**

Baking Powder

2   tsp. cream of tartar
1   tsp. baking soda

Mix together and use immediately. Mix into batter quickly and put in oven right away.

*If you want to mix ahead of time, add 1 tsp. cornstarch and store no longer than one month.

*If you have a recipe that calls for double-acting baking powder, use twice the amount.

Homemade baking powder starts to fizz and release carbon dioxide the minute it is added to liquid.

Buttermilk

3½ cups whole milk
½   cup buttermilk, room temperature

Mix and let sit out in warm spot for 24 hours and then you have a fresh batch of buttermilk! Works great. Don't forget to save a half cup at the end so you can make a new batch. It keeps going and going! Makes 1 quart.

Egg Substitute

1   heaping Tbsp. soy flour or powder
1   Tbsp. water

This is a great substitute for eggs in baking. Equals 1 egg.

Powdered Sugar

Combine 1 cup granulated sugar and 1 teaspoon cornstarch in a blender or food processor. Blend 1 minute or until powdered.

Self-Rising Flour

4   cups flour
2   tsp. salt
2   Tbsp. double-acting baking powder

Mix well and store in airtight container. Use in recipes calling for self-rising flour. Makes 4 cups.

Sweetened Condensed Milk

2   cups instant nonfat dry milk
2   cups sugar
1   cup boiling water
$\frac{1}{2}$ cup margarine, melted

Place ingredients in a bowl. With a hand blender, process until smooth. Refrigerate in covered container (mixture will thicken as it stands). One cup plus 2 tablespoons equals the 15 ounce can that most recipes require. Makes 3 cups.

Vanilla

2   vanilla beans cut lengthwise (but not in half)
¾   cup vodka

Combine the ingredients in a ½ pint jar and set aside to steep for 3 or 4 weeks. Use vanilla as usual. When the level of the vanilla drops below the vanilla beans add more vodka. You can get 4-5 large bottles worth of vanilla out of 2 beans.

Bouquet Garni Bags

bay leaf
sprig of thyme
parsley leaves

Place a few sprigs of each in a cheesecloth and tie. Use in stocks, soups, and stews.

Cajun Seasoning

1   Tbsp. paprika
2½   tsp. salt
1   tsp. onion powder
1   tsp. garlic powder
1   tsp. cayenne pepper
¾   tsp. white pepper
¾   tsp. black pepper
½   tsp. thyme leaves, dried
½   tsp. oregano, dried

Combine ingredients and mix well. Store in an airtight container.

Homemade Shake and Bake ™

4   cups flour
4   cups soda crackers, crushed
4   Tbsp. salt
2   Tbsp. sugar
2   tsp. garlic powder
2   tsp. onion powder
3   Tbsp. paprika
¼   cup vegetable oil

Mix well and store indefinitely in the refrigerator in a covered container. Moisten the chicken pieces with milk or water. Pour about 2 cups mixture, or more if needed, into a plastic bag. Place chicken pieces, one at a time, in the bag and shake until evenly coated. Bake coated chicken pieces in a greased shallow pan at 350° for 45-60 minutes. Discard plastic bag with unused coating. DO NOT reuse extra coating that has come into contact with raw chicken!

Italian Seasoning

¼   cup dried basil
2   Tbsp. dried marjoram
2   Tbsp. dried oregano
2   Tbsp. dried coriander
2   Tbsp. dried thyme
2   Tbsp. dried rosemary
2   tsp. garlic powder
1   tsp. sugar

Combine all the ingredients. Store in an airtight container in a cool dark place for up to 3 months.

Pumpkin Pie Spice

$\frac{1}{2}$	tsp. cinnamon
$\frac{1}{4}$	tsp. nutmeg
$\frac{1}{8}$	tsp. ginger
$\frac{1}{8}$	tsp. cloves

Mix well. Makes 1 teaspoon. Use in any recipe calling for pumpkin pie spice.

Seasoned Salt

8	Tbsp. salt
3	Tbsp. pepper
2	Tbsp. paprika
$\frac{1}{2}$	Tbsp. onion powder
$\frac{1}{2}$	Tbsp. garlic powder

Mix all ingredients in a bowl. Store in an airtight container.

Recipes reprinted with permission from The Complete Tightwad Gazette by Amy Dacyczyn.

Taco Seasoning

6	tsp. chili powder
$4\frac{1}{2}$	tsp. cumin
5	tsp. paprika
$\frac{1}{4}$	tsp. oregano
3	tsp. onion powder
$2\frac{1}{2}$	tsp. garlic powder
$\frac{1}{8}$-$\frac{1}{4}$	tsp. cayenne pepper

Mix all ingredients and store in an airtight container. One teaspoon of homemade taco seasoning equals 2 teaspoons store-bought.

Recipes reprinted with permission from The Complete Tightwad Gazette by Amy Dacyczyn.

Chili Sauce

1   gal. can tomatoes, diced
1-2 medium onions, diced
1   tsp. cinnamon
1   tsp. dry mustard
1   cup sugar
½   tsp. curry powder
½-1 cup vinegar
½   tsp. nutmeg
     chili powder (to taste)
5   tsp. salt

Cook tomatoes and onions until soft. Strain through a colander. Add the rest of the ingredients to a large pot and cook down to desired consistency. Can or freeze in 2-cup portions. Makes 10 pints.

Easy Barbecue Sauce

1   cup grape jelly
     garlic or garlic powder (to taste)
1   cup ketchup

Mix together and serve with ribs or chicken wings. Makes 2 cups.

Grandma's Barbecue Sauce

2   cups ketchup
1½   cups brown sugar
1   Tbsp. onion, finely chopped or ½ tsp. onion salt
½   tsp. garlic powder
2   Tbsp. liquid smoke

Mix all the ingredients in a bowl. Place in a jar and store in the refrigerator. Makes 3 cups.

Hickory Barbecue Sauce

1   (20 oz.) bottle ketchup
1   tsp. salt
½   cup water
1   tsp. onion powder
¼   cup cider vinegar
1-4 tsp. liquid smoke (to taste)
1   Tbsp. brown sugar, packed
⅛   tsp. garlic powder
1   Tbsp. Worcestershire sauce

Blend all the ingredients in a blender until smooth. Store in refrigerator. Use on anything you want a barbecue flavor. Makes 3½ cups.

Cranberry Sauce

1   (15 oz.) can jellied cranberry sauce
1   tsp. mustard
2   Tbsp. lemon juice
¼   tsp. ground cloves

Mix together. Makes a great topping for ham or turkey. Makes 1¼ cups.

Ketchup

1   (8 oz.) can tomato sauce
     very small dash of cinnamon
3   Tbsp. sugar
1   Tbsp. plus 1 tsp. vinegar

Pour tomato sauce into a small saucepan and boil away some of the water until it begins to thicken. Add the sugar, cinnamon and vinegar. Simmer for 3 to 4 minutes longer. Refrigerate. Warning: Go easy on the cinnamon because it's easy to put in too much. Makes 1 cup.

Ham Sauce

1   cup sour cream
2   Tbsp. prepared mustard
1   Tbsp. horseradish

Add horseradish and mustard to sour cream. Stir well. Serve with slow-cooked ham. Makes 1 cup.

Homemade Horseradish

fresh horseradish, peeled and chopped
water
vinegar

Place horseradish in a food processor. Process to the texture you desire. Add water and white vinegar as necessary. Store in covered jars in the refrigerator for several months.

Garlic Mayo

1   (½ quart) jar of mayonnaise
4-5 large cloves of garlic, pressed, or 1 tsp. garlic powder

Mix pressed garlic with mayonnaise. Refrigerate for at least one day before using. Great on sandwiches, chicken, fish or with vegetables. Makes 2 cups.

Dijon Mustard

2   cups dry wine
1   large onion, chopped
3   cloves garlic, pressed
1   cup dry mustard
3   Tbsp. honey
1   Tbsp. vegetable oil
2   tsp. salt

Combine wine, onion and garlic in a saucepan. Bring to a boil and simmer 5 minutes. Cool, strain and discard solids. Add mustard to the liquid and stir until smooth. Blend in honey, oil and salt. Return to saucepan and heat slowly until thickened, stirring constantly. Cool in the refrigerator in a covered jar. Age 6 to 8 weeks in a cool, dark place. Refrigerate after aging. Makes 2 cups.

Mustard

$\frac{1}{2}$ cup mustard seed
      dash of salt
      dash of turmeric
$\frac{1}{4}$ cup cider vinegar
$\frac{1}{2}$ cup water

Grind mustard seed, salt and turmeric in a food processor. Combine the mustard mixture with cider vinegar and water in the top of a double boiler. Cook and stir until smooth. Cool and thin as needed with water and/or cider vinegar. Makes $\frac{3}{4}$ cup.

Mustard Sauce

1 Tbsp. margarine
1 Tbsp. flour
¼ tsp. pepper
1 cup milk
3 Tbsp. prepared mustard
1 Tbsp. prepared horseradish

Heat margarine over low heat in a 1½ quart saucepan until melted. Stir in flour and pepper, stirring constantly until smooth and bubbly. Remove from heat. Stir in milk. Heat to boiling, stirring constantly. Boil and stir 1 minute. Stir in mustard and horseradish. Serve warm. Great with smoked sausage, steak bites, or cooked cabbage. Makes 1 cup.

Horseradish Mustard

1 cup dry mustard
1 Tbsp. lemon juice
¼ cup honey
¼ tsp. lemon peel, grated
½ tsp. salt
5 Tbsp. horseradish
½ cup vinegar
¼ cup oil

Combine all the ingredients in a food processor and mix well. Put mustard in jars and seal. Age 2-8 weeks in the refrigerator. Makes 1¼ cups.

Hot Mustard

1 cup dry mustard
2 Tbsp. honey
¼ tsp. corn oil
½ cup water

Mix ingredients. Seal in a jar. Age 2 weeks in a cool, dark place and then refrigerate. Makes 1¼ cups.

Hot Mustard Sauce

¼ cup ground mustard
¼ cup vinegar
¼ cup sugar
1 egg yolk
2 Tbsp. honey
  pretzels

In a small saucepan, combine mustard and vinegar. Let stand for 30 minutes. Whisk in the sugar and the egg yolk until smooth. Cook over medium heat, whisking constantly, just until mixture begins to simmer and is thickened (about 7 minutes). Remove from heat and whisk in the honey. Chill. Serve with pretzels. Store in the refrigerator. Makes ½ cup.

Salsa #1

4   cups canned tomatoes with juice
2-3 Tbsp. lime juice (to taste)
1   large onion, diced
¼   tsp. garlic powder
1   green pepper, chopped
2   Tbsp. cilantro, chopped
1   small, fresh jalapeno pepper, minced
      salt and pepper

Cook all the ingredients in a large saucepan on medium heat for 20 minutes. Pour into hot, sterile quart jars and seal. Process in a pressure canner for 25 minutes. We use salsa frequently enough that we don't have to can it. If you don't can it, store it in the refrigerator. Makes 3 pints.

Salsa #2

4   large ripe tomatoes
3   cans tomato paste
4   large green tomatoes, skinned
1½   cups vinegar
1   large green peppers, chopped
2   Tbsp. brown sugar
2   onions, chopped
12   jalapeno peppers, seeded and chopped--leave seeds in for hot flavor
4   tsp. garlic powder or 6-8 garlic cloves, chopped

Thoroughly process all ingredients in a food processor. Place in a large Dutch oven and bring to a boil. Can. If your family eats a lot of salsa there is no need to can it. Just refrigerate. Makes 6 pints.

Shrimp Cocktail

1 cup ketchup
¼ tsp. Worcestershire sauce (¼ tsp. more to taste)
1 tsp. lemon juice
1½ tsp. horseradish (more to taste)
1 Tbsp. honey

Mix ingredients together, stir well. Refrigerate any leftovers. Makes 1 cup.

Steak Dip

1 cup sour cream
1 tsp. lemon juice
2-4 Tbsp. horseradish (to taste)
½-1 tsp. garlic powder (to taste)
1 tsp. Worcestershire sauce

Mix together. Great for dipping pieces of slow-cooked round steak. Makes 1 cup.

Sweet and Sour Sauce

¼	cup brown sugar, packed
1	Tbsp. flour
2	Tbsp. white vinegar
2	Tbsp. soy sauce
¾	cup ketchup
⅓	cup reserved pineaple juice
1	can pineapple chunks (optional)

Mix the brown sugar and flour in a saucepan. Add the rest of the ingredients except the pineapple. Heat and stir until it boils and thickens. Great with pork or chicken. Makes 1¼ cups.

Tartar Sauce

1	cup salad dressing (Miracle Whip™)
¼	cup sweet relish

Combine ingredients. Mix well and refrigerate. Makes 1 cup.

It's often not a slow metabolism
that makes us put on weight,
but a fast fork.

Popcorn

2   Tbsp. vegetable oil
1½   cup popcorn

Heat oil in a large covered pan. Place 3 kernels popcorn in the pan. When the kernels pop, pour in the popcorn. Reduce heat to medium. Cover and shake until popping slows to 1 pop every 3-4 seconds. Remove from pan and season as desired. Makes 9-10 cups.

Popcorn Seasonings

Pour ¼ cup melted butter over popcorn and sprinkle with any of the following:

+ salt
+ Parmesan cheese
+ garlic powder
+ onion powder
+ chili powder
+ Cheddar cheese, finely grated

Barbecue Flavored Popcorn

2   tsp. dried parsley
2   tsp. paprika
½   tsp. hickory smoke salt
½   tsp. onion powder
¼   tsp. garlic powder

Mix and pour over popcorn.

Spiced Popcorn

1   tsp. paprika
½   tsp. crushed red pepper
½   tsp. ground cumin
⅓   cup Parmesan cheese
¼   cup butter, melted

Mix together and pour over popcorn.

Kettle Corn

½   cup popcorn
2   Tbsp. vegetable oil
3   Tbsp. white sugar

Heat oil in medium pan until hot. Add popcorn and sprinkle all of the sugar over it. Cover and shake continuously until popped.

✦ **Popcorn should be stored in the freezer. It lasts longer and pops more kernels.**

Roasted Sunflower Seeds

2	cups hulled sunflower seeds
1	Tbsp. oil or margarine, melted
1	tsp. Worcestershire sauce
1/4	tsp. salt
	garlic salt (to taste)
	onion salt (to taste)

Mix until blended well. Place a thin layer on a cookie sheet. Bake at 325° for 30 minutes, stirring occasionally. Seeds are done when they are lightly browned and crunchy. Makes 2 cups.

Roasted Pumpkin Seeds

Boil seeds in water for 5 minutes. Drain well. Sprinkle with salt or seasoned salt. Place a thin layer on a cookie sheet. Bake at 250°. Stir after 30 minutes. Bake 1/2-1 hour more or until crunchy.

*Squash seeds may also be used

Baked Tortilla Chips

corn tortillas
spray oil
salt
garlic powder (optional)
onion powder (optional)
chili powder (optional)

Heat oven to 275°. Very lightly spray tortillas with oil. Sprinkle with seasonings if desired. Place on oven rack and bake 20-30 minutes or until crispy. Sprinkle with salt and break apart into pieces when cooled. If you want more uniform pieces cut tortilla shells in quarters after spraying on the oil. Then bake on a cookie sheet. If you like flavor with garlic powder, onion powder or chili powder.

Fried Tortilla Chips

corn tortillas
oil for frying
salt (optional)

Cut tortillas into wedges. Heat 1 inch of oil in a frying pan. Fry several wedges until crisp on both sides. Remove with slotted spoon and drain on paper towels. Sprinkle with salt if desired.

Graham Crackers

2½-3 cups whole wheat flour
¼   cup brown sugar, packed
1   tsp. baking powder
½   tsp. baking soda
¼   tsp. salt
1   tsp. cinnamon
⅓   cup oil
⅓   cup honey
2   Tbsp. molasses or dark corn syrup
1   tsp. vanilla
¼-½   cup milk

Combine 2½ cups flour with brown sugar, baking powder, baking soda, salt and cinnamon in a large bowl. Mix oil, honey, molasses, vanilla and ¼ cup milk in a measuring cup or bowl. Add liquid ingredients to the dry mixture. Mix well. Use your hands to finish mixing. If the dough is too sticky, add ½ cup more flour. If dough is too dry, add ¼ cup milk. Form dough into a ball. Preheat oven to 300°. Divide dough in half. Roll dough directly onto greased cookie sheets to cover the entire sheet. Use a knife to cut dough into 2½ inch squares, but do not separate. Prick the surface with a fork. Bake for 15-25 minutes or until the edges are slightly browned. Remove from oven and let crackers cool before removing from cookie sheet. Store in airtight container. Makes 2-3 dozen.

Homemade Crackers

4	cups flour
3	Tbsp. sugar
1	tsp. salt
1/4	cup butter (1/2 stick)
1	cup milk

Sift together flour, sugar and salt. Cut in butter with 2 knives or a pastry blender until mixture looks like coarse crumbs. Stir in enough milk to make a stiff dough. Roll about 1/4 inch thick on a lightly floured surface. Cut into squares with a pizza cutter. Prick with a fork several times on each cracker and brush lightly with milk. Place on an ungreased baking sheet and bake at 425° for 15 minutes or until golden brown. Makes several dozen.

Soda Crackers

2	cups flour
1	tsp. salt
1/2	tsp. soda
1/4	cup margarine
1/2	cup buttermilk or sour milk
1	egg

Combine flour, salt and soda in a bowl. Cut in margarine with a pastry blender or two knives. Stir in buttermilk and egg. Form a ball and knead a few times. Divide dough into several pieces and roll out very thin on a floured board. Lay rolled-out dough on ungreased baking sheets. Sprinkle with salt and prick with a fork. Cut into 1½ inch squares with a pizza cutter or sharp knife. Bake at 400° for 10-12 minutes. Makes several dozen.

Wheat Crackers

3 cups all-purpose flour
1 cup whole wheat flour
1 tsp. baking powder
½ tsp. salt
¾ cup margarine, softened
1 egg, lightly beaten
  milk

Combine flour, whole wheat flour, baking powder and salt in a bowl. Cut in margarine with a pastry blender or two knives. Put egg in a measuring cup and add enough milk to make 1 cup liquid. Mix with dry ingredients and form into a ball. Knead lightly. Divide dough into 4 parts. Roll out thinly on floured board and place on greased cookie sheets. Cut with a pizza cutter into desired size crackers. Prick dough with a fork all over. Bake in an oven preheated to 425° for 7-10 minutes. Store in an airtight container. Makes several dozen.

Honey Butter

1 stick butter or margarine, softened
½ cup honey

Mix together until smooth. Store covered in the refrigerator. Great with corn bread, crackers or bread. Makes 1 cup.

Soft Butter or Margarine

½ cup cold milk or evaporated milk
1 lb. butter or margarine, softened

Soften margarine or butter to room temperature. Whip with milk. Store in the refrigerator. This is just like the store-bought "soft margarine". Makes 1 pound.

DO NOT use Soft Margarine for baking.

Diet Butter or Margarine

Use ½ cup cold water in place of the milk.

DO NOT use Diet Margarine for baking.

Garlic Butter

1 stick butter or margarine, softened
½ tsp. garlic powder or 2 cloves garlic, finely chopped

Mix together until smooth. Store in a covered container in the refrigerator. Makes ½ cup.

Cheese Spread

1   (12 ounce) can evaporated milk
1   lb. American cheese, grated
2   Tbsp. vinegar
½   tsp. dry mustard
½   tsp. salt
     dash cayenne pepper

Combine evaporated milk and cheese in a double boiler. Heat, stirring constantly until cheese melts. Remove from heat, add the rest of the ingredients and stir well. Stir occasionally as it cools. Store covered in the refrigerator. Keeps several weeks. Flavor the cheese with crumbled bacon, or onion or garlic salt and spices, if desired. Makes 2½ cups.

Chili Con Queso

24   slices American cheese
1   cup salsa
     green chilies or jalapenos, seeds removed, and chopped (to taste)*
¼-½   tsp. onion powder (to taste)
¼-½   tsp. garlic powder (to taste)

In a double boiler or in the microwave, heat cheese and salsa until cheese melts. Add the peppers, onion and garlic powder to taste. Serve immediately with tortilla chips, bread cubes, breadsticks or vegetables. Makes 2 cups.

*Leaving the seeds in the peppers makes the dip hotter.

Spiced Honey

1   lemon
12   whole cloves
3   sticks cinnamon
2⅔ cups honey

Cut lemon into 6 thin slices. Place all ingredients in a saucepan and bring to a boil, stirring occasionally. Remove lemon slices, discard cloves, and place 2 lemon slices and 1 cinnamon stick in each jar. Ladle hot honey into jars, leaving ¼ inch head space. Screw on lids and process for 10 minutes in boiling water canner. Makes 3 half-pints.

Better to remain silent
and be thought a fool
than to open your mouth
and remove all doubt!

Peanut Butter

2   cups roasted salted peanuts
1½ tsp. canola or peanut oil

Combine roasted peanuts and oil in food processor fitted with metal blade. Grind ingredients continuously for 2 to 3 minutes. The ground nuts will form a ball. As soon as the ball smoothes out, the peanut butter is ready. If necessary, stop machine and scrape down sides with rubber spatula. Pack into jar with tight-fitting lid. Store in refrigerator. Makes 1½ cups.

Chunky Peanut Butter

Add ¼ cup chopped peanuts to basic peanut butter recipe.

Honey Peanut Butter

Add 2 tablespoons honey to the processor when making basic peanut butter. Blend briefly until mixed.

Peanut Butter Syrup

½   cup creamy peanut butter
¼   cup corn syrup*

Mix until well blended. Great on crackers.

*More corn syrup could be added to make a syrup for pancakes. Makes ¾ cup.

Apple Butter

9-10 apples, cored, peeled and chopped
2   cups sugar
2   tsp. cinnamon
⅛   tsp. cloves
⅛   tsp. salt

Place everything into a crockpot. Stir, cover and cook on high 1 hour. Cook on low for 9-11 hours or until thick and dark brown. Stir occasionally. Uncover and cook on low 1 hour longer. Stir with whisk until smooth. Refrigerate or Freeze. Makes 2 pints.

Easy Orange Marmalade

1   organic orange*
1   Tbsp. water
½   cup sugar

Cut the unpeeled orange and blend in a blender or food processor with the water. Pour mixture into a saucepan with the sugar, and boil for 15 minutes. Makes ½ cup.

*If a non-organic orange is used, be sure to wash it very well with some dish soap and a vegetable brush before cutting into pieces.

Recipes reprinted with permission from The Complete Tightwad Gazette by Amy Dacyczyn.

Peach Jam

2   cups peaches
2   cups sugar
2   Tbsp. cornstarch

Peel and slice peaches. Put into a saucepan and boil the
peaches down to the pulp and juices. Add sugar and cornstarch
and boil until thickened. Refrigerate or freeze. This recipe may
be doubled or increased to whatever size you need.
Makes 2-3 cups.

Strawberry Jam

3   qts. fresh strawberries
¾   cup sugar
1   Tbsp. lemon juice

In large microwave-safe bowl, combine strawberries, sugar, and
lemon juice. Cover loosely and microwave on high 15 seconds.
Stir mixture to dissolve sugar. Microwave on high, uncovered, for
5 minutes. Stir mixture well and check to see if it is done by
putting a little on a spoon and placing it in the freezer for 5 minutes
uncovered. Look at the preserves on the spoon. They should be
thick but not hard. For slightly thicker preserves, microwave on
high for another 5 minutes. For sweeter preserves, stir in a little
more sugar then cook another minute. Spoon preserves into jars
and refrigerate or cool at room temperature; spoon into plastic
bags and freeze. Makes 7 cups.

✦ **When you have leftover jam or jelly, put ¾ cup of hot
water in the jar and shake well. Pour into popsicle
molds and freeze.**

Substitutions

&

Equivalents

Blessed are the flexible,
for they shall not be bent out of shape.

Substitutions

I didn't have potatoes...so I substituted rice,

I didn't have paprika...so I used another spice,

I didn't have tomato sauce... I used tomato paste,

A whole can...not half a can...I don't believe in waste!

A friend gave me the recipe

She said you couldn't beat it!

But there must be something wrong

As I couldn't even eat it ! ! !

Substitutions

Cheese

Cream cheese	=	cottage cheese blended smooth with butter or milk
Romano	=	Parmesan
Ricotta	=	cottage cheese

Eggs

1 egg	=	1 Tbsp. soy flour and 1 Tbsp. water

Flour

1 cup sifted cake flour	=	1 cup less 2 Tbsp. sifted all-purpose flour
1 Tbsp. cornstarch	=	2 Tbsp. flour for thickening sauces and gravies

Sugar

1 cup granulated sugar	=	1¾ cups powdered sugar or 1 cup packed light brown sugar or ¾ cup honey
1 cup powdered or confectioners sugar	=	½ cup plus 1 Tbsp. granulated sugar
1 cup brown sugar	=	1 cup sugar plus 2 Tbsp. molasses

Substitutions

Milk/Cream

1 cup milk = ⅓ cup dry milk plus 1 cup water or ½ cup evaporated milk plus ½ cup water

1 cup buttermilk = 1 cup plain yogurt or 1 Tbsp. lemon juice or vinegar plus enough milk to make 1 cup, let stand 5 minutes.

1 cup heavy cream or half and half = ⅞ cup whole milk plus 3 Tbsp. butter

1 cup light cream = ⅞ cup whole milk plus 1½ Tbsp. butter

1 cup sour cream (for baking) = 1 cup plain yogurt

1 cup sour milk = 1 cup plain yogurt or 1 Tbsp. lemon juice or vinegar plus enough milk to make 1 cup

1 cup whole milk = 1 cup skim milk plus 2 Tbsp. butter or margarine

Substitutions

Miscellaneous

1 pkg. active dry yeast	=	½ cake compressed yeast or 1 Tbsp. bulk yeast
1 tsp. baking powder	=	¼ tsp. cream of tartar plus ¼ tsp. baking soda
1 Tbsp. lemon juice	=	½ Tbsp. vinegar
1 cup chopped apples	=	1 cup chopped pears plus 1 Tbsp. lemon juice
1 cup dry bread crumbs	=	¾ cup cracker crumbs or 1 cup cornflake crumbs
1 cup butter	=	1 cup margarine or ⅞ cup vegetable oil
1 Tbsp. cornstarch	=	2 Tbsp. all purpose flour
1 cup dark corn syrup	=	¾ cup light corn syrup plus ¼ cup light molasses
1 chopped onion	=	1 Tbsp. instant minced onion
1 clove garlic	=	¼ tsp. garlic powder
1 cup tomato sauce	=	½ cup tomato paste plus ½ cup water
1 Tbsp. prepared mustard	=	1 tsp. dry mustard plus 1 Tbsp. water
1 tsp. dried herbs	=	1 Tbsp. fresh herbs
1 ounce unsweetened chocolate	=	3 Tbsp. unsweetened cocoa powder plus 1 Tbsp. butter, margarine or shortening

Healthy Substitutions for Recipes

Instead Of	Use
Bacon	Smoke flavoring, ham, Canadian bacon or bacon bits
Bread crumbs	French bread, dried and crushed
Butter, margarine or shortening in baking	Applesauce
Cream cheese	Neufchatel or low fat cream cheese
Canned Condensed Soup	White sauce made with skim milk
Cream of Chicken Soup	1¼ cups white sauce + 1 Tbsp. chicken bouillon
Cream of Mushroom Soup	1 cup white sauce + 1 can drained mushrooms
Egg (one)	2 egg whites
Ground beef	Ground turkey
Heavy cream, for whipping	Evaporated milk, freeze 30 mins. add ½ tsp. vanilla, whip
Heavy cream, in sauces and soups	Evaporated milk
Ricotta cheese	Low-fat cottage cheese, pureed
Sour cream	Yogurt
Whole milk	Skim milk
White flour	½ white and ½ wheat
White flour, for thickening	2 Tbsp. cornstarch
White rice	Brown rice

Equivalents

3 teaspoons . . . . . . = ... 1 tablespoon

4 tablespoons . . . . = ... ¼ cup

16 tablespoons . . . = ... 1 cup

1 gallon . . . . = ... 4 quarts

= . . . . 8 pints

= . . . . 16 cups

= . . . . 128 fluid ounces

1 quart . . . . = ... 2 pints

= . . . . 4 cups

= . . . . 32 fluid ounces

1 pint . . . . = ... 2 cups

= . . . . 16 fluid ounces

1 gill . . . . = ... ½ cup

= . . . . 4 fluid ounces

= . . . . 8 tablespoons

1 fluid ounce . . . . . = ... 2 tablespoons

1 tablespoon . . . . . = ... ½ fluid ounce

= . . . . 3 teaspoons

To convert **ounces** to **grams**, multiply ounces x 28.35

To convert **pounds** to **grams**, multiply pounds x 453.59

To convert **Fahrenheit degrees** to **Celsius degrees:**

$$°C = (°F-32) \times \tfrac{5}{9}$$

1 stick butter = **8** tablespoons = **4** ounces = ¼ pound

High Altitude Adjustments

Don't assume recipes won't work at high attitudes. Many of these recipes have been tested successfuly in altitudues up to 8,000 feet. I suggest making a recipe first before adjusting.
Deep Fat Frying-lower temperature 3° for every 1,000 above sea level to keep from burning food.

Cakes

3000-5,000 feet:
Reduce baking powder: for each tsp, decrease ⅛ tsp.
Reduce sugar: for each cup, decrease 0 to 1 tablespoon.
Increase liquid: for each cup, add 1 to 2 tablespoons.
Increase oven temperature by 25 degrees F.

5000-7,000 feet:
Reduce baking powder: for each tsp, decrease ⅛ to ¼ teaspoon.
Reduce sugar: for each cup, decrease 0 to 2 tablespoons.
Increase liquid: for each cup, add 2 to 4 tablespoons.
Increase oven temperature by 25 degrees F.

Adjustment for 7000+ feet:
Reduce baking powder: for each tsp, decrease ¼ teaspoon.
Reduce sugar: for each cup, decrease 1 to 3 tablespoons.
Increase liquid: for each cup, add 3 to 4 tablespoons.
Increase oven temperature by 25 degrees F.
Candy Making-decrease final temperature 2° for every 1,000 above sea level.

Yeast breads-2 risings may be needed. Once doubled punch down and let rise again.

Cookies-Decrease flour and increase baking temperature slightly. Most cookies work at high altitudes.

Mixes,
Gift Baskets
& Jars

Lord, help me to speak only words of love and kindness today.
For tomorrow I may have to eat my words.

Basket Tips

✦ **Dollar stores** are a great place to find small items to add to your basket.

✦ **Line baskets with white or colored tissue papers,** towels, baby blanket, leftover fabric, Easter grass or mixed nuts in the shell. The ideas are endless.

✦ **Wrap your baskets with cellophane** or tissue paper. Decorate the handle with a pretty bow, small jingle bells at Christmas, small pieces of wrapped candy, a tea ball, a small cluster of flowers-dried or real, or any item that will go with the theme of your basket.

✦ **Baskets don't have to be elaborate.** A teacup with a small package of tea mix or tea bags makes a simple but thoughtful gift. Tie a cluster of flowers on the handle.

Gift Ideas

✦ **One or two herbal tea bags** and 2 or 3 individually wrapped bath bombs in a tea cup make a nice gift.

✦ For the gardener, line a **terra cotta pot** with a washcloth and fill with bath products.

✦ **Cellophane bags** can be purchased from floral shops or party stores. They are inexpensive but make a great presentation for your gifts.

✦ **Give a nail care kit with cotton** balls, cotton swabs, polish, nail tools, cuticle cream, hand cream and polish remover.

✦ If your family loves to receive **perfume,** stock up after Christmas when gift sets are on clearance. Give for Mother's Day, birthdays, etc.

Ideas for Basket Filler

- Breadsticks
- Cheeses
- Cherries
- Chopped nuts
- Cluster of herbs
- Cookie cutters
- Croutons
- Flavored oils
- Fresh bread
- Fresh veggies
- Herb plant
- Homemade sauces
- Kitchen towels
- Maple syrup
- Mixed nuts
- Napkins
- Olive oil
- Peppercorns
- Popcorn
- Pot holders
- Potato chips
- Pretzels
- Small rolling pin
- Sun dried tomatoes
- Sundae dishes
- Tea ball
- Tea strainer
- Tortilla chips
- Towels
- Vinegars
- Wash cloths

Ideas for containers

- Baskets
- Bean crock
- Boxes covered with pretty wrapping paper
- Cake pans
- Clear containers
- Coffee cups
- Colanders
- Decorated tins
- Earthen ware bowl
- Fish bowl
- Ice buckets
- Jam jars
- Milk pail
- Muffin tins
- Mustard jars
- Salad bowls
- Salad spinner
- Soup bowls
- Soup terrine
- Stock pots
- Tea cups
- Teapots
- Terra cotta pots
- Water pitchers
- Wire basket

Gift Basket Suggestions

Tea & Cookies

Arrange in a basket lined with bright cellophane

Russian Tea (p.347)
Snickerdoodle Mix (p.357)
Oatmeal Cookie Mix (p.354)
Cookie cutters
Teacup
2 pot holders

Wrap mixes in cellophane bags or jars tied with ribbons

Pampered Princess

Wrap in a nice fluffy bath towel and tie with pretty cloth ribbon

Fluffy washcloth
Bath Bombs (p.421)
Almond Lotion (p.432)
Honey Lip Balm (p.434)
Massage Oil (p.423)
Nice book
Small candle

Peanut Butter & Chocolate Delight

Place in a decorated tin lined with tissue paper.

Chocolate Peanut Butter Cookie Mix (p.352)
Peanut Butter Cups or Peanut Butter Balls (p.266)
Mexican Hot Chocolate Mix (p.345)
Coffee Cup

Honeymoon Basket

Place in a box covered with red wrapping paper

Sparkling Cider
Can of whipped cream
Bottle of chocolate syrup
Jar of cherries
Bubble bath
Perfumed bath oil (p.422)
Energy bars
Clear shower curtain

Gardener Basket

Place in a terra cotta pot lined with tissue paper

  2 or 3 packages of seeds
  kneeling pad
  garden gloves
  trowel
  hand rake
  mister
  small potted plant

Chocolate Lover's Basket

Place in silver metal basket with gold tissue

  Chocolate Peanut Butter Cookie Mix (p.352)
  Mexican Hot Chocolate Mix (p.345)
  Brownie Mix (p.351)
  Party Mints (p.265)
  Small pkg. marshmallows

Kids Gift Basket

Place in a plastic pail. Tie ballons on handle
Plastic scoop
  Slime tied in a bag (p.384)
  Bubbles in a jar (p.378)
  Strawberry leather (p.377)
  Brightly dyed pasta in 4 or 5 colors (p.378)
  Finger paints, put each color in a baby food jar (p.381)
  Sidewalk chalk (p.383)
  Tub crayons (p.384)
  Coloring book
  Crayons

Get Well Basket

Place in basket that can be used as a magazine holder
  Turkey soup mix (p.358)
  Hot Chooolate Mix (p.344)
  Coffee Cup
  Crossword puzzle book
  Assorted magazines
  Stationery
  Perfumed body lotion (p.432)

Pasta Basket

Arrange in a colander. Wrap in cellophane or tissue paper with a large bow.

- Small cheese grater
- Fancy pasta
- Sun dried tomatoes (p.140)
- Flavored oil (p.154)
- Herbed vinegar (p.164)
- Napkins
- Napkin rings

Holiday Cheer Basket

Place in red holiday basket

- Holiday Muffin Mix (p.353)
- Chocolate Peanut Butter Cookies Mix (p. 352)
- Minted Coffee Mix (p.346)
- Sweet Christmas Potpourri (p. 366)
- Holiday Ornament
- Tis the Season sachet (p.368)

Small Gift Ideas

✦ Large soup mug and saucer with **soup mix** inside

✦ Small glass bowl with a package of **potpourri**

✦ Small frying pan with **corn bread mix** and a small jar of maple syrup

✦ Present several kinds of **mustard** in a pretty basket for a gift. Tie each jar with ribbon.

✦ **For the seamstress-**In a basket place 2 or 3 flour sack dish towels, embroidery thread, embroidery hoop, embroidery needles and iron-ons. You could also iron on the pattern for them.

✦ **Video buff-**In a box covered with wrapping paper place a video movie rental gift certificate, spiced popcorn (p.317), 2 candy bars, 2 cans of pop and glazed nuts (p.263).

Cafe Vienna Mix

½   cup instant coffee
⅔   cup sugar
⅔   cup nonfat dry milk
⅔   tsp. cinnamon
1   tsp. dried orange peel (optional)

Stir ingredients together. Process in a blender until powdered. Makes 1⅓ cups mix.

Attach this note to the jar:

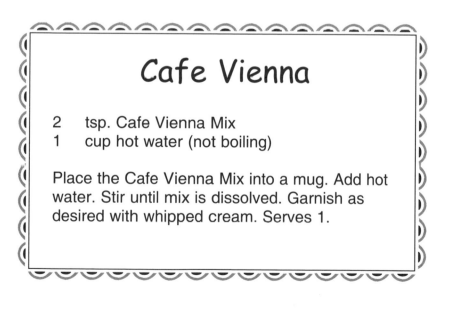

Cafe Vienna

2   tsp. Cafe Vienna Mix
1   cup hot water (not boiling)

Place the Cafe Vienna Mix into a mug. Add hot water. Stir until mix is dissolved. Garnish as desired with whipped cream. Serves 1.

Hot Chocolate Mix

8   cups dry milk
1¾   cups cocoa
1   sm. pkg. instant chocolate pudding mix
4¾   cups powdered sugar
1½   cup non-dairy creamer

Sift the ingredients into a large bowl. Place the mix into an airtight container.

Attach this note to the jar:

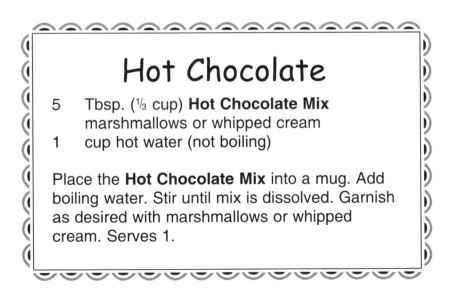

Hot Chocolate

5   Tbsp. (⅓ cup) **Hot Chocolate Mix**
     marshmallows or whipped cream
1   cup hot water (not boiling)

Place the **Hot Chocolate Mix** into a mug. Add boiling water. Stir until mix is dissolved. Garnish as desired with marshmallows or whipped cream. Serves 1.

Used with permission from Dawn Dobson, Valley City, OH

Mexican Hot Chocolate Mix

⅓   cup light brown sugar
½   tsp. cinnamon
¼   cup cocoa
2½   cups nonfat dry milk

Sift and mix ingredients in a small bowl. Store in an airtight container.

Attach this note to the jar:

Mexican Hot Chocolate

3   cups water
    Mexican Hot Chocolate Mix (to taste)
1   tsp. vanilla (optional)
    Cinnamon sticks for garnish

Heat the water to boiling and add the **Mexican Hot Chocolate Mix**. Add vanilla if desired. Stir with a whisk until the mixture is smooth. Garnish with cinnamon sticks. For a frothier hot chocolate, mix in a blender. Serves 6.

Minted Coffee Mix

¾ cup coffee creamer, powdered
½ cup sugar
¼ cup instant coffee
¼ cup cocoa
    dash salt
4   peppermint candies, crushed

Combine all ingredients in large bowl. Sift and mix well. Place in an airtight jar or container.

Attach this note to the jar:

Minted Coffee

2-3 Tbsp. **Minted Coffee Mix**
1   cup boiling water

Spoon **Minted Coffee Mix** into mug. Add boiling water and stir until blended. Serves 1.

✦ **When you find a gift item on sale, buy it. Keep a box going all year for good finds on gifts. The months of January and February are great times for bargain shopping for everything from clothes to toys to household linens and tableware.**

Russian Tea Mix

½   cup powdered orange drink
¼   cup instant tea
¼   cup lemonade or 1 pkg. lemon flavored drink mix
¾   cup sugar
⅛   tsp. cloves
¼   tsp. cinnamon

Mix all the ingredients in a bowl and store in an airtight container.

This is more expensive than plain Spiced Tea but it does make a good gift and it stores well. Makes 1¾ cups mix.

Attach this note to the jar:

Russian Tea

2-4 Tbsp. **Russian Tea Mix**
1   cup hot water

Place the **Russian Tea Mix** into a mug. Add boiling water. Stir until mix is dissolved. Serves 1.

Spiced Cocoa Mix

2¼ cups dry milk
⅓   cup cocoa
½   cup sugar
½   tsp. cinnamon
½   tsp. cloves
¼   tsp. nutmeg
¼   tsp. ginger

Combine all ingredients, and mix well. Store in an airtight container.

Attach this note to the jar:

Spiced Cocoa Mix

3   Tbsp. **Spiced Cocoa Mix**
1   cup boiling water

Spoon **Spiced Cocoa Mix** into mug. Add boiling water and stir until blended. Serves 1.

Swiss Mocha Mix

½   cup instant coffee
½   cup sugar
1   cup nonfat dry milk
2   Tbsp. cocoa
¼   tsp. vanilla

Stir ingredients together. Process in a blender until powdered. Makes 2 cups mix.

Attach this note to the jar:

Swiss Mocha

2   Tbsp. **Swiss Mocha Mix**
1   cup hot water

Place the **Swiss Mocha Mix** into a mug. Add hot water. Stir until mix is dissolved. Garnish as desired with whipped cream. Serves 1.

Apple Cinnamon Muffin Mix

2   cups flour
1   tsp. ground cinnamon
1   tsp. baking powder
½   tsp. baking soda
¼   tsp. salt
½   cup raisins and/or nuts

In a bowl, mix together first 5 ingredients. Place in an airtight container. Package raisins and nuts separately.

Topping

3   Tbsp. sugar
¼   tsp. nutmeg
¼   tsp. cinnamon

Mix topping ingredients in a bowl. Package in a small cellophane bag.

Attach this note to the jar:

Apple Cinnamon Muffin

1   cup apple juice   2 Tbsp. oil
½   cup applesauce   Margarine, melted
     raisins and/or nuts

Topping
Combine **Apple Cinnamon Muffin Mix** with next three ingredients until just combined. Spoon into lightly greased muffin tins. Bake in preheated 350° oven for 20-25 minutes until toothpick inserted in center comes out clean. While still warm, dip in melted margarine and then **Topping**. Makes 12-15 muffins.

Brownie Mix

6   cups sugar
3   cups flour
1½ cups cocoa

Place sugar, flour and cocoa in a large bowl and mix until ingredients are evenly distributed. Store in an airtight container.

Attach this note to the jar:

Brownies

4   eggs
½   cup butter or margarine melted
3 ½   cups **Brownie Mix**
½-¾ cup nuts, chopped (optional)

In a bowl mix **Brownie Mix** and butter. With a spoon, beat eggs into mix until batter is smooth. Stir in nuts if desired. Grease and flour a 9x13 pan. Spoon in batter and spread evenly. Bake in preheated 350° oven for 25-30 minutes or until knife inserted in center comes out clean. DO NOT OVER BAKE. Cool in pan. Frost if desired. Makes 18 brownies.

Chocolate Peanut Butter Cookie Mix

1½   cups flour
1   tsp. baking powder
¼   tsp. salt
1   cup brown sugar, packed
1½   cups powdered sugar, packed
¾   cup cocoa powder

In a bowl, mix first three ingredients. Beginning with flour mixture, layer ingredients in order given in a one quart wide-mouth canning jar. Press each layer firmly in place before adding next ingredient. Wipe jar after each layer.

Attach this note to the jar:

Chocolate Peanut Butter Cookies

Empty jar of **Chocolate Peanut Butter Cookie Mix** into large mixing bowl. Thoroughly mix.
Add: ¾   cup butter or margarine, softened
        ½   cup creamy or chunky peanut butter
        1   egg, slightly beaten
        1   tsp. vanilla

Mix until completely blended. Shape into balls the size of a quarter. Place 2 inches apart on greased baking sheets. Press balls down with a fork. Bake at 350° for 9-11 minutes (until edges are lightly browned). Cool 5 minutes on baking sheet. Makes 3 dozen cookies.

Holiday Muffin Mix

3	cups flour
1	cup sugar
1/2	cup dry milk
1	Tbsp. baking powder
1	tsp. salt
1/2	tsp. nutmeg
1 1/2	tsp. cinnamon
1/4	tsp. cloves

Combine all ingredients. Place mix in a one quart jar.

Attach this note to the jar:

Holiday Muffins

1   egg, slightly beaten
1 1/4   cup water
1/4   cup oil
1   jar **Holiday Muffin Mix**

Preheat oven to 400° and grease muffin tins. In a bowl, empty **Holiday Muffins Mix** with other ingredients until moistened. Do not overmix. Fill muffin tins 1/2 full. Bake 10-15 minutes or until toothpick inserted in center comes out clean. Immediately remove from pan and serve warm. Makes 15-18 muffins.

Oatmeal Cookie Mix

1	cup flour
1	tsp. cinnamon
½	tsp. nutmeg
1	tsp. baking soda
½	tsp. salt
½	cup brown sugar, packed
¾	cup sugar
1	cup raisins or chocolate chips
2	cups old-fashioned oats

In a bowl, mix flour, cinnamon, nutmeg, baking soda and salt. Set aside. Layer remaining ingredients in order given in a one quart wide-mouth canning jar. Pack down after each addition. Add flour mixture on top.

Attach this note to the jar:

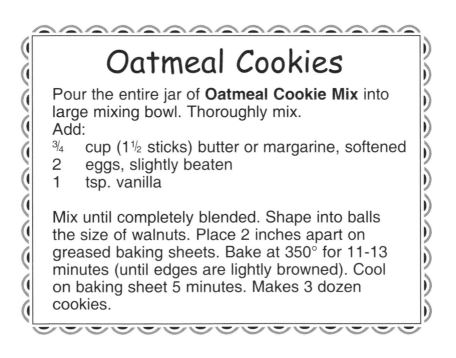

Oatmeal Cookies

Pour the entire jar of **Oatmeal Cookie Mix** into large mixing bowl. Thoroughly mix.
Add:

¾	cup (1½ sticks) butter or margarine, softened
2	eggs, slightly beaten
1	tsp. vanilla

Mix until completely blended. Shape into balls the size of walnuts. Place 2 inches apart on greased baking sheets. Bake at 350° for 11-13 minutes (until edges are lightly browned). Cool on baking sheet 5 minutes. Makes 3 dozen cookies.

Raisin Cookie Mix

½   cup sugar
¾   cup raisins or chocolate chips
1   cup flaked coconut, packed
1   cup corn flakes cereal, crushed
¾   cup brown sugar
¾   cup quick oats
1¼ cups flour
¾   tsp. baking soda
½   tsp. baking powder
¼   tsp. salt

In a bowl, mix flour, baking soda and baking powder and salt. Layer remaining ingredients, pressing firmly after each layer, in order given in one quart wide-mouth canning jar, ending with flour mixture.

Attach this note to the jar:

Raisin Cookies

Empty jar of **Raisin Cookie Mix** into mixing bowl. Thoroughly mix.
Add:
½   cup butter or margarine, softened
1   egg, slightly beaten
1   tsp. vanilla

Mix until completely blended. Shape into balls the size of walnuts. Place 2 inches apart on greased baking sheets. Bake at 350° for 10-12 minutes (until edges are lightly browned). Cool 5 minutes on baking sheet. Makes 2½ dozen cookies.

Shortbread Mix

1½ cups flour
¾   cup powdered sugar
¼   tsp. salt

In a bowl, combine ingredients, mixing well. Store in an airtight container.

Attach this note to the jar:

Shortbread

1   cup butter (2 sticks), softened
1   jar Shortbread Mix

Empty jar of **Shortbread Mix** into mixing bowl. Thoroughly blend. Knead butter into shortbread mix and press mixture firmly into an 8-inch pie plate. Bake in preheated 300° oven for 1 hour. Shortbread will be pale in color. Do not brown. While warm cut into wedges. Makes 12 pieces.

Snickerdoodle Mix

2¾ cups all-purpose flour
½ tsp. salt
1 tsp. baking soda
2 tsp. cream of tartar
1½ cups sugar

In a large bowl, combine the ingredients and mix well. Store the mix in an airtight container. Makes 1 batch.

Attach this note to the jar:

Snickerdoodles

1 cup shortening or butter
2 eggs
1 jar **Snickerdoodle Mix**
2 Tbsp. sugar
2 tsp. cinnamon

In a large bowl, cream the butter with a mixer until light. Add the eggs and beat on low speed until the mixture is smooth. Add the **Snickerdoodle Mix** and continue to beat on low speed until the dough begins to form. Combine the sugar and cinnamon in a small bowl. Shape the dough into quarter sized balls and roll in the cinnamon-sugar blend. Arrange on ungreased baking sheets 2 inches apart. Bake in preheated 400° oven for 8-10 minutes or until light brown. Cool on wire racks. Makes 5 dozen cookies.

Turkey Soup Mix

1   cup egg noodles, uncooked
1½   Tbsp. chicken bouillon
½   tsp. black pepper
¼   tsp. dried thyme
⅛   tsp. celery seeds
⅛   tsp. garlic powder
1   bay leaf
1   tsp. onion powder

Combine all ingredients. Place in a pint jar.

Attach this note to the jar:

Turkey Noodle Soup

1   jar **Turkey Soup Mix**
8   cups water
2   carrots, diced
2   stalks celery, diced
2   cups turkey, cooked and diced

Combine the **Turkey Soup Mix** and the water in a large stockpot. Add the carrots, celery, and onion and bring to a boil. Cover. Reduce heat and simmer 15 minutes. Remove bay leaf. Add turkey and simmer an additional 5 minutes. Serves 4.

Bean Soup Mix

¼ cup white beans
¼ cup kidney beans
¼ cup split peas
¼ cup pinto beans
½ Tbsp. barley

Seasoning packet

2 Tbsp. parsley
2 Tbsp. instant onions
1 bay leaf
2 Tbsp. beef bouillon, powdered

Layer beans in a jar. Mix seasonings and put in a plastic bag or wrap in plastic wrap and place on top.

Recipes reprinted with permission from The Complete Tightwad Gazette by Amy Dacyczyn.

Attach this note to the jar:

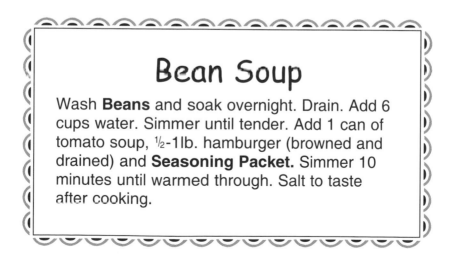

Bean Soup

Wash **Beans** and soak overnight. Drain. Add 6 cups water. Simmer until tender. Add 1 can of tomato soup, ½-1lb. hamburger (browned and drained) and **Seasoning Packet.** Simmer 10 minutes until warmed through. Salt to taste after cooking.

Cornbread Mix

2   cups baking mix (p.52)
½   cup cornmeal
½   cup sugar
1   tsp. baking powder

In a bowl stir all the ingredients together. Store in an airtight container.

Attach this note to the jar:

Cornbread

1   jar **Cornbread Mix**
2   eggs
1   cup milk
½   cup butter, melted

Empty **Cornbread Mix** in a large bowl. Add other ingredients Blend until smooth. Pour into a greased 8-inch pan and bake in preheated 350° for 30 minutes. Makes 9 pieces.

Curried Rice Mix

1 cup long grain rice
1 chicken bouillon cube, crumbled.
1 teaspoon onion powder
½ teaspoon curry powder

Layer the ingredients in a 1½ cup jar. Top with ¼ cup raisins, if desired.

Attach this to the jar:

Curried Rice

2½ cups water
1 tablespoons margarine
1 jar Curried Rice Mix

Bring water and margarine to a boil in a medium saucepan. Add rice mix. Cover and reduce heat and simmer for 20 minutes. Fluff with a fork before serving. Serve with chicken. Serves 6.

Caesar Dressing Mix

½   tsp. garlic powder
½   tsp. salt
½   tsp. pepper
½   tsp. sugar
¼   tsp. dry mustard

Combine all ingredients and stir until well blended. Put mixture into a 1-pint glass jar. Store in a cool dry place. Use within 4 months.

Attach this note to the jar:

Caesar Salad Dressing

Caesar Dressing Mix
¼   cup vegetable or olive oil
¼   cup lemon juice
¼   cup wine vinegar
     dash of Worcestershire sauce

In the jar combine all ingredients with the **Caesar Dressing Mix**. Shake until blended. Chill before serving. Pour on salad and top with Parmesan cheese and croutons. Makes ¾ cup.

Mexican Dip Mix

½   cup dried parsley
⅓   cup minced onion
¼   cup dried chives
⅓   cup chili powder
¼   cup ground cumin
¼   cup salt

Combine all ingredients in a bowl. Seal in a cellophane bag or jar.

Attach this note to the jar:

Mexican Dip

3   Tbsp. **Mexican Dip Mix**
1   cup sour cream or low-fat yogurt
1   cup mayonnaise or low-fat mayonnaise

In a bowl, combine **Mexican Dip Mix**, mayonnaise and sour cream. Blend until smooth. Refrigerate 4 hours. Makes 2 cups.

Lemon Pepper Mix

1 cup ground black pepper
¼ cup dried onion flakes
⅓ cup dried lemon peel, grated
¼ cup dried thyme
3 tablespoons coriander seeds

Mix all ingredients. Store in airtight container.

Attach this to the jar:

Grilled Lemon Chicken

¼ cup lemon juice
¼ cup vegetable oil or olive oil
2 teaspoons Lemon Pepper Mix
6 chicken breasts

Preheat broiler or barbecue grill. In a bowl, stir together lemon juice, oil, and Lemon Pepper Mix. Add chicken breasts and marinate in the refrigerator for 45 minutes. Grill or broil for 4 minutes on each side until done. Serves 6.

Ranch Dressing and Dip Mix

½   cup dried parsley
4   Tbsp. onion flakes
1   tsp. onion powder
1   tsp. garlic powder
1   tsp. paprika
½   tsp. cayenne pepper

In a medium bowl, combine all the ingredients. Store in an airtight container.

Attach this note to the jar:

Ranch Dressing

½   cup mayonnaise
½   cup buttermilk
1   Tbsp. **Ranch Dressing and Dip Mix**

In a large bowl, whisk together the mayonnaise, buttermilk and **Ranch Dressing and Dip Mix**. Refrigerate for one hour before serving. Makes 1 cup.

Ranch Dip

3   Tbsp. **Ranch Dressing and Dip Mix**
1   cup sour cream or low-fat yogurt
1   cup mayonnaise or low-fat mayonnaise

Combine **Ranch Dressing and Dip Mix** with mayonnaise and sour cream. Chill before serving. Great with raw vegetables, or as a topping for baked potatoes. Makes 2 cups.

Sweet Christmas Potpourri

3   Tbsp. whole cloves
2   bay leaves
3   cinnamon sticks
2   cups water
1   handful of pine needles
3   pieces dried orange or lemon rind

Mix all ingredients and place in a jar.

Attach this note to the jar:

Sweet Christmas Potpourri

Put **Sweet Christmas Potpourri Mix** in a saucepan. Add water. Bring to a boil, reduce heat and simmer all day if you wish. Add water as needed. When finished, refrigerate and reuse.

Funnel Cake Mix

1   cup sifted flour
1   tsp. baking powder
¼   tsp. salt
½   tsp. cinnamon
1   egg
1   cup milk
     vegetable oil

In a bowl, mix all dry ingredients. Store in an airtight container.

Attach this note to the jar:

Funnel Cake

Funnel Cake Mix
1   egg
1   cup milk
     vegetable oil

Put **Funnel Cake Mix** in a bowl. Add egg and milk. Stir until smooth. Pour oil into a skillet and heat to 375°. Holding finger over the end of a funnel, pour in ¼ cup batter. Holding over the hot oil, remove finger and let drizzle over the hot oil. As batter flows, move funnel in a circle to form a spiral cake. Fry about 2 minutes or each side, turning once, until golden brown. Remove from oil and drain. Sprinkle with powdered sugar, glaze, or nuts.   Makes 6 cakes.

"Tis the season" Sachets

1   qt. fir needles
2   cups coarse salt (not iodized)
2-4 bay leaves, coarsely crumbled
1   cup rosemary
½   cup basil
1   cup dried oranges, lemons, cranberries, thinly shredded
     (any combination)

Mix and pour into little calico bags. Makes 5 cups.

Place wherever you'd like to enjoy the scent of " Happy Holidays"

Christmas Scent

1 lemon
1 orange
3 (3 inch) cinnamon sticks
6 bay leaves
½ cup whole cloves
2 quarts water

Combine all ingredients except water in a clear bag or jar.

Attach this note to the jar:

Christmas Scent

Cut lemon and orange into slices or quarters. Combine fruit, spices and 2 quarts of water in a large saucepan. Bring to a boil and simmer. Add more water as needed. Cover any leftover mixture, refrigerate and reuse. Makes 8 cups.

Kids

The quickest way to make a tossed salad is to
feed vegetables to an 18-month old child.

Kid Tips

✦ **A child can hold a glass better** if 2 rubber bands are put on the glass about 1 inch apart.

✦ **Always fill a child's glass half full of milk or juice.** They usually don't need more than that, and half cup spilled milk is easier to clean up than a full cup.

✦ **Give children small portions of food.** Large amounts of food like other things can overwhelm them. Then if they want more give seconds.

✦ **Use terrycloth tablecloths**. If something is spilled it absorbs it quickly. I think more moms should enter 50 yard dashes. You can get pretty fast making that mad dash to the kitchen for a towel when something spills and you have 2 seconds to make it back before it starts rolling off the table on to the chair and another 2 seconds before it hits the floor. Terrycloth can be found at most fabric shops in the spring.

✦ **Use an old kiddie pool** with holes for a sandbox or an outside toy box.

✦ **When you get a splinter,** reach for the Scotch tape before resorting to tweezers or a needle. Simply put the Scotch tape over the splinter, then pull it off. Scotch tape removes most splinters painlessly and easily.

✦ **Clean up kids' spills right away.** Not only is it easier to clean up a fresh spill but the kids don't continue to spread it around.

✦ **Use an old shower curtain** under a high chair to catch toddlers spills.

✦ **If you only have one place setting of china,** use it for special occasions. If your child gets an A at school or it is someone's birthday, let them use the "special" china for dinner.

✦ Cut a **banana in half for one serving.** Save the other half. Later, trim off the browned part and eat.

Apple Snack

2   qts. apples, peeled, cored and halved

Coarsely grate apples. Place on a greased cookie sheet. Bake at 225° until dry. Remove from cookie sheet and break into pieces. Store in an airtight container.

Frozen Bananas

bananas
skewers (optional)

Cut bananas in half crosswise. Insert skewer in the thicker end. Place bananas on a tray and place in freezer. When frozen, move to a plastic bag and keep frozen until ready to use.

Toppings

yogurt
peanut butter
melted chocolate
wheat germ

nuts, finely chopped
applesauce
coconut

Allow bananas to thaw slightly. Put toppings in small bowls. Dip banana before each bite. Eat plain or roll or dip into any of the toppings. Use the wet topping first so the others will stick.

Frozen Grapes

Wash and separate the grapes. Drain and put on cookie sheet. Freeze. Store in freezer bags. Give to kids as frozen treats. Note: Do not thaw; grapes become mushy when thawed.

Peanut Butter Snacks

¼-½   cup honey or corn syrup (to taste)
½   cup peanut butter
1   cup dry milk

Combine all the ingredients and roll into 1-inch balls. These can then be rolled in coconut, sunflower seeds, granola or nuts. Store in an airtight container. Makes 1 dozen.

Pudding Pops

1   pkg. cook and serve pudding
3   cups milk

Combine 1 large package of pudding with 3 cups of milk. Mix only enough to blend well. Quickly pour into popsicle molds and freeze. Chocolate and vanilla pudding may be layered for a fun treat. Makes 8-10 popsicles.

*Regular homemade pudding may be used instead of store-bought pudding mix.

✦ **For popsicle molds, use small waxed paper cups. Insert sticks into paper cup molds when partially frozen. To serve peel off paper cup**.

Fudgesicles

½   sugar
2   Tbsp. cornstarch
3   Tbsp. cocoa
⅛   tsp. salt
2   eggs, slightly beaten
2½   cups milk
2   Tbsp butter or margarine (stick)
2   tsp. vanilla

Mix sugar, cornstarch, cocoa and salt in a 2 quart saucepan.
Add eggs to sugar mixture and slowly stir in milk until combined.
Cook over medium heat, stirring constantly, until mixture
thickens and boils. Boil and stir 1 minute. Remove from heat; stir
in margarine and vanilla. Quickly pour into popsicle molds and
freeze. Makes 8-10 fudgesicles.

Yogurt Popsicles

2   cups plain yogurt
6   ounce frozen orange juice concentrate
1   tsp. vanilla
6   ounce water

Blend together in blender and then freeze in popsicle molds.
Makes 8-10 popsicles.

Popsicle ideas:

- fruit, bananas, applesauce, blackberries, strawberries,
  raspberries
- yogurt
- gelatin
- syrup from canned fruit
- food coloring for added pizzazz

Easy Bake™ Oven Chocolate Cake Mix

1 cup sugar
3 Tbsp. cocoa
1½ cups flour
1 tsp. baking soda
½ tsp. salt
⅓ cup vegetable shortening

In a medium bowl, combine sugar, cocoa, flour, baking soda and salt. Stir until blended. Cut in shortening until mixture resembles corn meal. Store in an airtight container. Use within 12 weeks. Makes 11 cakes.

To Use:

cup Easy Bake cake mix
5-6 tsp. water

Mix together until smooth. Pour mixture into greased and floured 4 inch round baking pan. Follow directions for child's oven. Cool in pan for 5 minutes. Invert onto a small plate and remove pan. When cool, frost with Children's Chocolate Frosting. Makes 1 cake.

✦ **Make heart shaped cupcakes by placing a marble in between the muffin tin and muffin liner. Fill half full and bake as usual**

Easy Bake™ Chocolate or White Frosting

2   cups powdered sugar
3   Tbsp. dry milk
½   cup cocoa*
6   Tbsp. solid vegetable shortening

In a bowl, combine powdered sugar, dry milk and cocoa. Cut in shortening. Store in an airtight container. Use in 12 weeks.

*For white frosting omit cocoa.

To Use:

1   cup Chocolate Frosting mix
2-2½ tsp. water

In a small bowl, combine frosting mix and water. Stir with a fork until smooth. Makes about ¼ cup.

Preschool Prayer:

A,B,C,D,E,F,G
Thank you Lord for feeding me.

Snow Cones

snow, fresh and clean
1   pkg. flavored drink mix (flavor of your choice)

Mix drink mix half strength according to directions. Chill 1 hour.
Just before serving, go out and get some fresh, clean snow.
Pack snow into cups, pour chilled drink mix over the snow and
serve. You can also use fruit juice boiled down to half with food
coloring added.

Apple juice: green or red food coloring

Grape juice: purple food coloring

Snow Ice Cream

½   cup milk or cream
¼   cup sugar
¼   tsp. vanilla
2   cereal bowls fresh clean snow

Mix milk, sugar and vanilla together. Stir until vanilla is dissolved.
Add fresh snow and stir gently until it is thoroughly mixed. Serve
immediately. Serves 4.

Strawberry Leather

3   cups fresh or frozen strawberries*
1   Tbsp. lemon juice
1   Tbsp. light corn syrup

Place strawberries in a blender and process until smooth. Measure 2 cups of strawberry puree. Stir in lemon juice and corn syrup. Line a 15x10 inch jellyroll pan with heavy-duty plastic wrap and tape plastic wrap to the pan at the corners. Pour strawberry mixture in prepared pan and spread thin, leaving 1 inch on all sides. You can adjust this to fit your dehydrator or another pan; be sure it is spread thin on the pan. Dry in an oven or dehydrator at 150° for 7-8 hours or until surface is no longer sticky. Remove leather from pan while still warm and roll up jellyroll fashion. Cut into logs and wrap in plastic wrap. Makes five 2 inch logs.

*Any other fruit may be used in place of the strawberries.

Preserve Choice Children

1   large grassy field
2 or 3   small dogs
          Pinch of brooks and some pebbles
1 - 2   dozen children

Mix children and dogs together well and put them in the field, stirring constantly. Pour the brook over the pebbles, sprinkle the field with flowers; spread over all a deep blue sky and bake in the hot sun. When thoroughly brown, remove and set away to cool in a bathtub.

Brightly Dyed Pasta

Note: Do not eat! This is for art projects only!

2   cups (16 ounce bottle) rubbing alcohol
      food colors
      noodles, pasta or rice, uncooked

Pour alcohol into large bowl and add food color. Use ½ bottle food color for each bottle of alcohol for very bright colors. Add pasta or rice, stir and let set until desired color. Spoon out, onto newspapers using a slotted spoon. Spread to dry (about 2 hours). Store in plastic bags. Alcohol can be poured back into bottles and used again later to color more pasta.

Bubbles

¼   cup liquid dishwashing detergent
½   cup water
1   Tbsp. sugar

Put the dishwashing detergent in the water. Carefully stir in sugar trying to avoid suds. Take a regular drinking straw and cut into 4 pieces. Then dip into the solution and blow your bubbles. Tie a rope loop up to a foot in diameter on the end of a stick and make a gallon of bubbles. Dip the rope in the bubbles and run with them. This will give you giant bubbles.

✦ **Kids prefer quantity time with you, not quality time. Doing housework and yard work are great ways to spend time with your kids while teaching them life skills.**

Clay Christmas Ornaments

4   cups flour
1   cup salt
1   tsp. powdered alum
1½   cups water

Mix ingredients well in a large bowl. If the dough is too dry, work in another tablespoon of water with your hands. Dough can be rolled or molded and can be colored with a few drops of food coloring. To roll: Roll dough ⅛ inch thick on lightly floured board. Cut with cookie cutters dipped in flour. Insert wire or make hole in top about ¼ inch down for hanging. To mold: Shape dough no more than ½ inch thick. Bake ornaments on ungreased cookie sheet for 30 minutes in 250° oven.Turn and bake another 1½ hours until hard and dry. Remove and cool. When done, paint and seal with spray varnish. You can lightly sand before painting. *Alum can be found in the spice section of your store.

Crystal Gardens

bluing
water
ammonia
salt
liquid food coloring

Day #1: Place damp sponge pieces in a shallow glass or plastic bowl. Over sponge, pour 2 Tbsp. each of bluing, salt, water and ammonia. **Day #2:** Add 2 Tbsp. salt. **Day #3:** Add 2 Tbsp. each bluing, salt, water and ammonia. Avoid pouring on crystal growth.

Repeat Day #3 as needed to keep crystals growing. For color, add drops of food coloring.

*Bluing can be purchased in the laundry section at the store.

Natural Easter Egg Dyes

✦ **Yellow**-yellow onion skins, turmeric (½ tsp. per cup water) celery leaves

✦ **Orange**-any yellow dye plus beet juice

✦ **Red**-beets, paprika, red onion skins

✦ **Pink**-cranberry juice

✦ **Blue**-blackberries, grape juice concentrate, red cabbage

✦ **Brown**-black tea, white oak, juniper berry, coffee, barberry

✦ **Light purple**-blackberries, grapes, violets

✦ **Green**-alfalfa, spinach, kale, violet blossom plus ¼ tsp. baking soda, tansy, nettle, chervil, sorrel, parsley, carrot tops, beet tops or dip yellow egg in blue dye

Hard boil eggs with 1 tsp. vinegar in the water. Place dying ingredients in non-aluminum pans, cover with water and boil 5 minutes to 1 hour until desired color is achieved. Use enough material to make at least 1 cup dye. Crush ingredients as they boil to extract as much dye as possible. Strain the dye. Most dyes should be used hot. Let each egg sit in the dye until it reaches the desired color. Some dyes will take longer than others to make the desired colored on the egg. Remove the egg and let dry.

Face Paint

Note: This amount is for each color.

Mix all ingredients together in an old muffin pan and you are ready to paint.

1   tsp. corn starch
½   tsp. water
½   tsp. cold cream
      food coloring

Finger Paints

1	pkg. unflavored gelatin
½	cup cold water
½	cup cornstarch
1½	cups water
	liquid dish detergent
	food coloring

Dissolve gelatin in ½ cup water. Set aside. In a saucepan add cornstarch then slowly stir in 1½ cups water until well blended over medium heat. Cook until it boils, becomes smooth, thickens and turns clear. Add gelatin mixture and stir well. Pour into containers and add a drop of liquid dish detergent. Add food coloring until you get the desired shade. Store covered in the refrigerator 4-6 weeks.

Easy Finger Paints

¼	cup cornstarch
2	cups water

Mix in saucepan and boil until thick. Then pour into a jar and add food coloring until the desired shade is achieved. Store covered in the refrigerator.

> It's amazing how a boy
> who wasn't good enough to marry your daughter
> can be the father of the
> smartest grandchild in the world!

Play Dough

2   cups flour
1   cup salt
1   tsp. cream of tartar
2   Tbsp. oil
2   cups water
     food coloring

Mix together all ingredients except food coloring in a saucepan. Cook over medium heat, stirring constantly until mixture gathers on the spoon and forms dough (about 6 minutes). Dump onto waxed paper until cool enough to handle and knead until pliable. Store in a covered container or plastic bag. Add food coloring for different colors. Makes about 2 pounds.

Edible Play Dough

$\frac{1}{3}$ cup margarine
$\frac{1}{3}$ cup light corn syrup
$\frac{1}{2}$ tsp. salt
1   tsp. vanilla extract
1   lb. powdered sugar
     food coloring (optional)
     flavorings

Mix first 4 ingredients together. Add powdered sugar. Knead. Divide and add food coloring. Keep refrigerated to keep from spoiling when not in use. You can replace vanilla with flavored extracts to make other flavors.

Scented Cinnamon Ornaments

DO NOT EAT!

1   cup cinnamon
1   Tbsp. cloves
1   Tbsp. nutmeg
¾   cup applesauce
2   Tbsp. white glue
     ribbon

In a bowl, mix the spices. Add applesauce and glue, stirring until well blended. Work mixture until dough is smooth and ingredients are thoroughly mixed. Divide into 4 portions and roll each portion between 2 pieces of waxed paper to ¼ inch thickness. Cut dough with cookie cutters of desired shapes. Using a straw or toothpick, make a small hole in the top of each ornament. Place on wire racks and allow to dry at room temperature for several days. (For more uniform drying, turn ornaments over once each day.) Thread ribbon through holes to form garland. You can also glue to a wooden hoop, forming a wreath and decorate with ribbon as desired. Makes approximately 32 two-inch ornaments.

Sidewalk Chalk

2   qts. plaster of Paris
     water
     food colors

Mix plaster of Paris with 1 quart water. Mix in desired color. Pour into paper towel or toilet paper tubes (about 3 inches high). Let dry thoroughly (This may take several days). Remove from tubes and let the kids draw away.

Slime

½   cup white glue
6   Tbsp. water
    food coloring
1-4 tsp. Borax
1-4 Tbsp. water

Mix the glue, 6 Tbsp. water and food coloring until it is dissolved. In a separate bowl, dissolve 1 teaspoon borax into 1 tablespoon water. Add to the glue solution. You will get a very thick clump of slime when the two mix. Pull the clump of slime out of the glue mixture and put it in a separate bowl. Mix another batch of the borax solution and add to the remaining glue mixture. Repeat until all the glue mixture is used (about 3-4 times). With clean hands, knead the slime to mix. This will take about 10 minutes. If a looser, more slimy texture, is desired knead in a bit more water. The slime doesn't leave a residue and doesn't stick anything. Store in an airtight container.

Tub Crayons

5   cups soap flakes or grate bars of Ivory soap
¼   cup plus 1 Tbsp. hot water
    liquid food coloring

Put soap flakes in a large bowl and drop water into the soap flakes, stirring constantly. Spoon mixture into separate smaller bowls. Add food coloring by drops until the soap has the consistency of a very thick paste. Press soap into molds (ice cube tray, small plastic containers, etc...) and set in a dry place to harden. It should take 3-7 days to dry. When dry, remove from molds and allow to dry for a few more days before using.

Cleaning
Cents

Dirty Dishes Cause Debt

You have to organize your house before you can start to clean it.

Most people think their house is messy because of lack of storage when in reality it's just a lack of organization.

With that in mind, here's a quick start list for organizing and cleaning your home. Do as much as you can without getting overwhelmed or tired. It's taken quite a while for your house to become disorganized, so don't try to fix it in one day. After you have de-cluttered and picked up, the actual cleaning should only take 1-2 hours.

1. First, get dressed, comb your hair and put on a comfortable pair of shoes. You wouldn't show up at the office or work in your pajamas. Take your home and family's needs as seriously and get dressed!

2. Plan a schedule or a "to do" list that works for you, but don't spend all your time making the schedule or become a slave to it.

3. De-clutter, De-clutter, De-clutter-Oh, I forgot-did we tell you to De-clutter? Get rid of the junk you don't need. Half of what you have piled on the floor, the bed, the counter tops, and on your furniture is either trash or something you don't need. Toss it out or give it to charity - just get rid of it.

Here's a rule of thumb: If you haven't worn it, used it, eaten it, or played with it in the last year - you don't need it. Let it go.

4. If you're really in a bind, **get a friend to help.** Friends can be ruthless when it comes to getting rid of your junk. Just remember to return the favor and help them when the time comes. It's always a lot more fun to clean some one else's house than your own.

5. Pick up, Pick-up, Pick-up-Oh did we tell you to pick-up? You can either do this yourself or get your drill sergeant's whistle out and have the family help you. Although for some unknown reason (scientists have yet to find out the cause), husbands and children have a real problem developing in this area.

Walk through a room and just pick up whatever is out of place and return it to it's home. When you first start, this may seem like an overwhelming, daunting and miserable job, but when you finally do get it under control it becomes such a habit you don't realize you're doing it. **It's really simple to pick up things** as you enter each room and put them back where they belong.

6. Do one room at a time and if it is really bad one, do one closet at a time. **Clean closets and cabinets first** so you have a place to put the things that are piled in the room. Make three piles - one to keep, one to throw out, and one to donate to charity.

7. When you start putting things back in the closets, fold or stack them neatly. An item takes up much less room folded or stacked than when it is wadded and stuffed into place. **Put like items together.** Put all your underwear in one drawer, socks in another and so on. Give your husband and children a break. They have a hard enough time getting dressed in the morning without getting their socks out of one drawer and walking across the room to get their underwear out of another.

8. Use small amounts of time. While on the phone, clean out a desk drawer or your purse. Put away the tapes or DVD's that are piled around the TV. These small sorting projects can really make a huge difference in the amount of time you spend cleaning.

Organizing the Kitchen

Wash the dishes and clean your counter tops every day. When your kitchen is clean, your whole house seems cleaner and you will feel much better about picking up and keeping things in order.

Berry baskets make great storage containers for packages of spices, salad dressing, soups, and drink mixes.

Use strips of magnets to hang things like bottle openers or paring knives for storage.

Group like foods together in the pantry. Place all fruits, vegetables, soups, pasta, etc. together.

Need extra work space? Try pulling out a drawer and putting a baking sheet or cutting board on it.

If you run out of drawer space, **kitchen linens** can be stored on a pantry shelf. Remember to fold them neatly so they won't take up much space.

Store items close to where they will be used. **Keep dishes and silverware next to the dishwasher,** sink or eating area. Keep pans and baking utensils near the stove.

Store seldom used small appliances out of the way in the backs of cabinets or on the top shelf of the pantry.

Store frequently used utensils in a **nice crock on the counter.** This makes them easy to grab when needed.

Save your store-bought syrup bottles and use for homemade syrup, chocolate sauces and salad dressings.

To keep foods organized in the freezer, use **inexpensive baskets** in different colors for storage. Store each type of meat in a different color.

Make a place in a kitchen drawer to keep a **two-column list with the contents of your freezer itemized.** Use one column for cooked items and one for uncooked items. This way, you'll always know what you have and can plan meals in a snap.

Organize a baking center. Place mixing bowls, measuring cups and spoons, a mixer, spices for baking, a rolling pin, flour, sugar, brown sugar, confectioners' sugar and other baking supplies in one section of the kitchen, so baking is convenient.

If your recipe calls for **cheesecloth** and you don't have any, use a clean piece of an old pillowcase or flour sack dishtowel.

Buy restaurant sized aluminum foil, plastic wrap, and waxed paper. It is much cheaper and lasts longer.

Instead of paper napkins, buy an **inexpensive 12-pack of wash cloths** or small hand towels and use as dinner napkins. They wash easily and save money.

Gather all those **scraps of newspaper and recipes** pulled from magazines out of your junk drawer and put them in a nice photo album. If you really want to get organized, buy inexpensive colored tabs and make sections in the album.

If you are late getting dinner started, **set the table first.** Your family will know dinner is on the way and won't be so impatient.

Put a **turntable in your refrigerator** to keep things you use often close at hand.

Keep a **paper towel in your shortening.** Simply rub it on the pans to grease them. No need to wash a brush each time.

✦ **Ants? Well, they are said never to cross a chalk line. So, get your chalk out and draw a line on the floor or wherever ants tend to march. See for yourself.**

Mess Prevention - Stop It Before It Starts with These Great Ideas

If you **don't have time to clean** an entire room at one time, clean one kitchen drawer or cabinet while the noodles cook, or clean a shelf in the bathroom while supervising the kids in the bath. Wash one group of knick knacks each night while doing the dinner dishes. Do this with each room and you'll soon have things clean and organized.

Thinking of hanging **shelves?** They don't have to be fancy or expensive. Just get a cheap unfinished board at the lumberyard and cut it to length and attach it with some brackets. Paint or stain it only if you wish.

Place a **large flat tray by the door** to set boots and shoes on in the winter and rainy seasons.

Save **brown paper shopping bags** and use for trash sacks, wrapping paper, drawing paper for the kids, oil leaks under cars, etc.

In the pantry, place a **folded paper towel beneath your vegetable** oil and spices to catch spills.

Cut down **cereal boxes and use to store your magazines.** Decoupage with wrapping paper or spray paint to make them pretty.

Save bread bags and plastic shopping bags in an empty tissue box. The box fits nicely in most drawers and the opening in the box makes for easy removal of the bags.

Save cardboard oatmeal containers and put homemade granola, flour or sugar in them.

Over-the-door shoe hangers also work great on the inside of a closet to store small toys for kids craft supplies, craft articles and magazines, etc.

Cut down **shoe boxes to make drawer organizers** for your underwear and socks.

Re-fold your linens and clothing to see if another folding style takes up less room.

Use the space under beds. Add four coasters to the bottom of a an old dresser drawer. Then just slide the drawer under a bed for easy storage.

Fold extra blankets the long way and store between your bed and box springs

Use **zipper bags to organize** small objects such as art supplies, nuts and bolts, buttons, embroidery thread, sewing supplies, hair ribbons and small toys. This works for anything that is small and a little flat. Reinforce the bottom of the bag with clear shipping tape or contact paper and then punch holes in the bottom and store in a three ring binder. Use different size bags from the snack size to the freezer size to store many things.

Use extra **pony tail holders to wrap around extension cords.** The pony tails holders with plastic balls on the end work especially well for this.

A small pan or **kitty litter tray makes an easy store potting tray** for plants. Spills are contained in the tray making for easy clean up.

Keep like things together. All the dog grooming and pet supplies, all the supplies for cuts like Band-Aids and antibiotic ointment, shoe polish gear, manicure items etc. Small clear plastic containers work great for this.

Keep a **spray bottle of ammonia near the outside trash can.** Spray the can after each rain and it keeps the animals away.

Put a **turntable under your sink** to keep your cleaning supplies orderly and easy to reach.

Kids Can Do It Themselves!

(Or at least start to learn the right way…..)

To **help kids make their beds,** buy a sleeping bag to match the décor in their bedroom. Then, all they have to do is straighten the sleeping bag instead of a lot of blankets. They will also have a sleeping bag when they need one.

Kids can help with the housework. When trying to **teach kids** to make the bed, set the table or fold the laundry always work along side of them and show them.You may have to do this several times but they need to learn the proper way to do it so be patient.

Two weeks before Christmas and birthdays, **go through the toy box** and remove several of your children's toys, since they will soon be replaced. Let the kids play with half the their new toys each holiday and save the rest for them to play with later.

Have everyone make their own beds and pick up their rooms before they leave for school. I have found that the fastest way to get this done is to make sure that no one eats breakfast or turns on the TV until it's done. The Bible included this principle thousands of years ago and it still works today-If you don't work, you don't eat! When I first put this rule to the test, I went from one hour of nagging and accomplishing nothing to 15 minutes of peace and quiet with clean rooms and groomed children.

Use **plastic dishes when kids are little.** Let them help clear the table and wash the dishes.

Have a **family "dress" night** once a month. Dress for dinner as you would for a fancy restaurant or party. Set the table with a good tablecloth, your best china and silverware. Eat by candlelight. Teach the children to use their **best manners** - boys pull out the chair for mom, napkins in their laps, elbows off the table, proper use of silverware and correct language when asking for food or for permission to leave the table. This is not only fun but it teaches them manners **they will need in their every day adult life.**

Kids Can Do It Themselves!

(continued)

Make a box with each child's name on it. Put each child's clean laundry in the respective box and then have them put away their own laundry.

Draw a place setting for plate, glass, silverware and napkin **on a paper place mat.** Children can easily learn how to set the table by following your drawing. The place mat can also be laminated so you can use it over and over.

When your house looks like a bomb hit it

and company calls from a block away,

set your vacuum by the front door and say,

"Come on in ! I was just cleaning."

Dirty Dishes Cause Debt!

I was asked this question by a reader: **"Where do I start to get out of debt?"** After telling me of her huge credit card debt and how they eat out almost every night, the lady took a deep breath and said, "How do I save on laundry detergent and cleaning supplies?" Sometimes we can't see the forest for the trees. Even though **saving money on cleaning supplies does help** and should be done, that usually isn't where the biggest problem with the debt lies. This woman never once thought to ask me how to stop eating out so much. Most people don't want to face the real causes of their debt because their biggest problems are the things they like the most. **Going out to eat is one of the top five causes of debt.**

Get Those Dirty Dishes Out of the Sink!!

Keeping your kitchen empty of dirty dishes is the key to saving money. This is probably the #1 way to start getting out of debt. Most people are so overwhelmed with piled counter tops and dirty dishes that they would rather go out to eat than face a dirty kitchen. Do the dishes after every meal and keep hot soapy water in the sink while you are baking or cooking. Clean up as you go. If your sink is empty and the dishes are washed, your kitchen always looks good. This helps you save money because you have the time and space to cook.

✦ **To easily remove burnt on food from your skillet, add a drop or two of dish soap and enough water to cover the bottom of the pan. Bring water to a boil. he skillet is much easier to clean when cleaned immediately.**

✦ **To clean a burned pan, pour ¼ cup of baking soda into the pan. Fill with water and boil 30 minutes.**

Dishwashing Tips and Products

Use a **fresh dish** rag everyday. Keep a separate rag for cleaning the kids' hands and faces.

Use **inexpensive dishwasher detergent** (from the dollar store). Add a couple tablespoons of vinegar to your dishwasher and it will make the dishes sparkle.

Pour dish soap into a pump bottle and dilute with a quarter to a half cup water. This uses less soap but still gives great suds.

Place a nice rug in front of the kitchen sink. Put a piece of carpet pad under the rug. **The rug will keep your legs from getting tired** while you are doing the dishes.

Use a **toothbrush or small baby bottle nipple brush** to clean graters, can openers, blenders, rotary beaters and food processor parts.

Use your dishwasher to **clean things other than dishes,** such as: sponges, dish drainers, flower vases, soap dishes, metal sink drains, pet dishes, stove burner pans and microwave trays.

Don't forget to **clean your dish rack and drainer.** Spray with cleaner, let sit, then whip clean or place in the dishwasher.

Cut your **SOS pads in quarters or in half.** Store them in the freezer after each use to avoid rust.

Once a week, remove everything from kitchen and bathroom counter tops and clean thoroughly.

If an **old porcelain sink** is marked with metal scratches, use 400 grit wet/dry sand paper and lightly sand the markings out.

If you don't have a **dustpan** handy, dampen the edge of a **paper towel.** The wet edge sticks to the floor so you can sweep dust into the towel.

Pour a cup of **vinegar into the dishwasher** to remove soap scum.

Clean Your Kitchen in Seven Easy Steps

1. Put all dirty dishes in the dishwasher. Fill the sink with hot soapy water and put the hand washables in it to soak.

2. Wipe off counter tops and tables with hot soapy water. (This way, if you have unexpected company, at least your table and counters will be clean.)

3. Sweep the floor and shake throw rugs if needed.

4. Wash the dishes that have been soaking.

5. Wipe down the faucets and dry with a towel. (Be sure to wipe any sticky appliances, too.)

6. Put out a **clean dishcloth** and towel.

7. Take out the **trash.**

How to Clean the Refrigerator

Turn off refrigerator. Remove all food. Throw away moldy or spoiled food. Remove racks and clean with hot soapy water. Wipe out drawers and shelves. Remove drawers and clean any remaining food from underneath. Place paper towels in the bottom of each drawer before replacing in refrigerator. This will speed up your next cleaning. Wipe off door seal and door shelves. Replace food, cleaning any sticky bottles or jars before replacing. Wipe outside of refrigerator and dry.

Place a small amount of charcoal in the refrigerator or freezer to remove odors.

✦ **Use rubbing alcohol to shine appliances such as toasters or faucets.**

How to Clean your Oven and Stove Top

To clean the oven racks and stove top burner pans:

Remove oven racks and burner pans from the top of the stove. Place in a large plastic bag, spray with ammonia, tie the bag shut, and set out in the sun all day. At the end of the day, remove racks and burner pans from bag and rinse well,

To clean the oven:

Preheat oven to 200 degrees, then turn off. Fill a small glass bowl with ammonia, place inside the oven and let sit overnight. The next morning, wipe oven down with hot water, rinsing well. Replace racks.

To clean stove top:

Spray the stove top and area under burner pans with multi-purpose cleaner. Leave cleaner on surface for a few minutes to loosen grease. Wipe clean with hot water. Remove burner pans from plastic bag (see above) and wipe clean. Use a scouring pad to remove grease if necessary. Replace burner pans on stove top.

How to Clean the Microwave

Place a glass of water in the microwave. Cook until boiling. Then leave in microwave one hour. The steam will make it easier to clean. Wipe the microwave clean with hot soapy water. Dry. Rinse the turntable and dry. Replace turntable. Wipe outside door and dry.

Sanitize your WET sponge by placing it in the microwave once a day for one minute.

Clean Your Bathroom in Seven Easy Steps

1. Wipe hair out of the sink and tub with damp toilet tissue.

2. Spray disinfectant on the sink, tub and toilet. Either leave the disinfectant on the surfaces or wait 15 minutes before rinsing. Give the product time to work.

3. Wipe down counters and fixtures **with a dry soft cloth**.

4. Use a damp section of the same dry soft cloth to wipe down the mirror.

5. Empty trash cans and shake throw rugs.

6. Sweep the floor and wipe down with damp mop or rag.

7. Put out **clean towels.**

Save time by cleaning the bathroom sink and toilet while supervising bath time with the kids.

Shiny Shower-Use **car wax or lemon oil on a washrag to remove** residue on glass shower doors. Do not put on the shower floor or you could slip and fall.

Use **shaving cream as a cleaner** on your bathroom mirror. It will keep them from fogging up.

Use **dryer sheets to shine the chrome** on bathroom fixtures and use it pick up hair and lint off the floor.

Use air freshener to clean mirrors. It does a good job and better still, leaves a lovely smell to the shine.

Trade secret from professional housekeepers

Keep a stack of rags (used only for this purpose) or good paper towels and a spray bottle of disinfectant under the sink. Once a day, spray a rag with disinfectant and wipe down everything. Don't rinse. The most time consuming thing in cleaning is trying to rinse the product away. Professionals have been using this method for years. Some innovative companies have now put paper towels with disinfectant into a plastic container to be used to wipe things down. This is the same as my method-only more expensive.

Jill's best time saving tip for quick cleaning

This will work for those of you who cannot bring yourself to leave the disinfectant on surfaces without rinsing: Spray everything with disinfectant when you start cleaning a room. After you have sprayed everything, start with the area you sprayed first and then rinse. The idea is to make sure the cleaner stays on the surface long enough to act as a disinfectant. The cleaner needs to stay on the surfaces at least 15 minutes in order to work. So, if you must rinse, at least wait 15 minutes before doing so.

To clean your carpets:

Make a solution of ½ cup ammonia combined with ½ gallon of water. Use a rag to gently scrub the carpet. Repeat until clean. This may also be used in a carpet cleaner. Removes even the toughest spots. Test a hidden area first.

A note about household cleaners

NEVER MIX AMMONIA AND BLEACH. MIXING CHEMICALS CREATES A HARMFUL GAS THAT CAN BE FATAL!

If you don't want to make your own cleaning supplies, either **purchase the store brands at your dollar store** or buy in **bulk at a janitor supply.**

Buy **1 gallon of bubble bath** and use instead of liquid hand soap. It is much cheaper and smells better than regular hand soap.

Read the labels on any cleaning product you buy, even on common products that you, your mom and grandmother have used for years. For example for generations women have used ammonia to disinfect their kitchens, but ammonia is not a disinfectant, it is a de-greaser. It works great for that greasy grimy build-up on floors but it isn't actually disinfecting anything.

Mark your cleaning pail with fingernail polish to indicate the levels of water you usually use for your jobs (ie. ½ gal., 1 gal.)

When using cleansers, tear the tab back only part way. Then you only get half as much cleanser out and there is less to rinse down the drain.

Save on spray cleaners. **Spray the solution on a rag** and then wipe. This way the extra spray cleaner is not wasted and you save time by not having to rinse off the over spray.

Use fabric softener sheets to dust furniture and television screens. The sheets make your furniture smell lovely, but more importantly, eliminate static so dust won't be attracted to these surfaces.

An **inexpensive copper polish** is equal parts flour and salt made into a paste with vinegar or lemon juice. Store in the refrigerator.

Where to find the ingredients for some of the recipes

Fels Naptha Soap, Borax (20 Mule Team Borax) and Washing Soda (Arm and Hammer) can all be found in the laundry section of your grocery store. Sometimes Fels Naptha Soap will be in with the bar soaps.

Dishwasher Soap

1   Tbsp. baking soda
1   Tbsp. Borax

Mix and use in place of dishwasher detergent. You can mix larger batches to keep on hand.

In hard water areas you may still need to use dishwasher detergent. In that case, use equal parts baking soda, borax and dishwasher detergent. Use 2 Tbsp. for each load.

Counter-top Disinfectant

2   Tbsp. ammonia
$\frac{1}{2}$ cup rubbing alcohol
$\frac{1}{4}$ cup vinegar
    water

Put ammonia, alcohol and vinegar in a spray bottle and fill with water. This works especially good for counter-tops but may also be used to clean showers, toilets and sinks. Great for most cleaning needs.

Fruit and Vegetable Wash

You really don't need a special cleaner for your fruits and vegetables. Just wash them with a weak solution of dish detergent and a scrub brush. If you still insist on using a special wash, this is a good recipe that is the same as the "natural" stuff in the store.

1 Tbsp. lemon juice
2 Tbsp. baking soda
1 cup water

Put ingredients in a spray bottle. Be careful because it will foam up. Spray on vegetables, let sit 5 minutes then rinse with a scrub brush.

Drain Cleaner/Opener

1 cup baking soda
1 cup vinegar
4 cups boiling water

Pour baking soda into drain and then pour vinegar on top of it. Let it sit for 30 minutes. Pour boiling water down the drain. You may need to repeat this process if your drain doesn't come unclogged the first time. This will clean out a lot of clogs so try it first before running to the store to buy a commercial drain opener.

Don't throw away the baking soda used to freshen your fridge. Use it as a cleaning scrub or pour down your drain to clear clogs.

✦ **Use a fine tooth dog brush to remove dog and cat hair from furniture, carpet and bed comforters.**

Window Cleaner

½   cup ammonia
2   cups rubbing alcohol
    water
1   tsp. dishwashing liquid

In a one-gallon container, mix ammonia and rubbing alcohol. Fill almost to the top with water. Add dishwashing liquid and mix. Top off with water. Rated by Consumer Reports Magazine to work much better (and much cheaper) than most commercial window and kitchen sprays. Alcohol is the secret ingredient - it's what commercial window washers use.

*Safe on most, but not all, household surfaces.

All Purpose Cleaner

1   gallon water
1   cup ammonia
½   cup vinegar
½   cup baking soda

Combine all ingredients. Put in a spray bottle to clean showers, toilets, sinks and counters. Great for most cleaning needs.

Use all-purpose cleaner to clean your floors. Just spray on and wipe off as you would counter-tops.

✦ **Put your hand inside a plastic bag to pick up a sticky or gooey item. Then invert the bag and tie it shut.**

How to remove the wax
from your floor

Put ½ cup ammonia in a gallon of hot water. Get on the floor and scrub with a green kitchen scrubbie. Rinse with 1 cup vinegar in 1 gallon of water. You only need to do this every few months.

Ready Mop Cleaner Refill

1   gallon water
1   cup ammonia
½   cup vinegar
    water

Mix ingredients and pour use in your mops instead of buying commercial cleaner.

Tip: Use a piece of scrap fleece, scrap flannel or micro-fiber towels (purchased at automotive stores) to replace your Swifer™ or Clorox Ready Mop™ disposable pads. Cut several to size to have on hand. When soiled throw in the wash and launder as usual. Note: Don't use ammonia on wood floors. Just use vinegar and water or water and Murphy's oil soap.

An antique store sign:

Come in and buy

what your grandmother threw away.

Daily Shower Cleaner

8   ounces concentrated cleaner (Lysol is a good brand)
16 ounces isopropyl alcohol
    water

Pour cleaner and alcohol into a one-gallon bucket. Add enough water to make 1 gallon. Pour into spray bottle. Thorough clean shower before using. Spray on shower daily. Use daily to prevent water deposits and soap scum.

Homemade Cleaning Wipes

1   round baby wipe container*
1   roll of paper towels**
2-4 cups cleaning solution (homemade is fine)

Recycle a used round baby wipe container. Cut a roll of paper towel in half, (an electric or serrated knife works best for this.) Remove the center cardboard. Place ½ of the paper towels in the baby wipe container. Pour cleaning solution into the container. (The amount will depend of the absorbency of your paper towels.) This can be used for window cleaner, all purpose cleaner, or disinfectant cleaner. Pull the first paper towel out of the center of the roll, through the hole in the container lid. If the paper towels dry out before they are all used add more solution or some water.

*If you don't have a baby wipe container, you can use a round plastic container and just drill or punch a large hole in the center of the lid.

**It is best to use expensive, thick paper towels. The cheap ones won't hold up to scrubbing.

Outdoor Window Washer

3   Tbsp. liquid dishwashing soap
1   Tbsp. anti-spotting agent (Jet Dry™)

Put soap and anti-spotting agent into a spray bottle attachment for your garden hose. Spray upper windows and let them dry. This is for cleaning the higher windows on your house that you can't reach except with a ladder.

Tarnish Remover

½-1   cup baking soda or Borax
        aluminum pan (no substitutions)

Place aluminum pan in the sink and add your sterling or plated silver. Add enough baking soda or Borax™ to cover silverware. Pour boiling water to cover the utensils. When the tarnish disappears, remove silverware, and buff with a soft cotton cloth.

Tough Hand Cleaner

¼   cup Fels Naptha*, grated
2   Tbsp. mason's sand or pumice
1   cup water
2   cup plastic container (16 oz. cottage cheese container works great)

Place soap and water in a saucepan. Place over low heat; stir until soap is melted. After mixture cools, add mason's sand or pumice. Store in a cottage cheese container or margarine tub. Dip fingers into soap mixture and lather hands. Rinse well.

*Any grated bar of soap will work but Fels Naptha removes the stains better.

Misc. Tips

Keep a trash can in the garage by the car. Remove the trash every time you get out of the car. Just throw empty paper cups, napkins, wrappers, receipts and other junk in the trash-instead of taking it into the house.

To clean **silk flowers** place some salt in a paper bag add flowers and shake. The salt will remove the dust and dirt.

Disinfect and clean your telephone on a regular basis. This will help stop the spread of germs.

Save all of your plastic containers, jars and pie tins or buy some inexpensive ones at garage sales. When you need to **take a meal to a friend,** your friend can dispose of the containers and not worry about doing dishes or returning the containers to you

In a small inexpensive notebook, keep a simple **list of everyday Things to Do,** People to Call, Appointments and Bills to Pay. Also keep a running list of gift ideas for friends and family so that when you need a gift, you already have an idea about what to get.

To **prepare for the birth of you baby,** prepare several meals and freeze. Then your husband can just pull one out of the freezer and reheat for a home made meal after you come home with the baby. You won't have to cook a thing!

Sprinkle salt on an egg that has cracked on the floor. Let it sit 5 - 10 minutes. It should sweep up easily.

Use **Rit dye to stain furniture and wood.** Mix one package with a half gallon to one gallon of water, depending upon the color you want. Rit dye is less expensive than stain and allows you to have custom colors to match your décor.

Above all,
if it's not dirty - don't clean it.

Stain Removal Tips

Carpet stains: rub shaving cream on a stain. Wipe clean with a wet sponge.

Always test any stain remove on a hidden spot first.

Spray plastic containers with cooking spray before adding tomato products. The **oil will keep it from staining.**

Scuff marks on floor- use a pencil or pen eraser.

To **remove mildew** from clothes, dip stain in buttermilk and place in the sun.

www.crayola.com has about any problem you could have with crayons in their stain section.

Crayon stains in the dryer-Spray W-D 40 on a rag. Wipe the inside of the dryer drum until clean. Run a load of rags or old towels in the dryer for at least 30 minutes to remove any remaining crayon residue.

Crayon marks on walls-spray surface to be cleaned with WD-40 and wipe clean with a soft cloth. If residue remains add liquid dishwashing soap to water. Wash the surface with a sponge working in a circular motion and rinse.

Crayon stains on clothes-place item on an ironing board. Put 3-4 thickness of paper towel underneath and 2 thickness on top. Iron until crayon starts to melt. Move paper towel around until all the crayon is gone. Spray with W-D 40 on both sides and let sit for a few minutes. Treat with strain remover and launder as usual on longest cycle possible. Be sure to check before putting in the dryer as you may have to treat with stain remover again.

Lipstick-Use **make up remover** or face cleaner.

Stain Removal Tips

Ring around the collar-use shampoo. Rub into spot and launder as usual.

Permanent Marker-Wipe with rubbing alcohol until it's removed.

Ink-Spray area with hairspray and wipe off. Baby wipes also work. Just rub area with wipe until it's gone. This works on clothes, leather couches just about anything that has an ink stain.

Blood-use peroxide on a blood stain and the chemical reaction literally makes the stain disappear. Just pour enough peroxide on the stain to moisten and watch the "bubbles" eat the stain. If the stain is not gone when the bubbling stops, reapply. Repeat until the stain is gone. Since peroxide has a bleaching effect, you might want to test it on some colors first. Also if you get a **small spot of blood on an article from a pricked finger** like while your sewing, just splt on it and wipe off. It works great!

Rust-Mix lemon juice and salt together to make a paste. Just rub on spot and let sit over night. If it isn't all gone then repeat again. This works best on white clothes, linens and counter-tops.

Stain Pretreater

¹/₂ cup vinegar
¹/₂ cup ammonia
¹/₂ cup Wisk™
¹/₂ cup water

Mix all ingredients and store in a spray bottle. Spray on anything with grease or food spots. Wash as usual.

Laundry and Linens

Too many clothes mean too much laundry. Here's how to cut back on both:

Do you ever feel like your clothes are taking over and controlling your whole house? Like a blob from a horror movie, laundry is slowly consuming everything. It is piled on your couches, tables, beds and on every floor in the house. You shop for clothes, wash them, iron them, fold them and mend them. Usually, by the time you get that done you are too pooped to put them away, so you pile them right back where you started-the couch, table, bed and sometimes the floor.

One of the best ways to control this mess is to **limit the number of outfits** your family owns. I know it may be hard because there are so many cute outfits out there but you can do it! There is an awful lot of delicious chocolate out there, too, but that doesn't mean we buy all that we see. Why? Because it's not healthy and, of course, you could easily gain 100 pounds! In the same way, **owning too many clothes is not good for you.** The situation causes stress which is unhealthy and the resulting stress causes us to eat chocolate which causes us to gain weight forcing us to buy more clothes and then we're right back to where we started!

 Sit down and plan **how many outfits each member of your family needs.** Most families wash the laundry once a week or more. You don't need 15 pairs of jeans for each child. 3 or 4 pairs will work just fine.

You can **wear the same shirt or pair of jeans more than once** between washing if it isn't dirty or smelly. Make kids wear their clothes until they are dirty. If they are still clean, put them back in the closet. A newborn may need 10 pairs of pajamas since they live in them and spit up on them but a 10 year old only needs three or four pairs.

When possible, **hang your clothes out on a clothesline. I** know this may not always be possible or practical but it is better. Most people think it takes more time to do this but if you learn how to do it properly, it's as easy as drying in the dryer.

The reason I believe firmly in line drying, besides because it makes everything smell delicious, is that it can really save you money in the long run. The most obvious saving is of course in electricity for the dryer. There are many other ways it saves that we usually don't think about. For example wear and tear on clothes. Anything with **elastic** in it (underwear, socks, etc.) **becomes stretched and mis-shaped in the dryer** requiring more frequent replacement. Do you feel you need to buy new underwear every couple of weeks for your family? The dryer is the cause. Do your clothes seem to be wearing thin? What do you think all that **dryer lint** is?

I very **rarely have problems with stains.** The dryer sets stains terribly and line drying not only doesn't set them but sometimes helps fade lighter stains. With line drying, whites bleach out whiter and the stains you missed the first time around can be easily treated. How often have you had to throw away a perfectly good outfit because of stains? The worse your stains are, the more likely you will incur the added expense of trying dry cleaning or buying new clothes and as I mentioned, dryers tend to set stains.

An <u>optimist</u> sees the glass as half full...

The <u>pessimist</u> sees it as half empty...

A <u>realist</u> sees it as just
one more thing to wash.

Homemade Laundry Soap

I have discovered that people either love or hate this soap. I would suggest that you try it and see what you opinion is.

6 cups water
⅓ bar Fels Naptha Laundry Soap, grated
½ cup washing soda
½ cup Borax™

Heat 6 cups water and soap in a large pan until dissolved. Stir in washing soda and Borax. Mix and heat until dissolved. Boil 15 minutes. Remove from heat. (It will have the consistency of honey.*) In a 3 or 5 gallon bucket add 1 quart of hot water, then add the soap mixture. Mix. Add enough cold water to make 2 gallons mixture. Mix until well blended. Let sit 24 hours. The soap will gel*. Use ½ cup for each load.

Makes 2 gallons. (Approx. $ .40 per gallon)

*If the detergent doesn't gel up or reach honey consistency it will still work.

Notes:

Stir before each use as this does separate. Detergent can be stored in a liquid detergent bottle and then just shake it up each time you use it.

This detergent will not suds up in the washer, but it is still getting your clothes clean.

If you have extra hard water the soap may not clean as well. Add ½ cup borax or washing soda to the load and that may help.

Laundry Tips

To **make clothes wash more easily,** soak them overnight in cold soft water with one tablespoon of ammonia added for each bucket of water. ¼ cup works fine for a washer.

When **sheets get worn in the middle** cut the outer edges up and make pillowcases or cut into rags.

Place **dryer sheets in dresser drawers** or in your towels and linens to keep your clothes smelling clean.

Use a **shopping cart or TV tray to set a basket of clothes** on while hanging them outside.

Dye faded pants. You can also wash a faded pink shirts in with reds to give it a little more color. Faded navy colored items can be washed with new jeans for more color.

When jeans or any other **pants wear out in the knees** cut them off and wear shorts.

Dampen a washcloth with fabric softener and throw in the dryer with your clothes instead of buying fabric softener sheets.

Spray your ironing with water instead of spray starch. Clothing will still look starched and ironing is easier.

Clean stuffed animals by throwing them in the washer on the gentle cycle. They will come out looking great.

To remove soap scum from your washing machine, pour in a gallon of vinegar. Run washer through one cycle without clothes.

✦ **Sew a bath towel in half and use as a bath mat. It's cheap, matches your bathroom décor and doesn't fall apart in the wash.**

Odor Removal Tips

Use vinegar to **clean up urine on the floor,** clothes or furniture. Soak area with ½-1 cup of vinegar, place a thick towel on top and then weigh down with a heavy object for several hours until urine and vinegar are soaked up. Add ½ cup to toilet to break down urine smell.

Use vinegar or a solution of baking soda water to remove **odors from plastics like trash cans and diaper pails.** Spray sides of can with vinegar. Pour a little in the bottom of the can and let sit several hours. Rinse.

A **bacterial enzyme** from the janitor supply shop works to remove pet and urine odors.

Skunk Smell Remover

1   qt. hydrogen peroxide
¼   cup baking soda
1   tsp. dish detergent

Sponge on and let dry. Safe for use on cats and dogs.

Baby Wipes

1½ cups boiling water*
2   Tbsp. baby bath or shampoo
1   Tbsp. baby oil
1   roll paper towels

Mix the water, baby bath and baby oil in an empty round baby
wipe container. Cut the paper towels in ½ using an electric knife.
Remove core from the center. Place paper towels in wipe
container. Let the paper towels soak up the water solution. Turn
every few minutes to allow the solution to reach the middle of
the paper towels. If there is still a dry spot in the middle, add a
little more water and turn until soaked through. Pull the wipes
from the middle of the roll through the top of the wipe container.

*Keeps bacteria from growing.

✦ **Old cloth diapers make great rags for cleaning and
shining.**

✦ **An even less expensive baby wipe is to use wash cloths
and wash with your cloth diapers.**

✦ **Use cornstarch instead of baby powder. It is now sold as
"natural" baby powder in the stores. Put it in an old
spice bottle for a shaker.**

To Set a Table

Place a plate on top of a placemat. **To the right of the plate put the knife, blade turned in, and then the spoon. On the left, place your fork next to the plate and then the salad fork.** Place your glass at the tip of the knife. Fold the napkin and place it under the fork.

Use tablecloths, placemats and napkins for the season or holiday. Scavenge garage sales or go to a discount store for inexpensive material to use to make place settings. It is very simple to sew a straight line to make a tablecloth, place mat or napkin.

Only set the table with items that are needed. If you don't need knives for a particular meal, don't put them on the table.

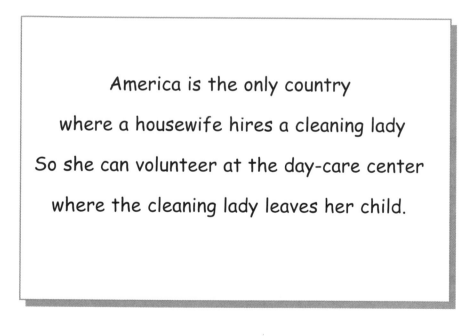

America is the only country

where a housewife hires a cleaning lady

So she can volunteer at the day-care center

where the cleaning lady leaves her child.

Pretty for
Pennies

Love is blind - marriage is an eye-opener.

Where to find the ingredients:

✦ Essential oils and flavored **oils can be found at health food stores,** on-line* and in some pharmacies.

✦ **Borax** is found in the **laundry section** of the grocery store. The brand name is 20 Mule Team Borax.

✦ **Citric acid, almond oil and beeswax** can also be found at health food stores but are **less expensive on-line*.**

✦ **Beeswax comes in blocks** or beads. The beads are easier to use but if you use blocks, you can simply grate the amount you need.

*These on-line sites offer the best prices that I have found:
www.wholesalesuppliesplus.com
www.thesage.com

Essential oils

You may use a variety of essential oils for lip balms, aromatherapy lotions and creams depending upon the mood you want to create. When making lotion you can use a teaspoon of your favorite perfume or cologne instead of essential oil. For unscented products, simply leave out the essential oils and perfumes.

Here is a guide to help you choose which oils to use:

Relaxing- Lavender, Rose, Sandalwood

Stimulating- Peppermint, Rosemary, Eucalyptus, Lemon

Uplifting- Orange, Jasmine, Rosemary

Antiseptic- Tea Tree, Eucalyptus, Peppermint, Lavender

Muscle Aches- Eucalyptus, Lavender, Rosemary

Bath and Relaxtion

Milk Bath

3   cups dry milk
5-6 drops essential or fragrance oil (optional)

Mix ingredients and add ½ cup to your bath water.

Scented Bath Bubbles

2   cups unscented dish soap (Ivory is a good brand)
10-15 drops essential oil

Mix ingredients. Let stand 1 week. Use ¼ cup per bath.

Bath Gel

¾   cup water
1   packet unflavored gelatin
½   cup baby shampoo, bubble bath or liquid soap
5-6 drops fragrance or essential oil

Heat the water to boiling, remove from heat and dissolve gelatin into it. Add the shampoo slowly and stir until combined. Pour mixture into jar and set in the refrigerator. Add little plastic fish or flowers before it sets for added charm. Scoop out a little as required for each bath.

Bath Sachet

¼   cup each lavender and rosebuds OR
     ¼ cup each peppermint and rosemary leaves*
2   cups Borax™
2   Tbsp. oatmeal

Put one tablespoon of mixture into a piece of cheesecloth and tie or use a tea ball. Use one bag per bath.

*Use lavender and rosebuds for a relaxing bath or peppermint and rosemary for a stimulating bath.

Bath Salts

½   gal. Epsom salts
1   cup baking soda
     A few drops of food coloring
     Vanilla, almond or peppermint extract or your favorite
     perfume

Place salts, baking soda, color, and scent into a bowl. Mix well and pour into a pretty jar with a ribbon.

Use ½ cup per bath.

✦ **You can use the salt for water softeners. It is much less expensive if you are making several jars of bath salts!**

✦ **Mix a half cup salt, sugar or cornmeal and a half cup vegetable oil. Stir and rub into skin. The graininess exfoliates the dead skin cells and the oil softens skin.**

Bath Bombs

1	cup baking soda
½	cup citric acid
½	cup cornstarch
2	Tbsp. plus 1 tsp. oil (almond, sunflower, coconut, mineral, canola or baby oil may be used)
2	tsp. water
1-2	tsp. essential or fragrance oil
¼	tsp. Borax™
	food coloring

Mix baking soda, citric acid and cornstarch. Mix the wet ingredients and the Borax™ and slowly add to the dry ingredients, mixing constantly. Mix slowly or it will bubble too much. Pack into mold; let set for a few minutes and then remove from molds. Let dry another 24 hours. In humid climates you may need to dry longer. Use 1-3 per bath. Store in an airtight container. Wrap in cellophane bags for a nice gift.

The mixture is very crumbly and dry. Mix as well as you can and then pack tightly into molds. If the bath bombs won't hold their shapes, add one teaspoon oil.

Bath Seeds

To make Bath Seeds mix ingredients above, omitting molds. Just place in a pretty jar and label. Use 2-4 tablespoons per bath.

✦ **Bubble bath keeps a ring from forming in the tub. If you're out of bubble bath put a squirt of shampoo in the tub instead.**

Oatmeal Scrub

1   cup oatmeal
3   drops essential oil (optional)

Mix ingredients together. Dampen with water and rub over skin in the shower. This is great for exfoliation.

Perfumed Body/Bath Oils

baby oil (cheap is best because it has less scent)
dried flowers
essential oils, liquid scent or favorite perfume

Place dried flowers, as few or as many as you like, into bottle and fill nearly full with baby oil. Add liquid scent to desired strength and gently shake to mix. Replace cap and let sit for a few days. Use a few capfuls in your bath for a soothing, relaxing bath. The scent will last for hours.

+ **If your blush crumbles, crush into a powder, add enough alcohol to make a paste and mix well. Pour back into container, leave open and let dry. It will be a cake again in a day or two.**
+ **Use shampoo as shower gel. Many of them smell wonderful (I love coconut) and cost ½ the price.**
+ **Try rubbing cocoa butter on your tummy and breasts while pregnant to help prevent stretch marks.**

Massage Cream

½   cup vegetable shortening
5-6 drops essential oil OR
      1 tsp. fragrance or cologne

Mix well. Makes a nice massage cream.

Massage Oil

6   tsp. oil (mineral, safflower, sunflower, or olive)
8   drops essential oil*

Mix well.

*Use lavender for a relaxing massage or peppermint and eucalyptus to rub sore muscles or sore back.

Steaming Facial

Add your choice of herbs to a boiling pan of water.

Add:

    Peppermint for colds
    Chamomile or lemon balm for relaxing
    Rosemary for uplifting

Remove pan from heat. Drape a towel over your head and bend over steam. **To avoid burning your face, do not put your head too close to the steam.**

This is a wonderful facial and really cleans out those pores! When I was in Sweden, we sat in the sauna every day. The steam from the sauna made my face clearer than it has ever been in my life. (That was when I was an acne-prone teenager, too!)

Herbal Foot Bath

Use any of the following dried herbs*:
    lavender
    rosemary
    sage

Mix herbs and place in a small cheesecloth. Fill a bucket full with warm water and add herbs. Soak away all the pains of the day! Make several at a time and keep on hand for use after a long day.

*A few drops of scented oil may be used instead.

Foot Massage Oil

1   Tbsp. almond oil
1   Tbsp. olive oil
1   Tbsp. sunflower oil
6-10   drops eucalyptus or peppermint essential oil

Combine ingredients. Stir well. Use to massage tired feet. Store in a cool dry place.

Rub a peppermint lotion or salve on your feet. Wrap a warm towel around your feet and enjoy.

✦ **You can make a nice toner by boiling two tablespoons of pine needles in a small amount of water. Strain and add to one cup of witch hazel.**

Hair and Nails

Hair Tips

✦ **Rinse hair with vinegar.** It gets rid of buildup and is gentle on your hair.

✦ Store **hair barrettes** on a pretty ribbon hanging on the back of your bathroom door.

✦ To **add highlights to hair:** Rub lemon juice on your hair. Then sit out in the sun for a half hour to a couple of hours.

✦ **Dilute** hair spray or shampoo half way with water. Save an old bottle for storing the other half.

✦ Only **shampoo once**-twice isn't really necessary.

✦ Mix 3 tablespoons of mayonnaise and 1 egg. Spread on hair and let sit for 30 minutes. A **great moisturizer!**

✦ **Dry Shampoo:** Sprinkle cornstarch in your hair. Let sit for a few minutes; then brush out. The cornstarch absorbs oils.

✦ Be sure to **wash your combs and brushes.** Put a squirt of shampoo in the sink with hot water. Let them soak a few minutes and then swish until clean.

A psychiatrist is a person who gives you expensive answers which your wife will give for free.

Hot Oil Treatment

2   Tbsp. olive oil*
2   Tbsp. vegetable oil

Heat ingredients just until warm. Spread on wet hair, especially the ends. (Place only on the ends if you have oily hair.) Wrap a warm, wet towel around hair for 30 minutes to one hour. Shampoo and rinse.

Alternatively, put this on before a shower and then put on a shower cap. Let the hot water from the shower run on your head to warm the oil.

You may also use a blow dryer instead of the shower. Be careful not to make it too hot.

*Other oils you could use are: sunflower oil, wheat germ oil, sesame oil, almond oil, avocado oil

✦ Use a hot oil treatment on your hair once a week to help moisturize dry hair.
✦ Rub a small amount of conditioner on the ends of your hair to keep it from frizzing.

There are two theories
to arguing with women.
Neither one works.

Leg Wax

(This is the same as the stuff you can buy in the store.)

1   cup sugar
2   Tbsp. lemon juice
2   Tbsp. water

Mix ingredients in a saucepan and boil for 8-15 minutes, or until mixture reaches 250° (soft ball stage). Then pour it into a container and let it cool down. Keep refrigerated. Heat in the microwave just until warm. Be careful not to make it too hot so that you don't burn yourself. Test on your hand first. Lightly powder the area you wish to wax. Pull skin taut and spread wax on using a tongue depressor or popsicle stick. Place a 3x5 piece of cotton cloth* over the area to remove hair. Pull off quickly against the grain of the hair. Cloths may be re-used simply by washing in hot water. I have not personally tried this recipe but friends say it works great. I have never had the courage to try and wax my legs. If you're not familiar with how to wax I would go to a beauty school and have them show you how to do it first.

*Old t-shirts or flour sack dish towels torn into strips work well.

✦ **Use conditioner instead of shaving cream for your legs.**
✦ **Dry your razor after each use. Water makes the blade dull and rusty. Put a small amount of mineral oil or petroleum jelly on the blade after drying it.**

Tips for Beautiful Nails and Hands

✦ To **soften hands or feet,** rub liberally with petroleum jelly, put on a pair of gloves or socks and wear overnight.

✦ Use a nail buffer to **shine nails between manicures.**

✦ **No-spill polish remover.** Cut a slit into the center of a sponge. Place sponge into a small container and fill with nail polish remover. Dip fingernail in slit and slide around to remove polish.

✦ Use an old toothbrush as a **nail brush.**

✦ **Go to the local beauty school to have manicures, pedicures and facials.** You can feel pampered without spending a fortune. Five bucks is a great deal for a facial!

✦ **To remove dry skin,** wash hands with a small amount of cornmeal or sugar mixed with water. (*Thanks to Cyndi in California*)

✦ **When finished eating a grapefruit or lemon,** place your elbows in the halves for 10-30 minutes to soften them. *Thanks to Erin in Washington.*

✦ **Purchase nail care kits after Christmas** at half price. You can get several polishes and tools for $2-$4.

✦ Thin thickened nail polish using **nail polish thinner** (not remover!). It's found by the nail polish remover.

✦ Soak nails in **lemon juice to remove stains.**

✦ **To remove the last bit of lotion** from a container, run the tightly closed lotion container under hot water. When the lotion melts, it will be easier to get it all. Also stand the lotion container on end.

✦ **Save the cotton** from aspirin bottles. Use for your face or for manicures.

✦ An easy way **to remove cuticles** is to rub them with oil. Then gently push back the cuticles.

Paraffin Bath

6   pounds of canning paraffin wax (Found in canning section of grocery store)
¼   cup baby or mineral oil
       a few drops of essential oil (optional)

Cut paraffin into chunks and heat over low in double boiler or crock pot. When melted, add mineral oil and essential oil. Mix well. Remove from stove and cool to 124° on a candy thermometer.

When cool, rub hands generously with lotion or salve. Dip one hand into the wax. Do not touch the bottom of the pan. Remove hand and allow wax to harden for a few seconds. Repeat 5-10 times for each hand. After last dip, let harden for a few seconds and then wrap in a plastic bag. (Old bread or newspaper bags work great!) Lay a heavy towel over the top of hands to insulate and leave on 20-30 minutes. Peel wax off when finished and place back in melting pan. The wax may be used again.

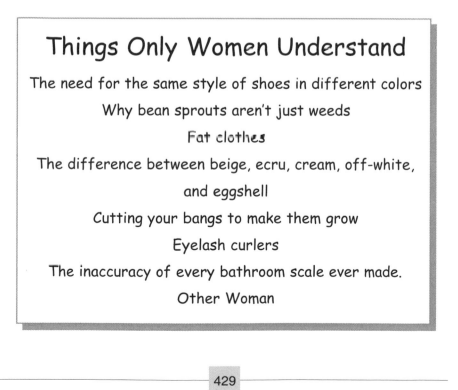

Things Only Women Understand

The need for the same style of shoes in different colors

Why bean sprouts aren't just weeds

Fat clothes

The difference between beige, ecru, cream, off-white,

and eggshell

Cutting your bangs to make them grow

Eyelash curlers

The inaccuracy of every bathroom scale ever made.

Other Woman

Beauty Tips

+ Dab a little baby oil on a piece of cotton ball and use to **remove make-up.**

+ **Wash your powder puff in the washer** and dryer and it will be fresh and clean!

+ Many stores will let you **return make-up** even if it's the wrong color. Ask before you buy it and save your receipt if they do take returns.

+ **If you purchase make-up that isn't the right color,** mix it with a lighter or darker shade until you get the color that is right for you. This works great for lipsticks and foundations.

+ For a **refreshing lemon toner,** add ½ cup lemon juice and ⅔ cup witch hazel to 1 cup distilled water.

+ About once a week I use baking soda to **exfoliate my face.** It's not too rough and makes a great face scrub. I keep a tub full of it in my shower all the time! *Thanks to Ingrid Cotner, VA*

+ Cucumber slices or tea bags on the eyes help **reduce puffiness.** Try it for half an hour.

+ Use baby wipes to remove **eye makeup.**

+ If you have **blemishes,** try any of the following:

> Toothpaste- dab on and leave overnight
>
> Diaper rash cream- dab on and leave overnight
>
> Aspirin- Smash one aspirin and make a paste with water. Put on a pimple and leave overnight.
>
> Visine- Soak a cotton ball with it and dab on pimples.
>
> Hydrogen peroxide- on a cotton ball and dab it on blemishes.

+ Put an ice cube **or teething gel (for babies) on eyebrows** before plucking to reduce pain.

After-Bath Splash

½   cup vodka
½   tsp. essential oil, fragrance oil or perfume
1   Tbsp. glycerin (optional)

Combine ingredients. Shake well before using.

Solid Perfume

2   Tbsp. beeswax
¼   cup almond oil
20 drops perfume

In a saucepan, melt beeswax and oil. Whisk in perfume. Pour into small jars or containers.

Bath Powder

½   cup cornstarch
2   Tbsp. arrowroot powder (optional)
15 drops favorite perfume or essential oil

Mix dry ingredients in a bowl. Add scented oil and stir until blended. Sift until smooth. Store in a powder box or cheese or spice shaker. Cover holes of cheese shaker with some tape so the powder doesn't come out so fast.

✦ **Add 2-3 tablespoons baby oil for a relaxing bath!**

Almond Lotion

½   cup almond oil
1   Tbsp. beeswax
¼   cup distilled water, boiling
⅛   tsp. Borax™
5-6 drops essential oil

Heat almond oil and beeswax together until melted. Combine water and borax. Slowly pour borax mixture into heated oil while stirring with a wire whisk. Add essential oil. Cool completely and place in a bottle. Makes about 1 cup.

This is my favorite lotion!

Lotion Bar

½   cup beeswax
1   cup of your favorite oil
     (palm, olive, almond, jojoba, or coconut)

Melt ingredients together in a pan on medium heat. Pour into bar molds (or whatever shape you want to make). When cool, remove from molds. Rub over body as needed.

Perfumed Lotion

Liquid scent or favorite perfume
Lotion, least expensive and unscented

Stir as much scent as you like into the lotion. Mix well and place into desired container. Small "travel size" squeeze bottles work great.

Lip Balm Basics

There are many ways to make lip balm. Basic lip balm contains oil, beeswax and flavoring (optional). I prefer a softer lip balm. If you want one that is a little more waxy add an additional teaspoon of beeswax. Experiment to see which you like the best.

Use any of the following oils in your lip balm:

+ coconut oil	+ castor oil	+ almond oil
+ sunflower oil	+ lanolin	+ jojoba oil
+ olive oil	+ shea butter	+ cocoa butter

Vitamin E is a preservative and is also thought to be healing for your skin.

Comfrey root and rosemary extracts may be used for their healing properties. If you wish to make your own extracts, you may boil comfrey and rosemary in sunflower oil for an hour or two. Strain oil before using in lip balms or creams.

Lip Balm

1   tsp. beeswax beads
1   tsp. sunflower oil
1   tsp. coconut oil
1   tsp. (total) comfrey and/or rosemary extract (optional)
2-5 drops flavoring (optional)- peppermint, cherry, grape, vanilla, orange or anything you like.
1   capsule Vitamin E

Heat oils and beeswax just until melted. Add the rest of the ingredients. Mix well. Use a dropper to place in tubes or small jars.

This is my favorite lip balm and I'm very picky about what kind I use.

Chocolate Lip Balm

1   tsp. cocoa butter
1   tsp. sweet almond oil
1   tsp. beeswax
1   capsule Vitamin E
3-6 chocolate chips

Heat cocoa butter, oil and beeswax just until melted. Add Vitamin E and chocolate chips. Mix well. Use a dropper to place in tubes or small jars.

Honey Lip Balm

2   tsp. beeswax
7   tsp. sweet almond oil
1   tsp. honey
5   drops flavoring (optional)
1   capsule Vitamin E

Heat beeswax and oil just until melted. Add the rest of the ingredients. Mix well. Use a dropper to place in tubes or small jars.

✦ **Save old lipstick and lip balm containers and put your homemade lip balms in them. Small mustard and jelly containers (the kind received in Christmas gift packs) are also great for storing lip balm.**

✦ **Put on lip liner, then lip gloss or petroleum jelly. This gives your lips a shine and makes it look like you are wearing lipstick.**

Lip Gloss

3   Tbsp. petroleum jelly
¼   tsp. lipstick*

Melt petroleum jelly and lipstick in the microwave just until melted. Mix well and place in a jar.

*Add more or less lipstick for desired shade. This is a great way to use up the last bit of lipstick in the tube.

Sparkling Lip Gloss

4   Tbsp. petroleum jelly
1-2   Tbsp. glitter or edible glitter*
½-1   tsp. lipstick
10   drops flavored oil

Melt petroleum jelly and lipstick. Add glitter and flavored oil. Omit lipstick for clear lip gloss.

* Edible glitter may be found at cake decorating stores.

✦ **Use a lip brush to get the last bits of lipstick out of the tube.**
✦ **When blotting lipstick, use 1 piece toilet tissue instead of an entire facial tissue.**
✦ **Use a lip liner pencil under your lipstick to make it last longer. Fill in the entire area of your lips with the pencil.**

Everything Else

After Shave

½   cup rubbing alcohol
½   cup water
1   tsp. cologne*

Mix rubbing alcohol and water. Add favorite cologne.

*Or add one or two little cotton cologne samples
(like Avon samples).

Toothpaste

1   tsp. baking soda
2   drops peppermint oil

In a bowl, mix baking soda and peppermint oil with a small
amount of water to form a paste. Dip toothbrush in paste and
brush as usual.

✦ **After putting store-bought toothpaste on your brush, dab
   brush into baking soda and brush. This whitens and
   brightens your teeth.** (*Thanks to Ang in Australia.*)
✦ **Wash your toothbrushes in the dishwasher once a week
   to sanitize them.**

Antiseptic Hand Cleaner

4   Tbsp. liquid soap (Dr. Bronners or Ivory)
      Water
20   drops tea tree oil

In a spray bottle, add liquid soap and tea tree oil. Fill bottle with water. Shake to mix.

Liquid Hand Soap

½   bar soap (leftover soap pieces, Ivory or Castile)
4   cups water
¼   cup Borax™ or washing soda

Grate soap. Place in a saucepan with water and heat. Do not boil. Add borax or washing soda. Stir until dissolved. Pour into a 2 gallon jug and top off with water. It will thicken as it cools. Place in a pump bottle.

✦ **Navy eyeliner makes the whites of your eyes appear whiter.**

✦ **If your blush doesn't stay on all day use cream blush and then top with powder blush.**

✦ **Use loose powder over your eye shadow and lip stick to set it in place.**

✦ **Use a deodorant stone instead of deodorant. A $5 stone lasts all year! Purchase at health food stores.** (*Thanks to Kassandra in Arizona*)

Heat Pads

Rice
Herbs
Essential oils

Add herbs or essential oils to dry rice. Mix in a bowl and let sit for a day or two before filling the pad.

Try using:

Allspice, cloves, cinnamon or nutmeg for an old-fashioned scent

Dried lavender to soothe headaches

Dried lavender and rosemary for body aches

Use an old sock, towel, washcloth, or scrap flannel or muslin for the outside of your heat pad. Sew into a desired shape. Usually a 10x30 inch rectangle sewn into a tube works well. Leave one end open to fill. Fill with dry rice mixture and then sew the pad closed.

To use: Spray lightly with water*. Place in microwave for 30 seconds to one minute. Use to soothe sore muscles.

*Be sure to spray with water before microwaving. This will make the heat pad last longer and will prevent it from burning in the microwave.

+ **Usen an old night gown or sheets to make great flannel heat pads.**

+ **An old cotton tube sock may be used for a no sew heat pad.**

Salve

1   cup olive OR almond oil
        Herbs*
2   tsp. beeswax
1   capsule Vitamin E
5-10   drops essential oil(s) as desired (rosemary, tea tree, eucalyptus & lavender are good choices)

Warm the oil and add herbs. Allow to simmer very gently for a couple of hours. Strain. Add beeswax and melt. Remove from heat and stir in Vitamin E and essential oils. Stir and cool until it barely starts to thicken. Pour into clean jars. Allow to cool. Label. Use on mild abrasions, on dry skin, or as a lip balm. This is a minimum recipe. Increase it as many times as you like.

*Suggested herbs to use:

Comfrey, calendula, lavender, pine needles, yarrow, chamomile

Leftover Soap?

✦ Use to mark darts and hems on washable fabric.

✦ Rub on gliders on drawers to make them slide easier.

✦ Rub on metal zippers to make them pull easier.

✦ Wet soap pieces and stick to a new bar of soap.

✦ Sew a pocket in a washcloth. Add soap slivers to make a soap glove. Or use an old sock: Put the soap slivers in and tie off the end.

How to Preserve a Husband

Be careful in the selection; do not choose too unripe or too old.

Best results are obtained if he has been reared in a healthy atmosphere.

Some insist upon keeping him in a pickle. Others prefer to keep him in hot water. However, such treatment makes the husband sour, hard, and sometimes bitter.

Many wives have found that even poor varieties can be rendered tender and good with a garnish of patience, the sweetening of a smile, and the flavoring of a kiss to taste.

Wrap him in a mantle of charity, place him over a warm, steady fire of domestic devotion and serve with peaches and cream.

Tip Index

A Dedication to Monty and James

If you can start the day without caffeine...

If you can get going without pep pills...

If you can always be cheerful, ignoring aches and pains...

If you can resist complaining and boring people with your troubles...

If you can eat the same food everyday and be grateful for it...

If you can understand when your loved ones are too busy to give you any time...

If you can overlook it when those who love you take it out on you, when through no fault of yours, something goes wrong...

If you can take criticism and blame without resentment...

If you can ignore a friend's limited education and never correct them...

If you can resist treating a rich friend better than a poor friend...

If you can face the world without lies and deceit...

If you can conquer tension without medical help...

If you can relax without liquor...

If you can sleep without the aid of drugs...

If you can say honestly that deep in your heart you have no prejudice against creed, color, religion, or politics...

Then, my friend, you are almost as good as you dog.

Author unknown.

T

U, V

W, X, Y, Z

Leftover Index

Thank God for dirty dishes,

They have a tale to tell.

While others may go hungry,

We are eating well.

With home, health and happiness,

I shouldn't want to fuss.

By the stack of evidence,

God's been very good to Us.

Try these recipes when you have leftover ingredients.

Recipe Index

For the Beginning Cook

You might want to plan cooking disasters to avoid rush hour. That way the fire department can get there in a timely manner.

Ask the fire department to use the back door and not to turn on their sirens if this is their third visit in the same week.

Do not be afraid to call the fire department even if it is the third time this week. Remember that putting out fires is their job. Volunteer firefighters might be tempted to avoid returning. However, you may convince them to return if you have a supply of emergency cookies.

The utility shed is a good place to store a back up supply of cookies. When erecting the shed, be certain it is not too close to the house. Be aware that several fires may cause your insurance company to become suspicious.

Know the shortest escape route before you start cooking.

If the dog turns up its' nose at your cooking, then you had better call the chemist.

Do not put the cookbook on top of the stove for easier viewing. This rule also applies to plastic containers and hot pads.

Written by Michael Kellam, while observing his wife, Tawra's, cooking.

In Great Appreciation

I would like to thank my husband Mike for all of his help. Thank you for all your patience when I was "panicking" about not getting this finished. Thank you for giving me a massage when I was in pain from my fibromyalgia and CFS from working too hard. Thank you for listening to me rattle on about "the book" for a year and helping me put it together so that it actually looks like a book. Thank you for helping me typeset and proofread into the night! Last but not least thank you for helping with the kids, faithfully doing the dishes and vacuuming while I was typing away!

Thank you to my brother David for faithfully doing all the artwork and for being our computer tech support. Thank you for being patient with me and staying up late nights to get it done. We wouldn't have been able to get this done without your help. To Sheala for donating David's time to help with my cookbook instead of reconstructing their home. And to my favorite nephew Cody, don't forget, www.notjustbeans.com

A great big thanks to Mom and Grandma for proofreading as you have never proofread before, for sharing all of your wonderful recipes with me and helping me figure out what I had done wrong when a recipe wouldn't work right.